STACKS

STACKS

*Interoperability
in Today's
Computer
Networks*

Carl Malamud

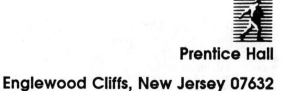

Prentice Hall

Englewood Cliffs, New Jersey 07632

Library of Congress Cataloging-in-Publication Data

MALAMUD, CARL,
   Stacks : interoperability in today's computer networks / Carl
Malamud.
   Includes bibliographical references and index.
   ISBN 0-13-484080-1
   1. Computer networks. 2. Computer networks—Security measures.
3. Computer networks—Standards. I. Title.
TK5105.5.M3575 1992   91-20647
004.6—dc20   CIP

Editorial/production supervision: **BARBARA MARTTINE**
Prepress buyer: **MARY MCCARTNEY**
Manufacturing buyer: **SUSAN BRUNKE**
Acquisition editor: **PAUL W. BECKER**

Published by Prentice-Hall, Inc.
A Simon & Schuster Company
Englewood Cliffs, New Jersey 07632

The publisher offers discounts on this book when ordered
in bulk quantities. For more information, write:
      Special Sales/College Marketing
      College Technical and Reference Division
      Prentice Hall
      Englewood Cliffs, New Jersey 07632

Diagrams of network topologies shown in Figures 2-1, 3-1 through 3-5, and 9-2 reprinted from
Analyzing Sun Networks by Carl Malamud. Copyright © Van Nostrand Reinhold (New York, 1991).
Reprinted with permission.

Printed in the United States of America

10 9 8 7 6 5 4 3 2 1

ISBN 0-13-484080-1

ISBN 0-13-484080-1

9 780134 840802

PRENTICE-HALL INTERNATIONAL (UK) LIMITED, *London*
PRENTICE-HALL OF AUSTRALIA PTY. LIMITED, *Sydney*
PRENTICE-HALL CANADA INC., *Toronto*
PRENTICE-HALL HISPANOAMERICANA, S.A., *Mexico*
PRENTICE-HALL OF INDIA PRIVATE LIMITED, *New Delhi*
PRENTICE-HALL OF JAPAN, INC., *Tokyo*
SIMON & SCHUSTER ASIA PTE. LTD., *Singapore*
EDITORA PRENTICE-HALL DO BRASIL, LTDA., *Rio de Janeiro*

Contents

Contents

Contents

Preface

This book looks at the question of interoperability within computer networks: how to turn components from different vendors into a coherent, transparent, and powerful computing environment. For our users, the best network is the one they see the least: The network doesn't break; and, it doesn't get in the way; it delivers resources when needed in the format that is the most useful. For those of us who make, run, buy, or otherwise busy ourselves with networks, life may not be quite so simple.

Interoperability is not a black-and-white issue. All computers are linked together in some fashion, even if it is something as rudimentary as running down the hall with floppy disks (the technical term for this process is SneakerNet). The question is not simply one of interoperability, but the level of interoperability.

We will look at interoperability from many different levels and perspectives. Sometimes, we will look at specific protocols: HIPPI and FDDI, for example, as protocols used in high-speed LANs. We'll look at SMDS and Frame Relay to provide similar services in a wide-area environment.

Periodically, however, we will take a step back and look at the forest instead of the trees. We will start, for example, with a look at the Internet and the maze of networks that form the global matrix. After looking at SMDS and other high-speed substratres, we will stop to see how they are applied in the national gigabit testbed program coordinated by the Corporation for National Research Initiatives.

Preface

To make networks interoperate, we need standards. Standards are a convention used by more than one vendor to allow pieces to plug and play. Standards may be official standards like OSI or de facto standards like Sun's Network File System. Throughout the book, we will concentrate on standards as the key to interoperability.

We start with the networking substrates: the mechanisms that actually move bits around. From early solutions like a wire between two computers, we have evolved to an environment with many different kinds of data link services.

Next, we will examine protocol stacks such as TCP/IP and OSI. We will look at how fast and big networks can be made. We will also look at dynamic and policy routing protocols to see how different kinds of networks can be connected together.

Next, we will look at three families of upper-level standards, meant to provide a powerful computing environment for the user. These three environments come from three very different types of standards organizations: the Open Software Foundation, Sun's Open Network Computing, and the ISO Open Systems Interconnection suite of standards. These environments combine with traditional applications, such as the TCP/IP FTP and Telnet protocols, to make up the services to the user.

Throughout the book we stop periodically and look at how the protocols are applied in the real world. We will look at supercomputer centers, gigabit testbeds, digital libraries, and other places where interoperability is becoming a reality.

If the key to interoperability is standards, the key to standards is being able to find out about them. This book finishes with a look at how standards are made and distributed. True interoperability—inexpensive and workable products that plug and play—requires a wide-spread dissemination of knowledge. We will look at how different types of standards bodies try to move the information about standards out to the people who make and use the equipment.

Preface

This book is liberally sprinkled with my opionions and covers a tremendous amount of ground. The aim is perspective, not detail. As Richard desJardins of the GOSIP Institute put it, this book is a "walk through the forest of interoperability." The path I have taken is only one of many possible routes—the aim of this book is not to encourage the reader to take my path but rather to develop his or her own view of the forest. I wish only—with a few notable exceptions—to inform, not to convert.

Carl Malamud
carl@malamud.com

ACK

A book such as this which covers such a wide selection of topics owes a particular debt to the people who are the real experts. These experts have been unusually gracious and generous in giving me access.

Dan Lynch and Ole Jacobsen of INTEROP, Inc. helped get this project underway and provided detailed reviews and considerable moral support. Mark Belinsky, Jackie Browning, Cynthia Candell, Wendy Gibson, and Christi R. Kraus of INTEROP, Inc. also contributed in many ways.

I would like to thank the many patient souls who took time out of their high-speed, packet-switched schedules to provide additional in-depth reviews of the manuscript. These experts don't necessarily agree with my opinions, but all were unfailingly generous in taking time out of their busy schedules to review drafts: M. Clayton Andrews of the Center for Telecommunications Research at Columbia University, D. James Bidzos and Kurt Stammberger of RSA Data Security, Inc., David Borman of Cray Research, Inc., Vinton Cerf of the Corporation for National Research Initiatives, Charles M. Corbalis of Stratacom, Richard desJardins of the GOSIP Institute, Jim Hughes of Network Systems Corporation, Clifford Lynch of the University of California, Office of the President, Gerard K. Newman of the San Diego Supercomputer Center, Brian Pawlowski of Sun Microsystems, Dr. Marshall Rose, Anthony Rutkowski of the International Telecommunications Union, Professor

ACK

Michael Schwartz of the University of Colorado, Daniel S. Stevenson of the Center for Communications, and Stephen Wolff of the National Science Foundation.

As always, despite the many people who gave me information, I would like to point out that the author is still the main bottleneck. If there are any errors because I have unsuccessfully digested this mass of information, I would like to take full credit for them.

Trademarks

PostScript is a trademark of Adobe Systems.

ANS is a trademark of Advanced Network and Services, Inc.

Apple, AppleTalk, Finder, LocalTalk, and Macintosh are trademarks of Apple Computer.

OPEN LOOK, STREAMS, Transport Layer Interface, UNIX, and UNIX System V Release 4 are trademarks of AT&T.

Knowbot is a registered trademark of the Corporation for National Research Initiatives.

Cray and UNICOS are registered trademarks and CRAY-2, CRAY X-MP, CRAY Y-MP and HSX are trademarks of Cray Research, Inc.

ARCNET is a registered trademark of DATAPOINT Corporation.

DEC, DECconnect, DECmcc, DECnet, DECnet-DOS, DECnet/OSI, DELNI, DNA, MAILbus, Message Router, MicroVAX, Ultrix, VAX, VAXBI, VAX Cluster, and VMS are trademarks of Digital Equipment Corporation.

Ingres is a trademark of ASK, Incorporated.

AS/400, DISOSS, IBM, IBM PC LAN, PC/AT, PC/XT, PROFS, SNA, SNADS, System/370, System/38, and 3270 Display Station are trademarks of International Business Machines, Inc.

INTEROP and ConneXions are registered trademarks of INTEROP, Inc.

Trademarks

Lotus 1-2-3 is a registered trademark of Lotus.

MS-DOS and Microsoft are registered trademarks of Microsoft.

Network General and Sniffer Analyzer are trademarks of Network General Corporation.

HYPERchannel is a trademark of Network Systems Corporation.

Novell and Netware are registered trademarks of Novell.

OSF, OSF/1, and Open Software Foundation are trademarks of the Open Software Foundation, Inc.

Retix is a trademark of Retix.

RSA is a registered trademark of RSA Data Security, Inc.

StrataCom is a registered trademark of StrataCom, Inc.

MAILbridge Server/MHS and Softswitch are trademarks of Softswitch.

Network File System, Open Network Computing, SPARC, Sun, SunOS, and TOPS are trademarks of Sun Microsystems, Inc.

Ultra and Ultranet are trademarks of Ultra.

Ethernet and Xerox are trademarks of Xerox.

Carl Malamud is a trademark of Carl Malamud.

– 1 –

Interoperability

Each workplace is unique. Consequently, the network needed to solve the problems in an environment will also be unique. No single network architecture will solve all problems—a series of modular components are needed that can be combined to provide effective, targeted solutions.

Take the universe of possible solutions—all the standards and all the implementations of those standards—and you don't have an architecture. Instead, you have many file cabinets full of standards. Likewise, if you take all the standards offered by one vendor, you still don't have an architecture, you have a marketing brochure.

Rather than buying all products from some all-encompassing universe (a process akin to furnishing a house by calling Sears and ordering one of each), we must carefully choose a subset of tools that will help us. We might pick Ethernet and telephone lines as data links, TCP/IP and OSI as transport service providers, and a few network services like FTAM, NFS, and FTP for data access. This subset of the possible universe of solutions becomes our network architecture.

The network architecture defines a series of components that work together to provide solutions. Each component provides a service. Ethernet, for example, will transmit a datagram from one node to another. Ethernet provides service to the network layer, which in turn provides service to the transport modules, until we have a stack of components all working together. Carefully choosing the blocks at each layer of the stack is the process of defining a network architecture.

Just because the architecture is a subset of available technology does not mean that it is narrow in scope. The architecture might include databases, 4GLs, and other tools that may or may not fit the traditional definition of a computer network. If we have excessive time on our hands or too many committees involved, we might even decide to drop the term network architecture for something broader like "information architecture." There is no difference between the two terms: you shouldn't do databases without networks and you certainly shouldn't be doing networks without thinking of the databases that run on them. Calling this collection of tools a network architecture or an information architecture is simply a matter of perspective (and marketing).

Choosing different subsets of the technologies available is the point behind open systems and interoperability. You have a generic framework, such as OSI, and different vendors making different parts of the framework. By connecting the pieces, you implicitly put your own network architecture together. A fundamental premise of this book is that the user should plan that architecture out—a house built with no blueprints is not going to be as nice as one where the architecture precedes the implementation.

Different pieces do not necessarily imply different vendors. For example, an architecture might specify that all open systems components be bought from IBM: X.25 software and controllers, Ethernet controllers, OSI network through session layers, FTAM, and X.400.

The fact that all the equipment comes from one vendor does not change the fact that there is a network architecture. The source of the products just happen to be all painted blue. Nor does a user network architecture necessarily imply open systems. A user may pick all SNA-based equipment from IBM. Even in the case of SNA, however, we have a very definite architecture. We can, if we wish, add more components to the architecture. We can even use the very well-defined interface to the SNA architecture to provide gateways to other environments, such as TCP/IP or DECnet.

Picking the appropriate pieces is the broad subject of this book. Choice is the theme. Technology has reached the point where users may configure networks to serve their own specific needs.

Not all choices will be mentioned in this book (not even a fraction, in fact). Instead, we will look at some emerging choices. The technologies picked are arbitrary—they represent one person's view (mine) of what is new and important.

The point of an arbitrary, selective survey of protocols is to try to separate the wheat from the chaff. Learning everything there is to know about one protocol is very important, but if that protocol does not work together with other protocols in the network, the exercise will have been wasted.

The reader should gain two things from this book. First, within this book are descriptions of many new protocols and research projects. Consider the descriptions of these projects and protocols as a first alert—readers who are interested in certain topics can then go on to more detailed descriptions.

The second point of this book is to put new technologies into perspective—to sort, categorize, and even flame a bit on the state of the Internet. Providing perspective serves as a basis for discussion. As Virginia Woolf observed in her classic *A Room of One's Own*:

> ... when a subject is highly controversial [she was talking about sex, but we shall instead substitute networks] one cannot hope to tell the truth. One can only show how one came to hold whatever opinion one does hold. One can only give one's audience the chance of drawing their own conclusions as they observe the limitations, the prejudices, the idiosyncrasies of the speaker.

This somewhat idiosyncratic view of the world is thus meant to serve as a basis for discussion. We leave the role of ultimate reference on a subject to other books and to standards documents. Instead, we try here to provide a map through the standards, allowing the reader to decide which portions are relevant to his or her own needs.

This selective view of the world is certainly not unique. I expect the reader to have his or her own views, perhaps radically different from the ones in this book. Two parties with different points of view, if both are based on a sophisticated, detailed analysis of the technology, can only serve to inform both parties. After all, what's the point of open systems without open discussion?

The Magic of Seven Layers

There is a law that applies to all books about computer networks. The law is that homage must be paid to the ISO seven-layer reference model (See Fig. 1-1). This law is certainly superior to the older law which required all books to explain how an RS-232 connection works.

An interesting illustration of the law in action is DECnet. DECnet formerly had six layers, with the functions of network management and "user applications" folded into the top layer of the architecture. After the reference model became popular, DEC split the upper layer into two to form the required number, seven. In the most recent phase of DECnet, Digital has gone even further, incorporating OSI (the ISO Open Systems Interconnection protocols) into the product name: DECnet has become DECnet/OSI.

The ISO seven-layer model has thus become a bit of a marketing tool. It is, of course, still a fundamentally useful abstraction on the network. However, to provide a bit of perspective on this abstraction, we propose another model as a basis for discussion. The model, as will be seen, has seven layers, with the bottom four incorporating the ISO reference model (see Fig. 1-2).

4

STACKS

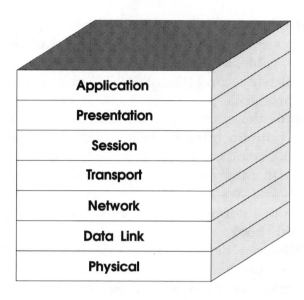

Figure 1-1 The ISO Reference Model

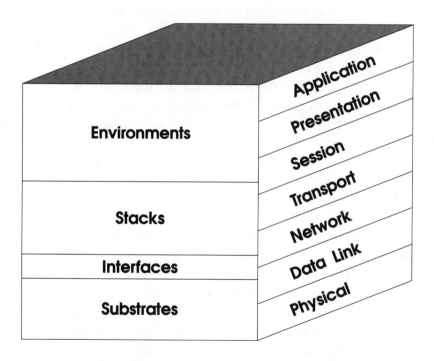

Figure 1-2 The Revised ISO Reference Model

5

Interoperability

At the bottom of our model, we have the concept of a substrate, a service that transmits data. A substrate might be an Ethernet cable, a 300-bps modem connection, a T3 line, or a 2.4 gigabit per second (Gbps) SONET link running the ATM switching protocol.

On top of the substrate is an interface. In the world of LANs, the common interface is the IEEE 802.2 protocol. Under the 802.2 standard are a variety of supported substrates, such as FDDI, Ethernet, token ring, and token bus. In the wide-area world, we have interfaces like X.25. We also have two emerging interfaces: SMDS and Frame Relay, both discussed in this book.

The difference between a substrate and an interface is a matter of perspective. The fast packet technology, ATM, that underlies many very fast wide-area networks is usually part of the substrate. However, some people are proposing to use ATM directly as a LAN, thus making it the interface.

On top of the interface is the protocol stack, the equivalent of the network and transport layers. The stack is where many books devote the bulk of their attention. Professor Douglas Comer's *Internetworking with TCP/IP*, for example, is an excellent introduction to the TCP/IP stack.

The reason we draw a line between substrates and stacks is that there may be many different stacks on a single substrate. Even within a single environment, we may see multiple stacks. A Novell network may have IPX/SPX and TCP/IP. A DEC network may have a Phase IV proprietary stack, an OSI-like Phase V stack, and TCP/IP.

Environments are on top of stacks. Environments are the mass of closely-aligned protocols that form the platform on which we build applications. The Open Software Foundation (OSF), for example, has an environment that consists of a naming service, a remote procedure call mechanism, the X Window System, the MOTIF look and feel, and a wide variety of other mechanisms. While we can carefully define the concepts of substrates, interfaces, and stacks, "environments" is our catchall layer for everything that sits on top of the transport layer.

This book considers the four layers from the bottom up. After a brief diversion to examine the Internet, we will discuss substrates in two chapters. First is the LAN. Here we examine how many different LAN technologies work together to provide a portfolio of substrates. Then we will discuss the question of wide-area access, particularly dynamic, high bandwidth links between different organizations over a public data network (or over a private data network within a large organization). Here, we examine the role of Broadband ISDN (B-ISDN) as an emerging architecture.

Next, we will examine protocol stacks from several perspectives. First, we will look at how protocol stacks are becoming fungible. OSI and TCP provide the same basic services and we will see how standards like the Transport Level Interface (TLI) and mechanisms like STREAMS are used to achieve independence from the particular stack in use.

We will also examine the sizing and scaling of protocol stacks. Mechanisms used in protocols like TCP, such as the retry mechanism when data is lost, have a very definite effect on speed of networks. If we are to use very fast networks (and we will) then we will need to make sure that the protocols that run on those fast networks can keep up.

Speed is one aspect of scaling, but so is the size of the system. We will discuss the question of routing protocols, the means by which a router is able to discover the route to a destination. Some routing protocols are dynamic, meant to allow quick discovery of routes to distant destinations, in a topology that may change very often. Another type of routing protocol we will examine addresses the issues of policy routing, making sure that packets take administratively appropriate routes through the maze of an internet.

Finally, at the top of the protocol stack, we will examine three emerging environments. The Open Software Foundation and Sun's Open Network Computing (ONC) are discussed because of the pitched marketing campaigns to capture the workstation's screen. OSI and GOSIP are also discussed to show how these environments serve a different purpose from OSF and ONC.

After discussing environments, stacks, interfaces, and substrates, we will pause to consider the question of security. Security is an issue that pervades the network architecture. In fact, it should be a fundamental question of protocol design just as efficiency, interoperability, and other issues are.

Once we have finished our tour of the bottom four layers of the protocol stack, we will describe how the components are being combined to form useful computer networks. We will examine the National Gigabit Testbed, a series of research projects that are making gigabit wide-area networks a reality. We will also discuss efforts to deploy national digital libraries.

The Revised Seven-Layer Model

The top three layers in our revised seven-layer model are the financial, political, and religious layers (see Fig. 1-3). This seven-layer model may seem a bit flip to some, but it is intended in all seriousness. It is important that solutions be both economically feasible and politically saleable.

It is just as important to avoid undue emphasis from the religious layer. It is too often tempting to try to address technical questions by the use of doctrine. The trend in some organizations to insist that all components be OSI (or SNA or TCP/IP or DECnet) is evidence of the use of doctrine.

Settling on one religion, such as OSI, doesn't solve any problems—it only precludes useful solutions for two reasons. First, any single family of protocols is so broad that it does not in and of itself provide a solution. For instance, relying on OSI as a Holy Grail only forestalls the type of detailed analysis necessary to provide solutions to real problems.

Second, there is no reason why protocols can't mix. If we are going to analyze the subsets of SNA that might provide a solution, why not also examine subsets of other protocol suites that might provide better solutions? Different network

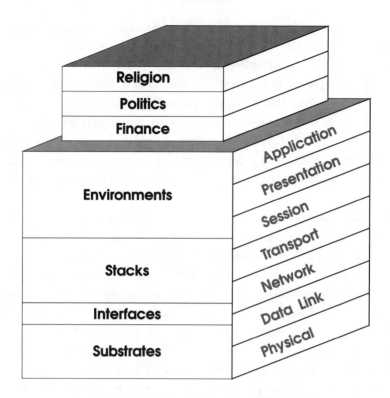

Figure 1-3 The 7 Layer Revised Model

architectures were designed with different models of computing in mind and thus a real world environment—one where many different models of work coexist—should need different models of networking.

Relying on OSI, SNA, or any other architecture to provide all the answers to a user's network architecture means that the user is trying to get away without doing the proper analysis. You can't use technology effectively unless you understand how it works and then apply it to your particular environment.

This statement doesn't mean that every problem requires analysis of the use of every possible protocol. Far from it. What we all need is a perspective on what the pieces are and how they fit together. Having a broad view of the architectures means that we know what the options are.

Interoperability

Armed with a knowledge of the possible options, we are in a position to do further research. We can go to trade shows and look for products, we can read standards to see how they compare, we can read the trade press for reviews, and (of course) buy books discussing the standards.

Based on a conscious awareness of the options and a bit of research, we can have a conscious architecture. Conscious choice is almost always a better choice, even if it just consists of picking from the options offered by a single-source vendor.

Interoperability means that the user can exercise choice. There are two important prerequisites to the exercise of this choice. The first is knowledge—the available choices must be known. Private standards, inaccessible processes for making standards, and the high prices and inaccessibility of standards documents are all factors that impede the spread of knowledge, and hence the spread of interoperability.

We will examine the question of access in the last chapter of this book. Even if knowledge is available, however, there must be a willingness to use it. There is a disturbing trend to try to oversimplify the world.

This trend towards oversimplification has always been present. I remember a large corporation that specified SNA as a network architecture. Not some subset of SNA, mind you, but just SNA. Of course, SNA is so broad that saying we have SNA as an architecture is like saying that our car is an "internal combustion." The corporation had a false sense of security because it had not performed the further analysis needed to decide which elements of SNA would fit into the organizational architecture.

Mangoes and Orangutans?

Flexibility and choice are very nice, some may argue, but it is more important to have standards. Basing an architecture on standards does not preclude flexibility. Let us examine this proposition in more detail by looking at a specific example—the choice of file access protocols for an enterprise-wide

10

network. To make the analysis even more concrete, we will use a straw man: "FTAM should be used to the exclusion of FTP and NFS in the enterprise-wide network."

There are a variety of ways to access data on a network. In the TCP/IP world of the Internet, the File Transfer Protocol (FTP) has long been used for bulk transfer of files. In more tightly-integrated distributed computing environments, Sun's Network File System (NFS) is often used.

FTP and NFS are not the only choices. If you have DECnet, you might use Digital's Data Access Protocol (DAP). If you are on an Apple network, you could use the AppleTalk Filing Protocol. We have not even begun to list all the choices, let alone examine alternative models of data access such as SQL-based relational database systems.

It is the diversity of proprietary data access mechanisms that has been largely responsible for the attractiveness of the Open Systems Interconnection (OSI) protocols. Diversity, if randomly applied without conscious direction, leads to a lack of interoperability. For an OSI network, File Transfer, Access, and Management (FTAM) is the standard protocol for remote file access.

Does this mean that FTAM should be used in addition to the other protocols or to their exclusion? The purpose of standards is to open up choice; to make increased levels of communication possible that were not possible before. Supporting FTP, NFS, FTAM (and even other mechanisms) helps open up more choice in the network.

We start first with the question of the venerable FTP, in use on many thousands of computers world-wide. One can, of course, compare the functionality of FTP to the more modern NFS and FTAM protocols.

The whole point of FTP in a modern computer network is that it is available on almost all computers: it forms a lowest common denominator of connectivity. It is certainly not the first choice for connectivity between two systems, but it makes a great last choice when all else fails.

Interoperability

Since an FTP implementation is a core part of any TCP/IP implementation, there is no real cost to support it (other than fielding user questions on arcane questions of syntax). Instead of discouraging the use of FTP, a more sensible course is to encourage the use of other protocols.

Let us look instead at FTAM and NFS.

It is tempting to see FTAM and NFS as competing protocols, both providing access to remote data. The network architect naturally wants to eliminate wasted effort caused by having two different groups solve the same problem in different ways.

On closer examination, however, we see that NFS and FTAM actually do very different things. Comparing NFS and FTAM is like comparing mangoes to orangutans. If you pick a high enough metaphysical viewpoint, they both serve the same function—both are carbon-based life forms. With a given set of criteria, one can easily compare the two and come up with a clear winner: "The mango is more portable and is thus preferable to the orangutan."

If you take a lower perspective, differences between the mango and the orangutan start to show up. The mango certainly tastes better, but you can't take a group of kids to the zoo to watch a mango and expect them to stay entertained.

It is easy to fall into the mango trap when looking at emerging standards like FTAM. When we see an international standard emerging, it is tempting to say that it will solve all problems and that it should be used to the exclusion of other protocols. After all, we don't want duplication of effort.

The issue is the universe used for the comparison. Analyzing enterprise-wide file access mechanisms to pick a winner requires some limitation of scope. Of course, one could compare Telnet (the TCP/IP service for interactive login) to FTAM and decide that FTAM is better: even die-hard FTAM fanatics would consider such an analysis silly.

In the area more traditionally known as file access mechanisms, one could pick a small subset, such as FTP, FTAM,

and NFS.   One could expand the analysis to also include
Carnegie Mellon's Andrew File System (AFS), Digital's Data
Access Protocol (DAP), and Novell's NetWare Core Protocols.
One could (but hopefully would not) even go so far as to
consider things like RJE over Bisync or custom COBOL pro-
grams over X.25 as candidates.

To illustrate why trying to pick a single winner from
these candidates, I would like to contribute another, imaginary, candidate—the Ultimate File System (UFS).   UFS is
clearly better than all other candidates: it is fast, efficient,
and powerful.   It slices, it dices, and can be implemented
quickly and easily.   It has an installed base only slightly
smaller than FTAM.

Because UFS is clearly better, one could do a blow by
blow comparison to FTAM and NFS. There is no doubt that,
given any set of criteria, one can find holes in each of them.
The basic problem with choosing a single enterprise-wide solution between candidates like UFS, NFS, and FTAM is that
they really perform different functions.

Let us look again at the top three layers of the revised
reference model.   If we perform the analysis of file access
mechanisms at the religious layer, the inclination is to pick a
single candidate for remote data access.   This single candidate for truth, beauty, and transparent access to remote data
is then deployed throughout the enterprise-wide network.

At the political layer, good reasons for employing multiple protocols begin to show up. No matter how widespread a
given standard becomes, there are always groups of people
who want to do things differently.

A single enterprise-wide file transfer mechanism has all
the disadvantages we've found with other forms of highly
centralized management decisions: inflexibility to change,
long lead times, and decision-making based on the lowest
common denominator. The whole point of distributed systems is to allow management tools to adapt to changing environments (which, by definition, change differently in different places).

Interoperability

At the financial layer, there are even more compelling reasons to allow multiple file access protocols. Take FTP vs. FTAM, for example. For the time being at least, one can make a strong argument that FTP is more efficient (and thus costs less) than FTAM for basic file transfer activity. In a local area environment, NFS is certainly more efficient (and significantly more transparent) than either FTP or FTAM.

There are other financial considerations besides performance (with the concomitant need for less hardware, software, and bandwidth). If you need a cheap, easy solution, mature protocols have more public domain implementations, making them more widely available to the general public. Vendors tend to bundle in older protocols with their operating systems, whereas the latest whiz-bang utility tends to require a separate purchase order.

A final financial consideration is the reality of the installed base. In many cases, a particular hardware or software platform dictates a particular networking solution—other solutions may be possible, but prohibitively expensive.

Even at lower layers, there are compelling reasons to use both FTAM and other protocols. It is clear that you can take FTAM and make it the basis of a distributed file system. You could build FTAM into ROM on diskless workstations and have network-based paging using FTAM—it seems likely that FTAM would be found lacking in these fields of application.

Likewise, there are functions that NFS doesn't perform as well. Because NFS is a means for extending a local file system, it is not as fully general as FTAM and, according to conventional wisdom, is harder to implement on all possible operating platforms. We can refer to this lack of generality as UNIXisms, but a better analysis would be to realize that NFS is a file service and FTAM is a record service.

Let's further our comparison of FTAM and NFS by examining the question of data independence across machine architectures. FTAM has the concept of document types. In theory, you can define any structure for data in a file and

14

have that data move transparently across machine architectures.

In reality, FTAM applications are limited to a few basic document types: straight uninterpreted binary, and text terminated by carriage returns at the end of the line are two common examples. The standard is extensible—groups can define new document types—but the key is not the theoretically possible document types, but the ones that have been implemented in the particular system with which you wish to communicate.

NFS has no concept of document types. NFS leaves the interpretation of the data to the client. Do you really want the operating system for your diskless VAXstation encoded so a Sun could read it? What would it do with it?

Why make the user of the data interpret the data stream instead of have the server structure the file as a series of records? For one, it certainly reduces server load. It also promotes the ability of a client to store arbitrary data on arbitrary servers as when a Sun workstation stores the binary image of its operating system on a VAX server. An uninterpreted byte stream also allows the client to access raw blocks at speeds much faster than with a structured access mechanism. File services are ideal for applications like diskless nodes where the client is accessing programs and not documents.

Just because the byte stream is not structured as a series of records does not necessarily imply that you can't have data independence on the network in NFS. The External Data Representation (XDR), the presentation layer under NFS, allows a user to take data structures and encode them for network presentation. This presentation layer function of encoding data is used by many applications, so that data stored on a server is readable by all clients. The choice of structuring data is left to the application that uses the file system in NFS, whereas it is built into FTAM.

Let's stop and look at this point again: NFS and FTAM perform different functions so they have different approaches to data representation. NFS is a file server: FTAM is based on a structured, record-oriented virtual file system.

There are some other differences between the two. FTAM uses a connection-oriented, stateful approach, whereas NFS is stateless and uses (at least in most implementations) the UDP transport layer in TCP/IP. A stateful approach means that locking, file open requests, or other information about the state of a user session is preserved between user requests. In a stateless protocol, each request is independent.

Again, the protocols do different things. FTAM is inherently stateful and has locking built into the protocols. NFS allows the locking mechanism to be an independent service. This doesn't mean that an operating system is going to allow multiple users to walk all over data: just because the NFS protocol is stateless doesn't mean that the server implementation doesn't keep state information.

Note that making NFS stateless simplifies its role as a file service, making crash recovery and other operations significantly easier. This doesn't mean that NFS can't work over a connection-oriented transport service: the Reno tape for the new Berkeley UNIX features a TCP-based implementation of NFS that works quite well in a wide-area environment.

Can NFS and FTAM coexist in a single network? It is not at all unusual to see DEC systems that use the Record Management Services (RMS) to tie together NFS, FTAM, DEC's Data Access Protocols, VAX Clusters, and DEC's Distributed File System into a single coherent view of data in a wide variety of environments. The local file access mechanism, in this case RMS, is responsible for masking the different protocols transparent to the client application.

Lists of Three

It is sometimes tempting to group all applications on all networks into three categories: data access, mail, and virtual terminals. Once this taxonomy is heard enough times, it starts to make sense. Every protocol is put into one of the three categories.

The next step is often to find the single best protocol in each of the three categories. The result is a list of the three standard protocols that make up a global solution to all our problems.

This approach is simplistic at best and can be quite destructive. Computer networks do many different things for many different populations of users. Picking a simple protocol is nice, but using it to the exclusion of complementary services just reduces the user's capability to accomplish useful work.

Picking FTAM as a single enterprise-wide data mechanism is reminiscent of the old COBOL wars, in which COBOL became a single enterprise-wide programming solution. Given a universe of COBOL, RPG II, and BASIC, standardizing on one helps. But specifying COBOL to the exclusion of other paradigms such as C, SQL, or Lotus 1-2-3 just ossifies the organization.

Let me give you an example. I used to work in the research division of the Board of Governors of the Federal Reserve System. We were trying to provide an alternative to IBM's MVS/TSO for econometric analysis and needed to hire some programmers to port our applications to UNIX and C.

Unfortunately, the centralized MIS group had decided that the standard language skill needed to work at the Board of Governors was a facility with COBOL. COBOL, being a Federal Information Processing Standard (FIPS), was the official way to write computer programs in MIS. Needless to say, writing econometric models in COBOL is a little tough.

Because MIS had decided Cobol was our enterprise-wide standard, Personnel wouldn't let us advertise for FORTRAN or C skills. Instead, we had to advertise for COBOL programmers and hope that somebody listed FORTRAN or C on his or her resume.

Enterprise-wide solutions should not attempt to provide a lowest common denominator or form a rigid model. Simplistic solutions to difficult problems don't help anybody. This doesn't mean we don't need standards. Standards are the basic requirement for interoperability. Standards should be a means to interoperability, however, not a corporate religion.

UFS+?

Let's return to the question of the Ultimate File System (UFS). I'm not going to recommend that you discard FTAM and NFS in favor of UFS, even though UFS is clearly better. Instead, I would begin implementing UFS on systems in tandem with FTAM and NFS. I might even make a UFS to FTAM gateway system to ease transition. As more and more of my users begin to use UFS, I might even make it one of several required applications for any host on my network.

But I certainly wouldn't say UFS was my network-wide, enterprise-wide solution. After all, UFS+ will be available soon.

Instead of looking for a single solution, we need to look at the universe of possible solutions and pick the pieces that provide solutions. How the pieces fit together provides the perspective from which we can analyze specific solutions. The rest of this book provides one such perspective.

For Further Reading

Throughout this book, we will suggest sources for further reading. This book should not be considered definitive: it is too short and too static to be a single source of information on a field this broad. The reader is highly encouraged to consult books and primary resource documents.

One of the best sources of information on networks is to read the standards documents that define them. Probably the best-written (and certainly the cheapest to obtain) are the Internet RFCs. To get an RFC, send electronic mail to service@nic.ddn.mil. On the subject line, put the word "RFC" followed by a space and the RFC number:

    To: service@nic.ddn.mil
    Subject: RFC 1194

Another source of RFCs is the CSnet "InfoServer." Send mail to info-server@sh.cs.net, and put the word "info" on the subject line. A message will be returned with information on RFCs and other documents, and directions to obtain them on-line. RFCs can also be obtained for $10 each from the Network Information Center (NIC) by calling (800) 235-3155.

For a user not on the Internet, you need to follow the instructions for sending mail between your own system and the Internet. See the "For Further Reading" suggestions in Chapter 2 for sources that explain how to move mail between networks.

– 2 –

The Core and the Periphery

It used to be that a network manager could take you into a room and point to a cable. "This is our network" he would proudly say. One can no longer point to "the" network—they have all merged together into one large mesh. This interconnected maze of systems is often referred to as the Internet, although we will see that connectivity has grown far beyond the official confines of the Internet itself, indeed it has grown beyond the bounds of the global TCP/IP internetwork to include other networks and internetworks.

There are very few networks today that do not have some form of link to this interconnected maze. The link can be very simple, consisting of a modem on a PC and an MCIMail account, allowing the user to send and receive mail. Alternatively, the link can be a full-fledged TCP/IP connection to a commercial provider like PSI or AlterNet. The link might even be to an organization's private network, such as NASA's Science Internet (NSI) or Sun's Wide Area Network (SWAN).

There are still anomolies—a local network consisting of an Ethernet, a Novell server, and a few PCs or a small Apple-Talk with no modems. Increasingly, even these little islands are being connected to the rest of the world. The question is no longer "are we linked to the outside world?" but "what level of functionality do our links provide?"

The Core and the Periphery

The Internet

The Internet (note the uppercase "I") is a network infrastructure that supports research, engineering, education, and commercial services. It is sponsored by a variety of federal agencies such as the National Science Foundation (NSF) and the Defense Advanced Research Projects Agency (DARPA). The word internet (with a lowercase "i") refers to any interconnected set of substrates (provided, of course, they are running an internetwork protocol such as IP).

The original ARPANET was built in 1969 and connected individual hosts. By 1975, individual groups had their own networks, built on Ethernet, packet radio, and packet satellite and the Internet came into being. Today, there are many different internets, many of them linked together.

The center of the Internet is a set of core backbones. The most prominent example is NSFnet, a set of T1 and T3 links connected by high-speed routers. Other backbones that are part of the Internet are the Energy Sciences Network (ESnet), the NASA Science Internet (NSI), and numerous national backbones, such as CA*net in Canada. There are also regional backbones, such as EUnet and NORDUnet in Europe and commercial backbones such as PSInet, ANSnet, CERFnet, and AlterNet.

Very few users are directly on the NSFnet: host computers do not get attached to the backbone. Instead, high speed routers (dedicated, specialized versions of general-purpose computers) are put on the core backbone and form the connection to routers on regional networks. These regional networks form the second level of the Internet.

Connected to the regional networks are the third level: local internetworks, which are operated by research labs, universities, corporations, and a wide variety of other groups. There are even a few individuals who have connected their home networks to a regional network.

The local internetwork may itself form a hierarchy. The University of Colorado, for example, is a large internetwork, which is in turn connected to the Colorado SuperNet, a statewide network, which is then connected to Westnet, the regional network.

These three tiers—the backbones, regionals, and local nets—are the switching fabric that make up the Internet. By submitting a packet with an Internet address to a neighboring router, a computer is able to send data to any other Internet computer.

The packet hits the router, which hands it to another router, and so on until it reaches the destination network—each router makes a decision on a hop-by-hop basis on which data link to use to move the packet one step closer to its destination. All this is transparent to the end systems. The Internet Protocol (IP)—or some other protocol such as the OSI network layer—shields the end systems from the intricacies of this maze.

We will see in Chapter 5 that the question of how to get from one network to another through the Internet is not necessarily a simple issue. As the number of networks and end systems continues to grow explosively, discovering a valid path from one node to another becomes increasingly difficult.

What is important to realize is that there are many paths and many backbones. In some cases, the regional networks are connected directly to each other, alleviating the need to cross a backbone link like the NSFnet.

So, what exactly is the Internet? The Internet is the collection of autonomously administered backbones and regional networks, and many thousands of local networks.

The key word is autonomous. Each net is run by a different group. They are members of the Internet because they are connected together. They happen to share the same protocols, currently TCP/IP, but we will see that even this common thread of unity is beginning to change as OSI and other protocols begin to play a role. Likewise, using TCP/IP does not necessarily mean that all computers can perform all functions: several core services are in use on most systems, but there are a wide variety of other protocols that make up the TCP/IP suite.

The above discussion brings us back again to the question of the Internet. This whole collection of autonomous systems is not run from any single location or administrative authority. There is no Internet Network Operations Center (though there are NOCs for individual core and regional networks), nor is there a Director of Operations. There is an Internet Activities Board (IAB), but this group rules more by a loose form of moral authority than by any direct control (the authority being loose, not necessarily the morals). The IAB has responsibility for the technical evolution of the Internet protocols, not for the operation of any of the constituent networks.

The job of the IAB is to develop standards for use in the Internet. Engineering and research task forces develop recommendations, and if the IAB believes that the recommendations are useful (and if the engineers have proved they can implement them), the recommendations become standards. Very few of these standards are adopted everywhere; most are adopted in some subset of systems.

The Internet has a fairly high degree of cohesion as far as networks go. Assuming two hosts both agree to use the same upper-level protocol, they are able to communicate with each other using that protocol over the Internet. It really does not matter where the hosts are located; the IP protocols move the packets back and forth.

The Internet has a wide variety of useful services (and broad connectivity at low cost so the services are widely available). Many research networks have mail protocols, but the Internet also offers file access, remote login, and a host of other functions. (See the "For Further Reading" section at the end of Chapter 5 for sources that explain the TCP/IP protocols and the applications built on top of TCP/IP that are used in the Internet.)

The Internet is very large—over five thousand different networks—but there are many other networks. We can con-

24

sider the Internet as a single meta-network because all the hosts share a common suite of protocols (although some of the hosts adopt more of the protocols than others).

If you think of the Internet as a core of connectivity, then we can quickly see that there can be other cores. Corporate networks, such as Digital's Easynet and Sun's SWAN are connected to the Internet, but form very large networks in their own right.

In the case of SWAN, the Sun network is based on the TCP/IP protocols. In addition to basic TCP/IP services, SWAN users have their own protocols, databases, and other services. SWAN tends to emphasize some services that are not necessarily used as much in other areas. A typical example is the Network File System (NFS). NFS is an optional Internet protocol, but plays a central role in the SWAN network allowing engineers to mount source code archives located across the country.

While SWAN uses TCP/IP, Digital's Easynet is based on (no surprise here) Digital's own DECnet protocols. Within Easynet, DECnet services are used between computers. To access the Internet, there needs to be a way of connecting the two protocol suites.

The connection can be made in two ways. While DECnet is used in most of Easynet, there is no reason why a particular computer cannot speak multiple network protocols. Ultrix nodes often speak TCP/IP as well as DECnet (or just TCP/IP in some cases). If a node does not speak TCP/IP, it can still access Internet services, but must do so via a gateway. Digital's software for connecting DECnet and TCP/IP is called the Ultrix Internet Gateway.

The key to this gateway is that it operates at the upper layers of the network. Rather than interconnecting all protocols at all levels, three target applications are picked: mail, virtual terminals, and file transfer.

Take mail, for example. A user can send mail using the DECnet Message Router to a gateway. If the mail has the proper address it is translated from Message Router format into the TCP/IP compatible format and then launched on its way.

The Ultrix Internet Gateway is software that performs this application-layer bridging function between two diverse environments. Digital has put a copy of this software in several key facilities on nodes at the edge of Easynet. These nodes act as the gateway between Digital's Easynet and the Internet.

The distinction between networking protocols (DECnet) and a particular instance of a protocol suite (Easynet) is crucial. There is no reason why, with the appropriate money and permissions, that another user couldn't put DECnet and an Internet gateway into his or her own corporate network.

We have seen a wide variety of networks. NSFnet is a network with no directly attached users; regional networks are connected to the NSFnet, Sun has SWAN, and DEC has Easynet.

The key is not whether or not there is connectivity between any two of these environments but the level of connectivity. Within SWAN, you can perform NFS mounts to make a remote file system appear locally attached (an Internet user could theoretically mount a SWAN file system, but various security mechanisms prevent unauthorized export of SWAN data to the outside world). Between SWAN and your typical Internet node, you use less functional protocols such as the File Transfer Protocol. Between Easynet and the Internet, you use application layer gateways.

While DECnet and TCP/IP are highly functional protocol suites, they are certainly not the only ones. In the area of full-fledged protocol suites, we must certainly include proprietary systems such as IBM's System Network Architecture or Novell's Netware (after all, if you count the number of computers, there are more Netware networks in the U.S. then any other protocol). And, of course, we do not want to forget Open Systems Interconnection (OSI).

There are also networks based on much simpler protocols. For example, consider MCIMail. This network originally did one thing: electronic mail. Like other mostly-mail networks (BITNET and AT&T Mail for example), MCIMail has expanded to offer other services such as access to the Dow Jones News/Retrieval service and private bulletin boards.

MCIMail, like the other systems, has gateways to other networks. Needless to say, the gateways are application layer gateways, since the only service MCIMail offers to its users is mail—an application.

Application layer gateways should not be underestimated, however. MCIMail users can send mail to any other users connected to the Internet, including all Internet users and users on any other network that have a gateway, such as BIT-NET, or Easynet. Other commercial systems, such as Compuserve or AT&T Mail are also available to MCIMail users via gateways.

In addition to gateways to other networks, MCIMail has links to other forms of communications: you can send electronic mail to a user who has a fax machine or a telex terminal, or even have the electronic mail printed on paper and delivered by the U.S. Post Office (sometimes referred to as the SnailMAIL network). You can also use mail as the basis for higher-level services, such as Electronic Data Interchange (EDI) of purchase orders, invoices, and other structured documents. Telex connections are especially valuable, allowing an electronic mail user to receive a telex.

At this point, the word network may be losing some of its meaning for the reader. We have seen core networks (NSF-net), generic network protocol suites (TCP/IP), corporate networks (SWAN), application layer networks (MCIMail), and meta-networks (the Internet). We're not done.

Just as MCIMail is a limited service application network, we also have limited service networks at a lower layer. These networks simply provide a connection from one point to another. An X.25 network such as Telenet or even a simple point to point connection with a pair of modems is an example of an access network. Access networks are simply commercial substrates. An access network, such as Com-

The Core and the Periphery

puNet, SprintNet, or my-modem-and-a-telephone-line-net can be used to allow a terminal to access a computer, but can also be used as a transport for network traffic. Instead of providing an X.25 interface to the user, these higher-level access networks provide a TCP/IP interface.

A simple example is PSInet. PSInet is a commercial TCP/IP network, connected to the Internet. How do you get to the edge of PSInet? You use a modem and a telephone to reach the edge, known as a point of presence (POP). Data link protocols such as the Point-to-Point Protocol (PPP) allow the telephone line to be used for real network protocols instead of just terminal emulation. The originating system transmits TCP/IP traffic, which then traverses the point-of-presence router into PSInet, and then on to the rest of the Internet.

The Matrix

All of these interconnected networks form what John Quarterman calls "The Matrix." The term, of course, comes from the wired world of cyberspace and cyberpunks popularized by William Gibson in his science fiction classic *Neuromancer*.

There are two important questions for the user of the Matrix (the real one, not the imaginary one of Gibson). First, we have to decide where to plug in. Where the connection is made will decide what level of service the user will get: what protocols are supported, how fast they operate, what level of security is available, and who else shares the network.

The second question is how to find other people and services. You hope that most of the people you communicate with are on your own type of network: it would not make sense to have one-half of your office on a TCP/IP network connected to PSI and the other half use UUCP connected to the UUnet host. Or would it?

One key premise of this book is that protocols are not sacred collections that must be used intact. A knowledge of what a service provides lets the user pick the appropriate mix for a particular situation.

STACKS

The appropriate mix of network protocols will be the subject of the remainder of this book. The reader will notice that no answers are given; only options. Any given environment will, if computers and networks are being used to their full potential, be different from any other.

The network manager thus has three issues to decide. First, there is the architecture of the internal networks. Second, there is the choice of which edge of the Matrix to hook onto. If your local, small network is part of a broader organization, this issue may already be decided; you hook onto your organization's backbone (which in turn has connections to other parts of the world).

Assuming you have some choice in the matter, you need to next decide how the local net and backbone get connected together. If your backbone is MCIMail, for example, you have two solutions. One is to equip the PC systems on the net with modems (or put the modems on a modem server) and have individual users place individual calls to their own accounts. The second option is to use the MCIMail EMS gateway, the interface used to connect a local messaging system to MCIMail system. The advantage of a gateway is that users can have a single interface for sending both local and remote mail.

Notice that the two interconnection options provide different levels of connectivity. If you want to connect instead to a TCP/IP service provider: a regional network, a commercial provider like PSInet or AlterNet, or your own TCP/IP-based backbone, there are also different levels of connectivity. The connection can be a simple TCP/IP-based router, leaving all Internet services intact. Alternatively, you might want to build a firewall between your internal and external traffic by placing a host at the periphery and using application-level gateways to provide services like file transfer or mail.

The Core and the Periphery

The NREN

The Internet is this international, amorphous creature consisting of multiple backbones, regional networks, corporate networks, and other networks merged together into a vague mesh. There is however, a portion of the network right near the core that is under very definite guidance.

Much of the research and educational community uses federally-subsidized networking facilities. When many people in these communities speak of the Internet, they speak of this "free" core. Of course, the core is not really free. The NSFnet is funded partially by the NSF, which is funded by the U.S. Congress, which is, in turn, funded by taxpayers. Access to the regional networks almost always costs money. What makes it appear free is that charges for the core do not usually make it back directly to the end users. Users located on university campuses, in government agencies, and at national laboratories all see an essentially free Internet. Even this situation is changing as more and more universities are beginning to push charges back down the chain to the departments and end users.

The focus of this research network has lately been the NSFnet, a core system originally operated by Merit, a nonprofit consortium that also runs the state network in Michigan and that was founded with strong backing from IBM and MCI. This may soon change.

For several years, Senator Albert Gore of Tennessee has introduced bills for a National Research and Education Network, known as the NREN. The exact details of the NREN—who would use it and who would run it—have always been the subject of considerable debate, but the general idea is to plow more money into NSFnet and expand it.

Because of the size of the NREN, organizations have been jockeying for position for several years. EDUCOM, a consortium of the computing centers for over 600 universities, has been jockeying to put more educational emphasis on the NREN ("the E in the NREN" as the lobbyists like to remind people). Others, such as the library community, have also attempted to find their role in the NREN.

Gore's NREN concept was coopted in 1990 by the Bush Administration when, through the Office of Management and Budget (OMB), the administration introduced its plan for a High Performance Computer and Communications (HPCC) program. HPCC has five parts, all framed in terms of grand challenges of science that will move us happily into the next century.

Some examples of these grand challenges are trying to forecast severe weather events or predicting new superconductors. The grand challenges all require at least an order of magnitude increase in the power of computers, data storage, networks, and perhaps, software complexity.

The HPCC plows a substantial amount of money into the five areas. This money is spread out over eight different federal agencies, including DARPA, NIST, NSF, and NASA. Of the five areas, two of the most significant are a high-speed network and computer technology that can perform over a trillion operations per second.

The networking money is split into two pieces. First, there is some research money that is used for a national gigabit testbed. NSF and DARPA, in order to get out ahead of the HPCC initiative, approved some preliminary funding for this project independent of the HPCC. This project is coordinated by the Corporation for National Research Initiatives (CNRI), the same group that provides many support functions for the Internet Activities Board (the standards-making body of the Internet) and the Internet Engineering Task Force.

CNRI started with $15.8 million seed money from NSF and DARPA and combined it with over $100 million in cooperative effort, goods, and services from private industry. Some of these gigabit testbeds are discussed in Chapter 9. The gigabit testbeds will help determine the technical feasibility of a gigabit NREN.

The other part of the networking money is for what is being called the interim NREN. The interim NREN is an enhanced version of the domestic cores of the Internet, such as the current T3-based NSFnet and the cores of other federal networks such as the NASA Science Internet and the Department of Energy's Energy Sciences Net (ESnet). While DARPA is the lead federal agency on the gigabit testbeds, the National Science Foundation is the lead for the interim NREN (NSF and DARPA jointly sponsor the current $15.8 million CNRI gigabit project).

A Commercial Core

Three commercial networks—CERFnet, PSInet, and AlterNet—connected themselves in March, 1991. Connecting commercial services together means that traffic may go from one commercial user directly to another without violating NSFnet or other core network policies on appropriate use which stipulate that the Internet is only for "education and scholarly research" or other non-commercial use.

The concept of a commercial core arose in several ways. Groups like PSInet and AlterNet are purely commercial service providers. There is a mix of traffic on these commercial networks, including research activities—there is no reason why an educational institute or other legitimate Internet user can't access the commercial providers instead of the regionals. Because NSFnet allows only non-commercial traffic (however that is defined), PSInet and AlterNet commercial customers were theoretically unable to communicate because they had to access the core to exchange packets. Routers have not been designed to enforce these policies, meaning that all and any packets were routed and enforcement of appropriate use was left to the users instead of the network layer of the protocol stack.

Regionals like CERFnet (see Fig. 2-1) and commercial providers like AlterNet are both full-service providers: they give the user an interface to the network at various levels of the protocol stack, allowing users to run any IP-based protocols on the network. Some providers also furnish selected

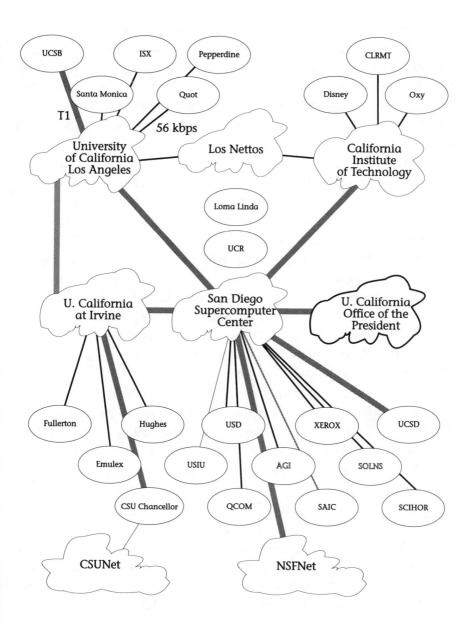

Figure 2-1 CERFnet

applications as in the case of PSI's X.500-based White Pages service.

There are several other types of groups prepared to provide services (as opposed to just products) in the commercial marketplace. Database and other information providers such as Dow Jones are already on-line and are trying to decide how best to integrate themselves into the Matrix. Dow Jones, for example, already has a Compuserve-based gateway in place.

Many information providers are investigating putting their systems directly on the Internet. Putting a service like Dow Jones on the Internet does not mean that the service is free, however. Access control can limit use by accounts and passwords and include billing for the services.

Instead of providing applications or other high-level services, other commercial providers simply provide a substrate. Here, the telephone companies are poised to increase their share of the market. In the U.S., substrates used to consist merely of leased lines. This is in contrast to most other countries, where public data networks based on X.25 are one of the few ways of moving packets.

The telcos are beginning to provide more switched services, appropriate for the bursty nature of most data flows. A T1 line is nice if you have 1 Mbps or more of sustained throughput. Putting 1 Mbps through during peaks, but leaving the pipe empty most of the remaining time can be an expensive proposition.

Technologies like the Switched Multi-megabit Data Service (SMDS) and Frame Relay are allowing the telcos to provide a bursty service to match bursty data. Many of the telephone companies are positioning themselves to provide service on a very large scale, as in the case of operating a regional or commercial network over an SMDS public data network.

Finally, there is a rather strange non-profit entity poised to try to offer commercial backbone services. This non-profit corporation, founded by IBM and MCI and run by a former

IBM vice-president, is known as Advanced Networks and Services (ANS). ANS purchases T3 lines from the telephone companies and then sells the bandwidth to NSFnet.

In addition to being the substrate provider for NSFnet, a research and educational network, ANS provides a commercial point of presence to large customers. A university, for example, may decide that it is spending too much money with its regional network and would instead ask to connect directly to a backbone.

NSFnet thus shares its facilities with commercial traffic added into the network by the ANS points of presence. How can we tell "free" traffic for NSFnet from "paid" traffic from ANS? How can we guarantee that the NSFnet gets adequate bandwidth during periods of peak demand? These are some of the questions raised by layering a non-commercial backbone over a commercial network.

ANS is clearly poised to try to provide backbone service for the new NREN. The NREN architecture is based on cost-recovery from users along with some federal subsidies. The explicit goal of NREN is to reduce those subsidies, making the NREN a potentially lucrative service for a network services company.

To provide this commercialization of the Internet, the NREN will buy service from commercial backbone service providers. ANS, as the service provider for the NSFnet, is in a good position to bid for the NREN contract when it becomes available.

Notice that ANS is a non-profit corporation, an essential status given the large federal government interest in the Internet. However, it was started with considerable financing from companies like MCI and IBM. Why would MCI and IBM start a non-profit corporation like ANS? Well, one can presume that if ANS gets an NREN contract it is going to need to use many high-speed communications lines and buy an awfully large number of routers.

The Core and the Periphery

Navigation Tools

A Matrix provides the interconnectivity, but the whole point of that connectivity is to communicate information. Finding other people (and other objects) becomes crucial as the mesh expands.

Let us focus for a few minutes on how to locate other people. Let's say we have a user on the Internet who wants to send electronic mail to a user on BITNET. Let us also assume that the user's BITNET address is known (finding the address is another issue, covered in the discussion of resource discovery in Chapter 10). Just having the address of a user on the destination network is not nearly enough—you still have to know how to format the address in such a way that your mail message will make it through the Matrix. Think of it as having the address of somebody in Thailand, but the address is in the Thai script. You need a transliteration of the address (or at least the country name portion of the address) so that the United States Postal Office knows what to do with the message.

Three books provide the basic information needed for finding how to move mail from one user to another. John Quarterman's *The Matrix* is the starting point. It is a wealth of information on major and minor topics. Need to know which computer network serves Bulgaria? Quarterman will tell you.

Even if the question of Bulgarian interconnection is low on your list, *The Matrix* is still useful. It contains descriptions of what many major networks are and how to get to them. Interested in reaching BITNET? Quarterman describes what BITNET is, the services it provides, and how Internet and other users should address mail to have it successfully reach BITNET.

The Matrix is a good source of information on how the networks were formed, what technology they use, and even who uses them. It thus provides a fascinating starting point for somebody trying to learn what kinds of networks exist.

A related reference book is *!%@:: A Directory of Electronic Mail* by Donalyn Frey and Rick Adams. Adams is the founder of UUnet, which helped transform UUCP mail delivery from a haphazard service into a dependable, commercial offering.

!%@:: is more strictly a reference work than *The Matrix*. The body of the book lists each network, how an address is formed, which networks the network is connected to, and lists of contacts for more information.

For example, in a telephone call with a Spanish colleague, the colleague may tell you that he has recently been given an account at his university. Looking in *!%@::* we see that the university is probably a node on IRIS, the Spanish National Research and Development Network. We see that IRIS is connected to HEPnet (the High Energy Physics Network), EARN (the European BITNET), and EUnet (a European UUCP-based network which is moving towards TCP/IP). We also see that if we are sending mail to IRIS from the Internet, the address we should use is:

surname@subdomain.ES

We learn that IRIS is built on top of the public X.25 network (Iberpac), supports operating systems ranging from UNIX to VMS to AOS and NOS. We also get the email, snail mail, and phone numbers for the network manager.

This information makes establishing connectivity between two users fairly straightforward. We start by just trying to send mail. If this first attempt fails, we send mail to postmaster@iris.es asking for help. If that fails, we send mail to the network manager listed in the directory.

You can use this same procedure to establish connections between any other systems. Say you need to go from the Internet to AT&Tmail? We learn that we simply send mail to accountname@attmail.com.

Tracey LaQuey has written the third essential book for people navigating the Matrix, *The User's Directory of Computer Networks*, which contains a variety of very useful lists. The book has chapters on the major network infrastructures, including BITNET, UUCP, the Internet, JANET (the British Internet), and networks based on DECnet, such as the HEPnet.

LaQuey's *User's Directory* is one of the more complete reference works around. It contains, for example, a list of all BITNET hosts at the time of printing and their capabilities. All three books, however, suffer from the same problem: they quickly go out of date. However, having an out-of-date copy is still better than having no copy as the core of the network tends to stay the same even if it gets bigger or faster.

How do we get this information on-line? Currently, there is no on-line, world-wide, all-encompassing, user-flexible directory system. The books are the places to start. There are, however, some efforts underway to try and solve these directory type problems on the network. We will look at some of the efforts for resource discovery and directory services again in Chapter 10.

For Further Reading

Cerf, V., *Thoughts on the National Research and Education Network*. RFC 1167, July 1990; 8 pp.

Frey, Donalyn, and Adams, Rick, *!%@:: A Directory of Electronic Mail* (2nd ed.). Sebastopol, CA: O'Reilly & Associates, 1990.

Gibson, William, *Neuromancer*. New York, N.Y.: Ace Books, 1984.

LaQuey, Tracey L., ed., *The User's Directory of Computer Networks*. Maynard, Mass: Digital Press, 1990.

Office of Technology Assessment (U.S. Congress), *Seeking Solutions: High-Performance Computing for Science*. S/N 052-003-01227-8. Call (202) 783-3238 for ordering information.

Quarterman, John S., *The Matrix*. Maynard, Mass: Digital Press, 1990.

Westine, A., DeSchon, A., Postel, J., and Ward, C.E., *Intermail and Commercial Mail Relay Services*. RFC 1168, July 1990.

– 3 –

A Portfolio of LANs

The debate on Ethernet vs. token ring was the second great war in the field of networks (asynchronous vs. synchronous terminals was the first). Let us look at the question of Ethernet versus token ring.

The Ethernet contingent, notably Digital and the raft of then small companies that make UNIX workstations, argued that Ethernet was the medium of choice for the modern network. Their primary argument was scaling: because Ethernet has no token to pass around, adding a node does not reduce access by other nodes (unless, of course, they all need to send at the same time). The token ring contingent, notably PC LAN companies and IBM, argued that the token ring is more deterministic, ensuring fair access to the network by all.

The network world split into these two camps. If you had Digital computers, you had the choice of Ethernet. If you had IBM mid-range systems, you had the choice of token ring. Even if you could somehow jam a token ring adapter into your VAX, you still didn't have upper-level support for the token ring in DECnet.

We revisit these tired issues to show that matters that appear to be of great importance at the time may end up being less relevant later (IBM, for example, has for some time had an Ethernet card for their mainframes). The differences between the technologies pale beside their similarities. Both token ring and Ethernet are appropriate interfaces for work groups and mid-size networks. They are both supported in open architectures like OSI and TCP/IP.

When we broaden our horizons to look at other substrates, we see that token ring and Ethernet look even more alike. Take speed, for example. They both operate at approximately the same order of magnitude: 10 Mbps for Ethernet, 4 Mbps, or sometimes 16 Mbps, for token ring.

When you compare two things, you need a baseline. We can compare two runners, see that one is faster than the other, and determine that the key to speed is, say, some particular brand of tennis shoe. However, when we see a car drive by, our attention may be drawn to the fact that shoes can only make so much difference in speed. Comparing Ethernet and token ring is like arguing about old tennis shoes.

In the world of LANs, two generations of technology are beginning to provide order of magnitude increases in speed:

• FDDI operates at 100 Mbps.
• HIPPI operates at 800 or 1600 Mbps.

Just because FDDI is faster than Ethernet does not spell the end of Ethernet; nor does the even faster speed of HIPPI spell the end of FDDI. The lesson learned from the token ring/Ethernet war was that we can have multiple types of data links working together to provide a coherent network.

The key to a coherent network is a portfolio of substrates, each used for a different, appropriate purpose. Few organizations are so specialized that a single substrate, even Ethernet, will suffice. Even if a local work group can easily fit on a small Ethernet, when that work group gets connected to a regional network or corporate backbone, other technologies will have to play a part.

Of course, the eventual solution to a detailed analysis of a particular environment may end up being a series of Ethernet networks joined together with routers. Notice the difference: it is important to consider the alternatives, not necessarily to choose them. The important point is that a conscious analysis is being made.

STACKS

In this chapter, we will discuss briefly how FDDI and HIPPI work. (After all, unless we know something about the protocols and architecture, we are unable to understand how to apply them.) Then, we will look at how two high-end installations have chosen to configure their networks. Both are supercomputer centers with extensive wide-area access from the Internet. These centers have many of the characteristics today that all networks will have tomorrow.

A Common Interface

If we accept the classification of all bit pipes into substrates with some interface on top, then the world of LANs is quite simple. There is basically one interface, with a wide variety of underlying substrates. The interface to most LAN substrates is the IEEE 802.2 standard. The IEEE, when attempting to reconcile the conflicting needs of token ring and Ethernet, decided to split the data link layer into two components:

- Logical Link Control (LLC)
- Medium Access Control (MAC)

The MAC sublayer contains any medium-dependent mechanisms, such as the carrier sense and collision detection mechanism in Ethernet, for example, or the token passing methodology underlying the token ring MAC. It is the physical layer portion of the medium that pushes the bits and the MAC sublayer that controls the pushing of the bits.

The Logical Link Control provides a common interface to the user of the LAN. The basic LLC service is the connectionless, best-effort data service; the datagram. A user, the network layer of a stack for example, submits a datagram to the LLC. The datagram contains data, an LLC address (technically, a packet type that identifies the upper-layer user), and a MAC address.

The MAC address identifies some user of the subnetwork, such as an Ethernet interface on a cable. The Ethernet interface is connected to some host which accepts the incoming

41

datagram. The LLC interface identifies the user of the data link service; the IP module of a TCP/IP stack, the DECnet routing layer, or some other network service provider.

This interface may seem exceedingly simple, but it is exceedingly powerful. As long as the network layer knows the MAC address of a user, the network layer can simply submit datagrams. The fact that the datagram has to wait until the medium is free, a token is received, or any of the other details of the underlying MAC sublayer are irrelevant. The power of this architecture is that new mechanisms can easily be added. A particular TCP/IP implementation starts out with support for Ethernet. Adding FDDI support is a trivial task because both Ethernet and FDDI use the LLC 802.2 interface.

For those schooled in LANs, the idea of a common interface may seem obvious. We will see, however, that in wide-area networks, the common interface has been a long time coming. If you want TCP/IP to work with X.25, you need to provide an interface between IP and X.25. If you want Frame Relay, you need to provide an interface between IP and Frame Relay. In the LAN world, the LLC standard provided a common interface and encapsulation was used to deal with variations, making the underlying substrate transparent to the Internet Protocol (just as IP provides that function to its own upper-layer users).

More, More, More

No matter what technology is currently in use, one can safely assume that a network manager has at least two pressing needs:

- More nodes
- More bandwidth

Technology like Ethernet can be scaled to form a LAN of up to 8000 nodes by connecting large multi-segment Ethernets with repeaters, and then using MAC-level bridges to connect all the Ethernets into one extended LAN.

Extensive or exclusive use of MAC-level bridges, however, has many disadvantages. For example, a broadcast to 100 nodes may be an appropriate way to find a service provider, but on a network with 8000 nodes the number of answers to the broadcast could quickly overwhelm the network. Using MAC-level bridges to build a very large LAN is like providing office space by dumping a bunch of desks in a warehouse—it may be cheaper, but computer networks, like groups of people, work best if tasks can be isolated in separate work areas.

Rather than scale a single network, many sites have opted to keep many small LANs and connect them together using some form of backbone. Keeping a LAN small means keeping more bandwidth available for local traffic. If the local traffic comes from diskless workstations or graphics-intensive X Windows applications, it makes sense to localize the traffic onto a small network. The topology then becomes a series of Ethernets, one of which is designated the backbone. Connected to the backbone are a series of routers, each one connecting a different work group to the backbone.

The San Diego Supercomputer Center

Figure 3-1 shows a simplified form of the network topology at the San Diego Supercomputer Center (SDSC). SDSC is one of the NSF-funded supercomputer centers on the Internet (national laboratories and research centers have many other supercomputers on the network as well). The NSF supercomputer centers were funded to provide general access to scientists all over the country.

In addition to extensive WAN access, SDSC has a considerable amount of work on-site. Corporate customers often use the facilities to do high-end work. A company that pioneered animation in the movies, for example, did some of their work on the SDSC Cray with the results piped over to an output device that produces studio-quality film. Another corporate customer used the SDSC Cray to simulate a wind tunnel: The actual application was a bird strike simulation—the computer equivalent of firing a frozen chicken at a working prototype of an engine to see if it breaks (the engine, not the chicken).

Notice in the map in Fig. 3-1 that three kinds of networks are used:

- Many Ethernets
- Ultranet
- HYPERchannel

HYPERchannel and Ultranet are both proprietary networks operating at speeds of 100 Mbps and 1 Gbps, respectively. Only a few of the Ethernet systems are used for what many consider to be their primary purpose—putting a user with a workstation on the network.

There are a few users on the network, of course. At the top of the diagram is an Ethernet visualization network. The results of a program run on a Cray can be shipped over the network to frame buffers, or moved over to a user's screen on a Sun or Silicon Graphics workstation.

Most of the network, however, is devoted to various back-end functions and to access. The back-end networks hold the servers. Some of the servers are general-purpose computers, such as a Cray YMP or XMP system. Other computers are specialized, as in the case of the Amdahl 5860, which functions solely as a file server. It is no typical file server, of course, having access to an automated tape library with three terabytes of storage (three terabytes, for the intellectually curious, is a stack of 3 ½" floppy disks over eight miles high).

Other servers on the network are a series of VAX minicomputers. These VAXen are the hosts for interactive users coming in over the Internet. They also act as output servers, holding various printers, film recorders, and other similar devices.

Two of the Ethernets are used to provide access to the outside world. Notice that both bridges and multiprotocol routers are being used. The multiprotocol routers can handle DECnet and TCP/IP connections, while the bridges are used for protocols like Digital's LAT protocols.

44

STACKS

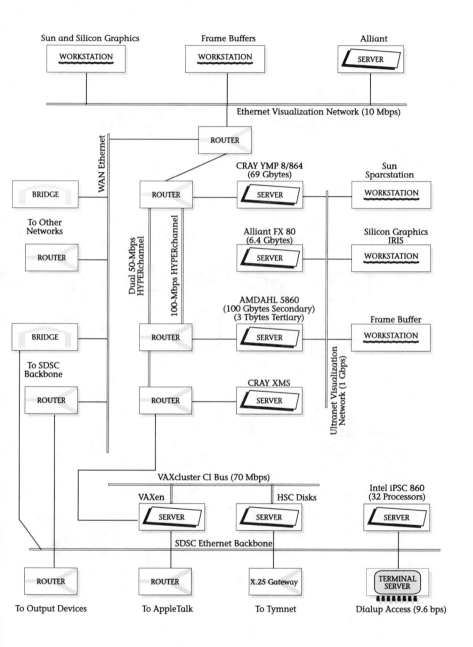

Figure 3-1 SDSC LANs

A Portfolio of LANs

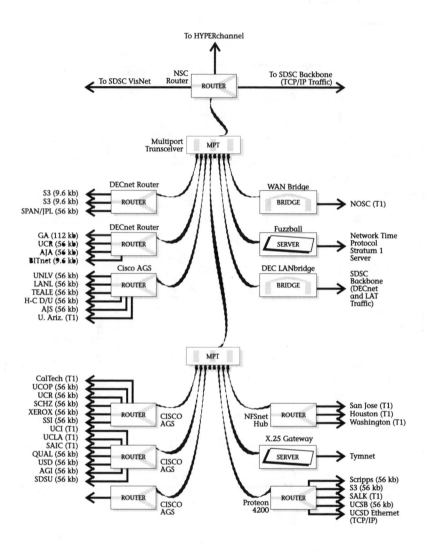

Figure 3-2 SDSC WAN Connections

46

Figure 3-2 shows the wide-area access in a bit more detail. Note that there is no Ethernet cable; a multi-port transceiver ("Ethernet in a can") is being used instead. A large number of 56 kbps, T1 (1.544 Mbps) and other WAN connections are set up to various client sites. The links to the client sites are actually CERFnet sites, because SDSC is one of the main CERFnet hubs. In addition to being a CERFnet hub, SDSC is one of the main NSFnet sites as well.

Notice the Network Time Protocol (NTP) server also on the system. In addition to routing packets for Internet nodes, SDSC is one source of accurate time for the Internet. The NTP server provides the correct time to other servers lower in the hierarchy. Coordinated time is important in a distributed environment where time is used to order events (as in the case of a database system or routing updates).

Several different Ethernet systems have links to this WAN backbone. The Naval Ocean Systems Center (NOSC) has a bridge which provides a T1 link. The SDSC backbone is on the system with both routers and bridges, and there are links to the visualization network (VISnet).

The WAN network thus provides two functions. First, it is the road in and out of the supercomputer center, for both local and remote users. A NOSC user, for example, could address a computer on the SDSC backbone through the two bridges. The second function it serves is as a switching node, routing traffic for Internet nodes, CERFnet nodes, and any other packets that happen to come through this hub.

Figure 3-3 shows a similar configuration, this time at the Center for Numerical Aerodynamic Simulation (NAS). NAS, located at the NASA-Ames research center at Moffet Field, California, is a major supercomputer site in the NASA system.

Notice that the network architecture is similar. There are several different Ethernets, each dedicated to a single function. Some Ethernets are for file servers, others are for WAN access. There are also HYPERchannel and Ultranet networks used to connect the back-end servers.

A Portfolio of LANs

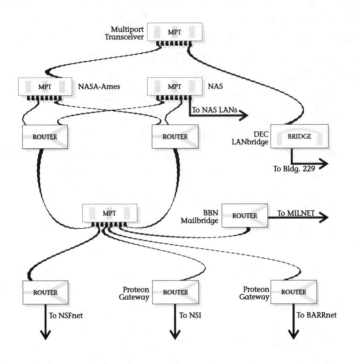

Figure 3-3 NASA-Ames WAN Connections

Figure 3-4 shows the switching system used at NASA-Ames for access to the outside world. NAS is one of several different important activities at NASA-Ames. Notice that there are, once again, multiport transceivers used to connect the devices, allowing all the components to be neatly packaged in racks in the machine room.

NASA-Ames serves as a hub for the NSFnet, the NASA Science Internet, and is a gateway into the military MILNET. It is also one of the main sites for the Bay Area Regional Research Network (BARRnet) and links different federal networks together at a router called a Federal Information Exchange (FIX). When users from these different networks

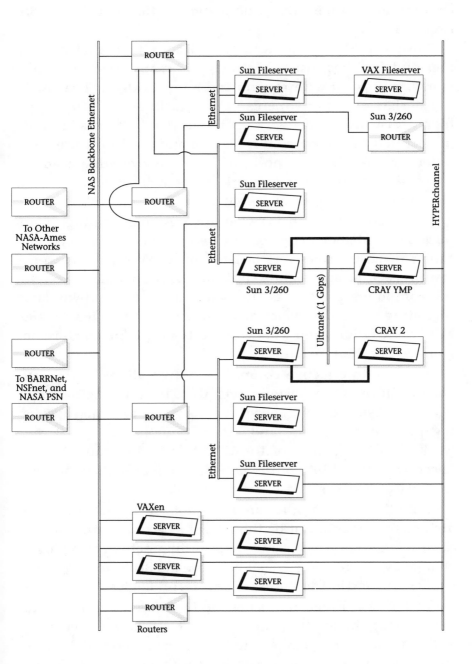

Figure 3-4 SDSC LANs

49

communicate, their traffic often passes through the NASA-Ames routers.

Both the SDSC and NASA-Ames sites (and many other high-end facilities) use this strategy of many specialized networks, connected with routers and a few bridges. The key to the design of these supercomputer facilities is a modular, highly distributed network. At this point the reader may protest that this discussion is all well and good for supercomputer facilities, but has no bearing on the everyday needs of a corporate or research network in the real world. After all, we cannot all be so lucky as to work at SDSC or NASA-Ames.

The architectures of SDSC and NASA-Ames are highly applicable to smaller networks for two reasons. First, specialization of tasks on servers isolated on work group networks can proceed at any facility, but on a smaller scale. Second, the computers used in facilities like these will quickly start migrating down to smaller environments. If you have a 100-MIP workstation (and you will), a 10-Mbps Ethernet is not going to cut the mustard.

The key to effective computer configurations has always been balance. On a system level, the CPU must be balanced with the disk size and speed, memory size and speed, floating point coprocessors, and other components. On a network level, the ability of the CPU to do work must be balanced with the ability of the network to deliver the work and take back the results.

Both these case studies are snapshots of the networks. An architecture should not be thought of as a stable, unchanging document; architectures and the resulting network topologies change over time. Fig. 3-5 shows how the SDSC topology will evolve during 1991 to embrace new technologies.

In Fig. 3-5, Ethernet backbones have been replaced with FDDI. This change from Ethernet to FDDI is not necessarily a difficult one. Remember, multiport transceivers ("Ethernet in a can") were usually used for backbones. To make the switch, the multiport transceiver is taken out and an FDDI multistation access unit (MAU) is put into the rack instead.

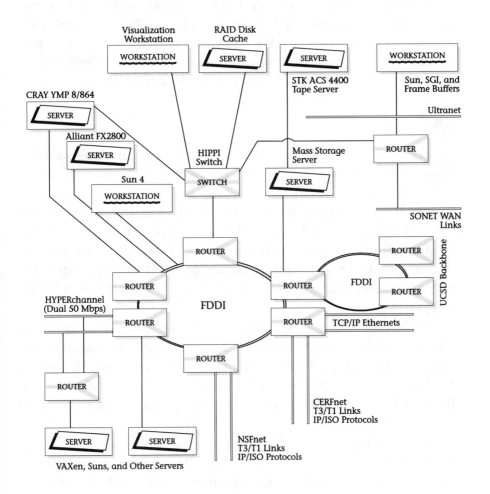

Figure 3-5 SDSC LAN Migration

Then, Ethernet controllers are taken out of the routers and bridges and FDDI controllers are substituted instead.

The Ultra network, formerly the high-end network for the back-end servers, has been moved over to be a work group visualization network. Instead of Ultranet, a HIPPI switch is installed. The HIPPI switch connects main memory caches, mass storage servers, various computer servers, and even one or two workstations.

A Portfolio of LANs

Having received a cook's tour of these two facilities, we now dig a bit deeper to look at HIPPI and FDDI. FDDI, rapidly coming on the market and being installed in campus settings, is helping to upgrade many overtaxed backbones. HIPPI is being used as a high-end, back-end network.

FDDI

FDDI is a 100-Mbps LAN, no different in functionality from other LANs. Nodes can connect directly to the FDDI network and perform their work, but at very fast speeds. However, many sites look to FDDI for another purpose—to form a campus backbone. Because FDDI can span fairly large distances (even with repeaters, Ethernets are usually under 1 km), is fast, and is stable under load, it is an ideal way of connecting several buildings, each with its own building LANs.

FDDI is a token ring system. A token circulates the ring; when a node sees a token, it has the right to capture the token, substituting data in its place. After holding the token for the specified maximum amount of time, the token is put back onto the ring and the next node has the opportunity to send data.

A full FDDI configuration is based on dual fiber rings (FDDI is also available on other media such as copper wire). Data are meant to flow on a primary ring, with the second ring acting as a backup in case of failure. If there is a failure, the ring wraps itself around using the second piece of fiber to reform the loop.

Thinking of FDDI as a ring is a bit of a misnomer. Several configurations are available. To start, let us look at the basic FDDI equipment. We can put an FDDI network together with just a series of computers communicating with each other. Each computer has an FDDI controller on which there are four connections.

Each connection has a piece of fiber connected to a neighbor. There are two neighbors, upstream and downstream.

For each neighbor there are two pieces of fiber, primary and backup.

The basic operation for an FDDI node is to take all data coming from an upstream neighbor and copy it back out to the downstream neighbor. This operation is the default. If two nodes on the opposite side of the ring wish to communicate, the controllers for all intermediate nodes must copy that data through their controllers.

To send data, a node looks for a special data pattern, the token, to be received from an upstream neighbor. Instead of copying that token back out, we send a data frame. Data frames in FDDI can be up to 4500 octets long.

When we send data through the network, they must contain an address, based on the IEEE 48-bit addressing scheme. Each node that copies data through also scans frames for its address. If it sees its own address a node does two things. First, it copies the data through to the downstream neighbor. Second, the node also copies the frame into a local buffer to be handed to upper-layer protocols.

When data are copied into the local buffer, there is a "copied" bit which is flipped before the frame is sent downstream. When the data reach the original source host, the source sees the copied bit flipped and thus knows that the frame was received.

The original host does not continue to copy the data through, or the data would stay on the ring forever. Instead, the data are removed from the ring and a token is put back on. The token goes downstream, allowing the next node to send. (Actually, the token is sent downstream before the original data are received, allowing multiple data streams to be present on the ring at once).

If we take the number of nodes on the network and the amount of time it takes each node to send data, we see that each node is assured of receiving a token within a bounded period of time. In this sense, FDDI is a deterministic protocol because a node is assured of receiving a certain amount of throughput. If other nodes do not capture the token to send data, the token circulates faster, allowing a faster than minimum throughput rate.

FDDI controllers typically also include a bypass function, an optical switch, which is used when the station is not active. The bypass function allows the ring to keep operating despite the missing link. Note that the bypass function means that the signal is not being regenerated, and is thus attenuating. If too many consecutive stations are in bypass mode, the signal becomes too weak.

An FDDI configuration can have up to 1000 physical links on a total fiber path of 200 km. If dual rings are being used, this amount is equivalent to 500 nodes on a 100-km (dual) ring. The FDDI limits are based on a single parameter, the maximum ring latency, which is 1.617 ms. The maximum ring latency is the time it takes for a starting delimiter to circulate the ring. From this parameter, the total number of nodes, the maximum distance, and a variety of other ring parameters can be derived.

For example, assume we have a total path length of 200 km. At the speed of 5085 ns/km, a latency of 1.017 ms is introduced. For 1000 physical connections, each with a latency of 600 ns, there is a further latency of 0.6 ms. Thus, the total latency of a 200 km, 1000-connection ring is 1.617 ms, equal to the maximum ring latency parameter.

While it is possible to put nodes directly on an FDDI ring, many vendors use a Multistation Access Unit (MAU) as a concentrator. The MAU is a node on the dual ring or can operate in stand-alone mode as a "ring in a can." Coming out of the MAU are (typically) 8 or 16 ports. If a station is inoperative, there is no problem with the signal attenuating because the bypass function is provided at the MAU.

One big advantage of the concentrator is that it is cheaper to provide single-ring controllers for workstations and servers than it is to provide a dual-ring attachment. In a typical concentrator-based configuration, there might be a few stations that are directly attached to the main ring. Most stations, however, are attached to the multistation access unit.

STACKS

Modes of Operation

An FDDI ring operates in two modes:

• Synchronous mode guarantees a certain amount of bandwidth and response time to nodes.
• Asynchronous mode provides dynamic bandwidth sharing.

Asynchronous mode is instantaneously allocated via the token, while synchronous bandwidth is allocated ahead of time using Station Management (SMT) protocols. Most initial FDDI implementations do not make use of synchronous mode.

Synchronous bandwidth is allocated as a percentage of the Target Token Rotation Time (TTRT), which, if every node captures the token and sends data, is equivalent to the total bandwidth on the ring. Needless to say, the sum of the synchronous allocations should be less than or equal to 100%.

Each node with a non-zero bandwidth is allowed to transmit data frames for a period of time, without starting the token rotation timer. If, after all nodes are finished with their synchronous transmissions, there is still some remaining bandwidth, nodes can do asynchronous transmission up to the limit of the token-holding timer.

Asynchronous transmission is a two-tier allocation of the bandwidth:

• Non-restricted mode provides time-slicing among all nodes that wish to send data.
• Restricted mode is dedicated to a single extended dialogue.

Normal operation is in non-restricted mode. In this mode, allocation of the token is based on a priority scheme. The priority scheme is based on the amount of time it takes for the token to circulate the ring. Each priority level has a threshold Token Rotation Time (TRT).

As the TRT gets longer and longer, lower priority levels are cut off. Nodes can then only send data of higher priorities. As the token goes around the ring with a high priority, eventually all nodes will have sent their high priority data, meaning that the token will go around the ring more quickly, allowing lower priority data frames to be transmitted.

The target token rotation timer is the total bandwidth available on the ring. After the synchronous transmission is finished, a certain amount of bandwidth remains, symbolized by the token rotation timer. The difference between the current TRT and the target TRT is thus the available asynchronous bandwidth—the minimum value of the TRT is equivalent to no synchronous traffic.

Restricted mode is entered by two nodes when a nonrestricted token is received. The first node sends an initial batch of data, and then issues a restricted token. The receiving node sends its data, then sends the restricted token back out.

Restricted mode prevents all unrestricted asynchronous traffic (including basic station management tasks such as exchanging neighbor IDs). The decision to enter, terminate, or continue a restricted dialogue is up to the higher layers that are using FDDI. Because synchronous transmission is unaffected by the token, it is unaffected by the restricted mode.

One of the functions of station management is to negotiate a maximum restricted mode time. Note that in restricted mode, there is really no need to obey the token holding timer—by its very nature, restricted mode has already preempted fairness with other nodes.

Extensions to FDDI

The dual-ring FDDI uses multi-mode optical fiber, which allows a single link to be up to two kilometers in length. There can be a total of 2000 connections to this ring, allowing a total of 1000 dual-attach stations.

An extension to the FDDI standard allows the use of single-mode optical fiber, which allows a single link to extend up to 60 kilometers in length. In addition, there are a variety of extensions proposed that would allow an FDDI-SONET mapping for bridging FDDI rings over common carrier facilities.

One extension to FDDI currently going through the standards process is known as FDDI-II. The basic FDDI is strictly packet switching: a node gets a token and sends a packet of data. FDDI-II allows a circuit switching capability to be added onto the ring through the use of synchronous mode. Each synchronous allocation is known as a Wideband Channel (WBC). The channels are 6.144 Mbps, allowing a total of 16 channels on a ring.

It is not necessary to assign all channels. If only eight channels are assigned, for example, then 49.920 Mbps would be dedicated to circuits. The remainder would be available for token-based packet switching.

HIPPI

HIPPI, the High Performance Parallel Interface, is a LAN that operates at 800 Mbps or 1600 Mbps. HIPPI has its roots in the Cray Supercomputer which uses a proprietary HSX channel operating at 800 Mbps to communicate with peripheral devices.

The original purpose of HIPPI standards was to open this HSX channel to provide support for devices like frame buffers. If a Cray is doing scientific visualization, a large amount of data will spew from the innards of the Cray which then need to be displayed on a screen. The data rate is both too fast for the limited bus speed of the workstation and too much for the limited buffer space in the workstation. The frame buffer is an alternative output device, accepting data at rates of up to 75 Mbytes per second (using an Ultra frame buffer on an Ultranet).

HIPPI is a point-to-point simplex interface. The interface is one-way: if you want full duplex communication you must set up dual connections. Point-to-point means that the inter-face is quite different than multiple access LANs. In fact, HIPPI is a circuit-oriented system (although we will see that the circuit is usually of one-packet duration).

What makes HIPPI attractive to many users is that it is fairly simple. It does not use fiber, at least in the native im-plementation. Rather, it is based on twisted pair wires. While twisted pair limits the reach of a HIPPI network to about 25 meters, it certainly makes implementations cheaper.

The basic interface is a 100-wire cable, based on fifty pairs of twisted pair wire. The interface is parallel, with 32 wires used to carry the actual data. The word size is thus 32 bits. An extension to HIPPI uses two cables—64 data lines—and operates at twice the speed, or 1600 Mbps.

The physical wires used for a HIPPI interface is in many ways just a souped-up version of other physical interfaces like RS-232. Each line is under the control of one side of the connection.

The request line, for example, is asserted by the host. When a host wants to set up a connection, it asserts the re-quest line. The connect line is asserted by the slave. When both lines are asserted, a connection is made to the switch. The switch will interpret the first data to cross the connec-tion to determine the final destination for the circuit.

In addition to the 32 data lines, there are four lines for parity checking. For every eight data lines, one parity line is calculated. The remaining lines are used to control the con-nection. The ready line is a credit mechanism. Every time the ready line is asserted, the master is able to send a burst of data. The slave can assert the ready line multiple times, allowing the master to save up credits.

The packet and burst lines are used to delineate data from the slave. HIPPI uses a framing format at the next layer that divides a packet into multiple bursts. By asserting these two lines, the host indicates that it has sent a complete packet or a complete burst.

STACKS

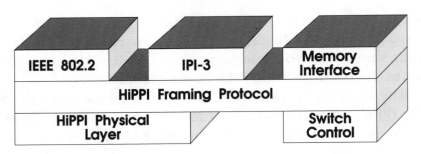

Figure 3-6 A HIPPI Stack

The remaining three lines are quite simple. The clock is used for synchronization. HIPPI uses a 40-nanosecond clock, which at 32 bits per clock cycle yields a throughput of 800 Mbps. The remaining two signals are interconnect signals which indicate that the interface is up and running.

Physical lines are simply used for transmitting data across a line. As such, this allows a permanent network of two—a host and a slave. While this is appropriate for a dedicated link on a Cray HSX channel, it is not a very useful network.

The HIPPI Standard

HIPPI takes the physical HSX definition described above and adds a few enhancements to make it a useful network. In the middle of the network is a switch. Typical switches have 8 to 32 ports on them.

To regulate the switching process and the format of the data, the HIPPI standards specify several layers on top of the physical interface (see Fig. 3-6). The framing protocol defines how packets of data are sent from one device to another. Three different upper-level protocols are used, depending on the type of device.

The upper-level protocol we see in a LAN environment, for computer to computer communications, is link encapsulation. This protocol makes the HIPPI switch appear like any other 802.2-compatible device.

Two other protocols reflect the use of HIPPI as a peripheral interface. The memory interface allows a remote coproc-

59

essor to access main memory on a host. The master (the out-board machine) initiates a HIPPI connection to the host, reads some data from memory, processes the data, and then writes the result back into the host's main memory.

The IPI-3 standard is the Intelligent Peripheral Interface. The IPI standard allows a host to treat disk drives, such as a Redundant Array of Intelligent Drives (RAID), as an extension of the systems bus.

The Framing Protocol

At the packet level, HIPPI is quite simple. It starts by making a connection, followed by one or more packets. In most implementations, the connection is automatically taken down by the switch after a single packet, but this is certainly not required by the standard.

A packet is separated into a series of bursts, each burst separated by an optional, variable wait period. A full burst is defined as 256 words. In HIPPI version one, a word is 32 bits, yielding a burst size of two megabytes.

A packet is defined as many full bursts and one short burst. The short burst is (logically enough) anywhere from one to 255 words. The short burst is either at the beginning or end of the packet, but not in both locations. Each burst, short or full, is terminated by a length/longitudinal redundancy check to ensure the data have not been corrupted.

Switch Control

HIPPI is a simplex connection between two points. To make this design useful we need a way of establishing a connection between multiple points. This is the function of the switch control portion of the protocol.

It is possible to set up a HIPPI circuit involving multiple switches. There are two ways to specify the path between two different end points in a switch environment, source-provided routing and destination addressing (where the source provides a logical destination address and the intermediate switches determine how to reach that destination).

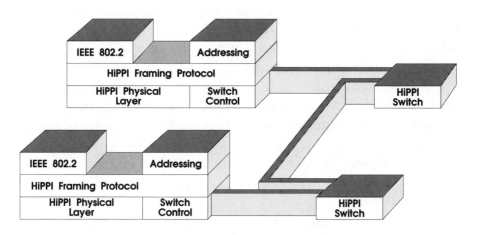

Figure 3-7 Multiple HIPPI Switches

Source-provided routing is a bit easier to implement since switches don't need routing tables. When a connection is established, the first piece of data to cross the line to the first witch is an I-field, consisting of a series of addresses. The first piece of the address sets up the first connection. In a simple single-switch environment, this information is enough to set up the connection to the end point. In a multi-switch configuration, the remaining portion of the source-provided address is handed to the second switch and so on until we run out of addresses and have a complete circuit.

The other method of addressing is to hand the first switch the name of the ultimate destination. The first switch "knows" how to set up the connection to the relevant end point, and either passes the request through to other switches that also know how to reach the ultimate destination. Routing decisions are made on a manually configured table or a background routing protocol.

The first HIPPI implementations are based on the source-provided addressing method. A node that wishes to start up a connection sends a connection request to a switch (see Fig.

3-7). The first byte is a control flag that indicates the size of data words (32 or 64 bits), the type of addressing, and various other pieces of information (such as the camp-on bit which indicates that if the connection is not available the switch should keep on trying).

After the control byte is a string which represents the address. In the case of source-provided addressing, the length of each address segment varies: it is up to the switch to know how long a particular address is. A typical source-provided address segment is four bits, allowing for 16 addresses in the route to the final destination (an unlikely diameter for a HIPPI network).

Addresses are listed in reverse order. The last address is the one that the first switch looks at. After the switch has used an address, it strips the address. This procedure shifts the addresses so that the next address is now the last one.

In addition to stripping off a used address, a switch will take the address of the source port and put it at the head of the string of addresses. By the time the connection request has gone through a series of switches and the last destination has been pulled, the address byte consists of a string of source ports, allowing the destination to reconstruct the path back to the origin.

Once a connection is set up, the source node will send a packet. The first word of the packet is for header control and includes the identification of the upper layer protocol used, such as the link encapsulation protocol.

The frame itself is split into two pieces, known as the D1 and D2 areas. The D1 area is intended for upper layer header control information, such as 802.2 LLC. The D2 area is intended for user data, as in the case of data to be written to a disk drive or the header and data items for the TCP and IP protocols (considered user data by a data link service). Separating the D1 and D2 areas allows for more efficient implementation, because the receiving end is able to place the data straight into a memory buffer without an intermediate copy operation.

The D1 data area has a size of zero to 1016 bytes. After the D1 area is an offset of zero to seven bytes, allowing the D2 to be properly aligned. The D2 area can be anywhere from zero to almost four Gbytes in length (or even infinite length if the bits of the length field are all set).

This whole packet is sent as a series of bursts, with the D1 area sometimes conforming to the first burst. If D1 is a separate burst, it may be padded with zero to 2047 bytes of fill so that the D2 will conform to a full burst.

Using HIPPI

HIPPI cannot be the basis for a single organizational LAN. Rather, it is one of many different data paths. HIPPI is used for high-volume, high-speed data bursts. A separate network would be used for other tasks.

It is not uncommon to use another network, such as FDDI, to set up a control connection between two different hosts. A workstation, for example, would set up a TCP connection to a Cray computer.

The TCP connection would be used to submit a job to be executed. Included in the job instructions would be a request to have the results dumped into a frame buffer. The Cray would then use HIPPI to set up a connection to the frame buffer and dump the results. The workstation would then set up a connection to the frame buffer to retrieve the results.

LAN Portfolios

The normal HIPPI configuration is circuit-switched: the user requests a connection to some destination and then sends one or more packets of data, each consisting of one or more bursts. Notice however, that most HIPPI implementations release the connection after the first packet is sent.

In practice therefore, HIPPI is used to send a burst of data—a datagram. Granted, the datagram is potentially very long, ranging from 64 kbytes for a maximum length TCP packet, up to 4.3 Gbytes or more for a memory or peripheral dump.

FDDI, in its basic configuration is packet-oriented. You get the token, send a packet of data, and release the token. Notice, however, that there is a circuit option through the use of wide band channels in FDDI-II.

There are some other significant differences between HIPPI and FDDI. FDDI was formulated to be used in very large local area networks. In fact, the limits of tens of kilometers for a normal FDDI dual ring means that FDDI is really a metropolitan area network (MAN) masquerading as a LAN. When you add single mode fiber options, FDDI becomes a viable backbone for a very large campus setting.

However, not all FDDI rings will be huge. As with Ethernet (which can also span fairly large distances) many of FDDI's uses are confined to a single machine room as a way of connecting back-end computers together.

It is important to understand that the choice of one LAN over another depends on the situation, not on some inherent superiority of one mechanism over the other. Because both FDDI and HIPPI use the IEEE interface, taking one out and putting the other in does not change the operation of the stacks that run over it (with the exception of a few games necessary to handle addressing and switch control in HIPPI).

Deciding which mix of technologies to use is more of an art than a science. While some vendors try and turn it into a science (witness DECconnect or the IBM Cabling System) this is really just a convenience for the user.

The best place to see how to practice this art is to look at real networks. Because the desktop computers of tomorrow are the supercomputers of today, it makes sense to look and see how supercomputer centers are configuring their LANs. These high-end computing facilities are tackling many of the issues that will be in the mainstream very soon.

For Further Reading

ANSI, "High-Performance Parallel Interface— Framing Protocol (HIPPI-FP)." X3T9.3/89-146, X3T9.3/89-013, Rev. 3.1, January 23, 1991.

——, "High-Performance Parallel Interface—Encapsulation of ISO 8802-2 (IEEE Std 802.2) Logical Link Control Protocol Data Units (HIPPI-LE)." X3T9.3/119-Rev. 2.0, December 3, 1990.

——, "High-Performance Parallel Interface—Physical Switch Control (HIPPI-SC)." X3T9.3/90-Rev. 1.6, February 28, 1991.

Lang, Lawrence J., and Watson, James, "Connecting Remote FDDI Installations" *Computer Communication Review*, Volume 20, Number 3, July 1990, p. 72.

Malamud, Carl, *Analyzing DECnet/OSI Phase V.* New York: Van Nostrand Reinhold, 1991. Includes discussions of Ethernet and FDDI.

——, *Analyzing Novell Networks.* New York: Van Nostrand Reinhold, 1990. Includes discussions of ARCnet and Token Ring.

Ross, Floyd E., et. al., "FDDI: A LAN among MANs" *Computer Communication Review*, Volume 20, Number 3, July, 1990, p. 16.

-4-

A Switching Fabric

For many years, X.25 networks and dedicated point-to-point links have been the two means available to establish wide-area links. In many countries where telecommunications is strictly regulated by the PTTs, X.25 has often been the only choice.

X.25 is an interface to a wide-area, packet-switched network. What happens when a packet enters the network is not defined: The network simply delivers the packet to the edge of the network closest to its destination, where the X.25 protocols are used to interact with the destination node.

Because X.25 is an interface with the internals undefined, X.25 is usually represented as a cloud. Figure 4-1 shows the layers of an X.25 network (with the X.25 cloud represented as blocks, which the reader can consider to be a square form of cloud). A physical layer protocol such as RS-232 or V.35 is used to form a connection between a node (such as a router that connects an Ethernet to X.25) and the edge of the X.25 cloud. The HDLC LAPB protocols are a data link protocol used to transfer data and the upper-layer X.25 protocols are used to establish and tear-down circuits and perform other control functions.

Just like Ethernet, the X.25 service is basic; it simply delivers packets. X.25 differs from Ethernet, however, in that it is based on virtual circuits. When a virtual circuit is set up, the X.25 network is informed that data will be coming for a particular destination. The X.25 network can then set up any

A Switching Fabric

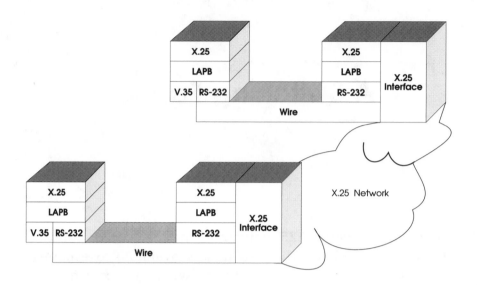

Figure 4-1 X.25

internal paths that are needed to support the virtual circuit. X.25 is also a network that guarantees the reliable delivery of data, reflecting its wide-area roots (Ethernet does not guarantee the reliable delivery of data, but it has such a low error rate that the effect is the same as if it did).

X.25 serves as a transport for two kinds of traffic. First, X.25 can be a simple packet-oriented substrate, no different, once the connection is in place, from Ethernet. X.25 is slower (the U.K. has links running at 2 Mbps and 64 kbps is a more typical maximum speed), and it is a point-to-point instead of multiple access link. Still, the basic service is the same—delivery of datagrams for the network layer.

The other use of X.25 is as a transport for terminal traffic. Here, three additional protocols, X.3, X.28, and X.29, define how a Packet Assembler/Disassembler (PAD) works. The PAD is a special user of the network that allows a character-oriented terminal to make use of a packet oriented network, essentially a wide-area terminal server. The X.3 standard defines the operation of the PAD itself, X.28 is the interface between the terminal and the PAD, and X.29 defines a protocol for a host on the X.25 network to control characteristics of the terminal session.

In the United States, X.25 is used, but only as a supplement to leased lines. If the amount of traffic between two sites is fairly large, U.S. tariffs usually make it desirable to use a leased line instead of the commercial X.25 service providers. If the number of sites linked with leased lines is large enough, it is possible to use the X.25 protocol inside of the private network.

Leased lines are not necessarily available in every country. Leased lines are frowned upon by many PTTs and in many countries the lead time of six months to a year makes planning impractical. In many places, even the use of modems on public lines is illegal. This may seem strange to those used to plugging in a modem from any location, but the message of the PTTs in many countries is clear: "Use a Modem, Go to Jail." The ubiquitous spread of fax machines has helped change the PTTs, but these are organizations that change slowly.

X.25 is fairly old technology and has served its purpose well. It has, however, begun to show its age. X.25 is a heavyweight protocol. X.25 has many bells and whistles (known as features or functions in more formal documents). These options slow it down from the basic service of delivering datagrams.

Two related efforts are taking place to supplement X.25 with other forms of wide-area, common carrier networks. First is Frame Relay, which is essentially a simplification of the X.25 protocol but run over faster facilities. Second is the Broadband Integrated Services Digital Network (B-ISDN), an architecture that will provide access to wide-area facilities at 51, 155, and 622 Mbps and, eventually, to 2.4 Gbps per channel.

Frame Relay is actually a part of the B-ISDN definition. However, to provide immediate access to Frame Relay while

A Switching Fabric

B-ISDN is being defined, vendors have lifted the interface to Frame Relay and moved it over to existing X.25 networks.

In addition to Frame Relay, another service is starting to be gain attention. The Switched Multi-megabit Data Service (SMDS), developed by the Bell Operating Companies through their research arm, Bell Communications Research (Bellcore), shares many of the characteristics of B-ISDN and is thus discussed within that framework although it is a slightly different service.

Where is ISDN?

ISDN, the Integrated Services Digital Network, has long been touted as the interface of the future to the public telecommunications network. ISDN is what a subscriber uses (assuming you can get it) to request services from a service provider.

ISDN is more than just a telephone line with a dial tone; ISDN is based on an integrated network where voice, video, data, and other services can all share a common pipe. ISDN defines a series of channels. The basic configuration, known as a Basic Rate Interface (BRI), is intended for the home user and is sometimes referred to as 2B+D.

2B+D means that the subscriber gets three pipes. Two of the channels operate at the B rate of 64 kbps. The third channel, the 16 kbps D channel, is used for signalling. If you need to make a voice call, the D channel is used to set up the call. One of the B channels then carries the traffic.

There are other variants of this basic ISDN interface. The so-called primary interface consists of 23 B channels, plus a 64 kbps signalling D channel (23B+D). This set of 64 kbps pipes is collectively known as narrowband ISDN because it is compatible with the existing copper wire going into homes.

Notice that the 23B+D has a total capacity which roughly corresponds to a T1 line. However, that capacity is divided into the individual channels. To have a single circuit with a large bandwidth, the channel would require an upper-level protocol to divide the traffic into 64 kbps channels and reassemble the data at the remote end.

Narrowband ISDN has suffered from two problems. First, there is a developing consensus that 64 kbps D pipes are of use only for low-volume applications. After the 9.6–19.2 kbps available over voice-grade phone lines, many argue there is a gap of usable bandwidth until rates of 1.544 Mbps (T1) are reached.

Consider a low-resolution PC screen, for example. If you are transferring multiple VGA screens, a 64 kbps pipe will quickly fill up. A VGA screen on a PC is 640 x 480 dots, each dot being eight bits, representing 256 simultaneous colors. Even this fairly primitive graphics interface requires 2.4 Mbits per screen. In other words, with narrowband ISDN, one screen can be transmitted every 38 seconds, suitable only for the most rudimentary application. It should be noted that some experiments with data compression over narrowband ISDN have yielded promising results, but even these data compression techniques would not provide the order of magnitude increases necessary for animation or other high-speed applications.

Another problem with narrowband ISDN is deployment. Many people argue that narrowband ISDN is compatible with the existing wiring plant and is thus "easy" to deploy. The telephone companies, however, have been fairly slow to deploy ISDN. There have been limited field trials, and a few companies are beginning to use ISDN actively. We are a long way, however, from broad deployment in the user base.

The promise of ISDN is as the standard interface for the personal communications terminal, the successor to today's telephone. Narrowband ISDN works on the existing physical plant of twisted-pair copper wires that go into almost every home. However, to move to narrowband ISDN, the user terminal needs to be upgraded, as do the switches at the RBOC (Regional Bell Operating Companies) central offices. In addition, switch-to-switch protocols, such as Signalling System 7 (SS7), need to be widely deployed to make the service useful.

All this upgrading takes time. Remember, telephone companies amortize capital expenditures over periods as long as

A Switching Fabric

30 years, a policy not conducive to rapid deployment of new equipment. Before the RBOCs will undertake wide deployment of ISDN, the different interpretations of the standards must interoperate. The Corporation for Open Systems (COS) has begun a program to solidify ISDN as a standard so user terminals and switches from different vendors can interoperate.

The key to narrowband ISDN will be to bring the price for user terminals down to the point where it is affordable. In 1991, ISDN terminals cost enough to make them only workable in select environments, such as telemarketing service centers. Widespread demand for the service will not occur until the ISDN terminal begins to approach the cost of other communications devices, such as 2400 bps modems.

Narrowband ISDN will spread a bit like facsimile services did. At first, facsimile terminals cost several thousand dollars and were only available to large corporate groups. Now, the cost of facsimile terminals are down to a few hundred dollars for stand-alone units and a hundred dollars for a PC-based fax modem.

ISDN terminals will operate the same way. Users will be able to purchase a device that controls the 2B+D lines and connects them to peripheral devices like the telephone or the computer.

Larger ISDN pipes, such as 23B+D, will be useful for small businesses. This is not necessarily how a credit card verification center might do business, but 23B+D, or a few multiples thereof, would be fine for many small and medium business, such as your local neighborhood electronic mail service center or the EDI service run by your local pizza parlor.

Broadband ISDN

An emerging standard is a variant of ISDN based on broadband technology. Broadband ISDN (B-ISDN) greatly increases the size of the pipe going to the subscriber. Initial B-ISDN subscriber interfaces will operate at 51, 155, or 622 Mbps. Because of the high speed, fiber must be used to the user termi-

STACKS

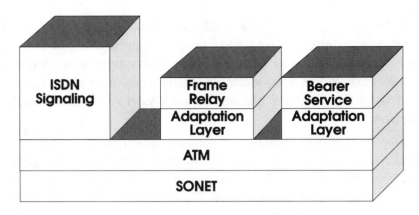

Figure 4-2 Broadband ISDN

nal instead of the existing twisted-pair physical plant. B-ISDN will first appear in dedicated campus environments or densely populated areas like lower Manhattan.

B-ISDN, like the narrowband version, provides the basis for a wide variety of different services. A user might be sending video across the link, high-speed data, teleconferencing, or any of a wide variety of other applications.

The substrate used to transmit the high-speed B-ISDN data is based on two underlying services:

• Asynchronous Transfer Mode (ATM)
• Synchronous Optical Networks (SONET).

Both ATM and SONET are beginning to be deployed (or at least widely discussed). Full B-ISDN is a bit further down the road, but the underlying technologies will be used for a variety of specialized applications.

Figure 4-2 shows the basic architecture for a B-ISDN network. At the bottom is SONET, which provides raw bandwidth at speeds up to 48 Gbps. On top of SONET is Asynchronous Transfer Mode (ATM), a switching technique which splits data into small cells and switches them between SONET links. Finally, there are the end-to-end services that use the underlying switching fabric.

A Switching Fabric

Most services, such as X.25 or Frame Relay are bearer services, available to the user for applications such as moving data between LANs or sending video signals to a workstation screen. There are also signalling services, used to handle incoming calls, allocate channels, and perform other control functions.

The adaptation layers allow upper level protocols to work within the ATM switching format. For example, a packet-oriented service would have an adaptation layer that would break a datagram into many small cells. The adaptation layer would contain the sequence numbers that would allow the remote node to reassemble the datagram (or send an error when cells are missing).

Before we look in more detail at how ATM and SONET provide these very fast services in the substrate, we will first look at Frame Relay. It is important to note Frame Relay, like X.25, is an interface to a network. That network could be a Broadband ISDN network, but it could be any other system that provides for the delivery of the frame to the indicated destination address.

The Frame Relay Compromise

Frame Relay is one of the services that will be offered on B-ISDN networks. Frame Relay is very similar to X.25, offering users the ability to send packets of bursty data across a network without tying up bandwidth during silent periods.

Although Frame Relay will eventually be offered on B-ISDN networks, it is now being deployed as an upgrade to X.25 networks. Frame Relay has some significant advantages over X.25, including speeds that go up to 1.544 Mbps and possibly higher (there is some debate as to whether Frame Relay will be able to operate at higher speeds). The similarity of the Frame Relay interface to X.25 means that routers can be easily upgraded, although the X.25 switches inside of the network need to be significantly changed to handle the faster speeds of most Frame Relay offerings.

74

STACKS

The definition of Frame Relay in the 1988 *Blue Book*, the official documents of the CCITT, is very vague. It indicates that on top of a broadband ISDN network there may be various services, of which a frame-oriented datagram service may be one of them. How that service is to be realized is left to future standards.

This fairly vague definition was taken up by a consortium of four companies, Stratacom, DEC, Northern Telecom, and Cisco, and expanded by the T1S1.2 subcommittee into a concrete interface definition. This interface definition was subsequently adopted by most other vendors in the industry and has formed the basis for ANSI standardization efforts.

The Stratacom Frame Relay specification is based on the a priori existence of permanent virtual circuits. Once the circuit is in place between two points, Frame Relay allows the transmission of bursty traffic without the overhead of extensive error detection or additional call setup.

The service is quite simple. The Frame Relay frame has a Data Link Connection Identifier (DLCI) which identifies the permanent virtual circuit, a frame check sequence, and a user data field. User data sizes vary by network, but because initial deployment is for interconnection of LANs (particularly Ethernets), a frame size of 1600 is not unusual. The DLCI addresses are usually locally administered within a single network, although there is a provision in the standard for global addressing. Flags in the Frame Relay frame provide for congestion notification, loss priority, and extending the address field.

The basic specification is thus quite simple. Issues like multicasting, address resolution protocols (to find a DLCI if one knows the network layer address of the remote node) and global addressing have been added on, but the basic network just takes a frame of data, relays it through the substrate, and delivers it to the other end of the congestion.

Built on top of Frame Relay are specifications for how different network layers should use the service. The IETF, for example, has defined Frame Relay over IP, including the definition of an Address Resolution Protocols (ARP) so a router can find the DLCI associated with a remote IP address.

Frame Relay, unlike X.25, does not guarantee error-free transmission meaning that, in a relatively error-free environment, switches inside of the network can be much faster. Because permanent virtual circuits are assigned out-of-band, there is no overhead in the protocol implementation for establishing circuits.

Frame Relay is thus ideal for connecting two LANs. To do so, a user would approach the Frame Relay service provider (e.g., companies like Sprint or MCI). The service provider would then set up the permanent virtual circuit between the two interconnection points and give the user back virtual circuit identifiers.

Once this information is in place, the user would install (or upgrade) two routers to include Frame Relay interfaces. This is typically a simple line card in the router. The routers then move data between the LANs as needed.

Alternatively, a user could establish a private Frame Relay network by leasing T1 lines from a telephone company, and then purchasing termination equipment that supports a Frame Relay interface. For example, Stratacom sells a nodal processor, a device that uses Stratacom's FastPacket (a switching technique similar to ATM) and presents interfaces to Frame Relay, voice traffic, and other users. Again, routers would need to be upgraded to use the Frame Relay interface.

Notice that Frame Relay has some limits. Initial offerings are based on permanent virtual circuits, although the specification does allow switched virtual circuits and multicasting. Nor is Frame Relay intended to scale up to extremely high speeds—most people envision Frame Relay providing service in the range of 64 Kbps up to T1 (1.544 Mbps) although there are no technical reasons why the standard could not run faster.

Frame Relay is thus X.25 stripped of much of the overhead that is not needed for simple LAN interconnection. If you have an X.25 network in place, the internals of that network are not specified by the standards, only the interface. Adding Frame Relay is simply upgrading that interface.

Is Frame Relay the "Path to Broadband ISDN" as many of its supporters claim? It is a long-needed upgrade to X.25, but does not have the flexibility, at least as deployed today, to provide the types of services we will eventually need from a public data network. Frame Relay makes sense any time a private, wide-area subnetwork is needed.

It should be noted that Frame Relay and B-ISDN are not incompatible. However, attention should be paid to the underlying substrate that a particular Frame Relay offering is implemented on. For example, the Stratacom Frame Relay interface is built on top of their IPX nodal processor, an ATM switch. In this case, Frame Relay would certainly position an organization to move into a B-ISDN world. Frame Relay itself is not necessarily the "Path to Broadband ISDN" but certain implementations may be.

Asynchronous Transfer Mode

ATM is a technology not a product. It forms the basis for different types of products. ATM is based on an assumption that a network may carry different kinds of traffic. It is possible to dedicate a separate circuit for each kind of traffic, but dedicated bandwidth wastes resources for any traffic that is bursty.

Take voice, for example. Voice typically requires a circuit of 32–64 kbps (possibly less with compression techniques). When a person is not speaking, however, he or she needs zero bandwidth. During normal speech, there are many pauses in conversation and between words—wasted bandwidth on the circuit.

During these gaps, a dedicated circuit is essentially wasted bandwidth. The bits are going across the pipe, but they are not carrying any traffic. Data are also bursty in nature. At times, datagrams are being sent and large amounts of bandwidth are needed. At other times, the pipe is empty.

77

A Switching Fabric

ATM takes all of this traffic and splits it up into small cells of 48 bytes. Two ATM devices communicate with a constant stream of cells. If somebody has traffic to send, the cell carries traffic. If not, no cell is transmitted.

An ATM switch thus accepts traffic from a wide variety of users. Because the cells are small, the switch is able to provide statistical multiplexing for different data sources over a single physical link.

The size of the cell for ATM was the subject of much debate in the standards committees. The telephone companies wanted very small cells, because with small cells there is a greater chance that cells will be available as needed and thus reduces delay for voice traffic. If voice is delayed more then around 10 ms, the result is an annoying echo which is expensive to fix.

The data people, on the other hand, wanted big cells. Big cells mean that there is less overhead in splitting up the datagrams into little pieces. Big cells, however, mean that there are fewer cells per second, and thus introduces more variable delay for voice or video traffic.

After great debate, the committees finally coalesced into two camps: one advocating 32-byte cells, the other advocating 64-byte cells. In the spirit of technical compromise, a 48-byte ATM payload was finally agreed upon.

Each ATM cell is preceded by a five-byte header. The header identifies where the cell is meant to go. It is possible that a single cell will traverse a variety of different links and go through many different switches. The header information is the basis for providing that switching.

ATM is a cell division technique. Before sending cells off to the switch, however, there needs to be some method of finding out where the cells will go. In the setup phase, the ATM switch assigns each user a virtual circuit ID. The virtual circuit ID identifies a stream of data.

A user can potentially generate many different circuits. These circuits could be for different higher-level entities such as data, voice, video, and other traffic. All these circuits from the user to at least the first ATM switch will share the same link. All traffic over a given link is identified by a second identifier, the virtual path ID.

A virtual path contains many different circuits. Based on the virtual circuit ID and virtual path ID, the switch knows where a cell should go. It takes the cell and sends it out to another link, either an end-user or another switch.

Adaptation Layers

Different users of the ATM service have different needs. Built on top of ATM are adaptation layers. Different adaptation layers provide different functions. For constant bit rate services, such as voice, the adaptation layer compensates for the variable delay in the network to make the voice come back out at a constant rate.

For variable bit rate services, such as data, the adaptation layer handles functions such as segmenting blocks into cells, handling partially-filled cells, loss of cells, and other functions. Frame Relay is defined as Class 3, one of three adaption layers for variable bit rate traffic. We will see another example of an adaptation layer shortly when we look at SMDS.

ATM as a LAN?

ATM is a technique that breaks data up into small cells to transport data. This architecture seems ideal for a wide-area environment with many different users, but a few computer companies are actually considering using ATM as the basis for local area networks.

Most current LANs (HIPPI being the exception) are based on a datagram service. As such, there are really no service guarantees. If there is a constant data rate, as in the case of full-motion video, a packet-switched network may introduce considerable jitter, delivering some packets quickly and others slowly.

When very powerful workstations are coupled to super-computers and frame buffers, there is a need for very high bandwidth. It often makes sense to set up a circuit for that traffic, guaranteeing the bandwidth to the workstation by reserving capacity at possible delay points. When data are ready to send, a circuit is set up, the data sent, and then the circuit is taken down.

There is also a need to support different kinds of traffic. Workstations are increasingly being used for sending video traffic to the desktop, as in the case of scientific visualization or medical imaging. Multiple data streams at very high volumes argue for techniques similar to ATM.

Several switch manufacturers, in conjunction with workstation companies, are examining the use of ATM as a LAN switching fabric. The workstation would send cells into a switch, much as SMDS does. Fiber would deliver cells to the workstation, although a simpler protocol than SONET would probably be used.

SONET

SONET is the Synchronous Optical Network, a standard developed by Bellcore for a point-to-point link on very high-speed optical fiber lines. SONET is being widely deployed in the telephone networks and is the target physical transmission mode for B-ISDN.

SONET defines a hierarchy of speeds, corresponding to the underlying speed of the optical carrier (OC). These OC rates operate in multiples of 51.840 Mbps. Several levels of OC rates have currently been defined:

- OC-1 (51.840 Mbps)
- OC-3 (155.520 Mbps)
- OC-9 (466.560 Mbps)
- OC-12 (622.080 Mbps)
- OC-18 (933.120 Mbps)
- OC-24 (1244.160 Mbps)
- OC-36 (1866.240 Mbps)
- OC-48 (2488.320 Mbps).

Many of the first uses of SONET will be based on OC-3 and OC-12. It is also possible for the OC-1 rate to be used to provide a counterpart to today's DS3 (45 Mbps) links. The OC-24 and OC-48 rates will be used for higher-speed requirements. In theory, the hierarchy allows up to OC-240 (12.4416 Gbps), but rates higher than OC-48 require, as they say in the standards documents, "further study."

Built on top of the optical carrier hierarchy is the electrical equivalent, known as the Synchronous Transport Signal (STS). STS signals are equivalent to their OC counterparts; STS-1 operates at 51.840 Mbps, for example. When looking at SONET operation, we usually use the STS-1 signal as a frame of reference.

An STS-1 frame is a 125-microsecond signal. The frame itself consists of 9 rows of 90 bytes for a total of 810 bytes. Of that 810 bytes, 27 bytes are reserved for overhead functions; nine bytes are for section overhead; 18 bytes are for line overhead (explained below); thus leaving a payload of 783 bytes.

The frame payload is called the synchronous payload envelope (SPE). Inside of that envelope, is a payload 87 bytes wide by nine rows deep, with nine bytes reserved for path overhead. The remaining payload available to the user is thus 774 bytes.

One function of the transport overhead is to point to the beginning of the actual payload within the payload envelope. Payloads are not necessarily aligned within frames: a payload can overlap frame boundaries. The pointer thus signals the beginning of the actual payload.

Likewise, the actual data inside of the payload itself may not begin at the beginning of the payload. A path overhead pointer signals where the real data begin. The concept of pointers is very important as they allow data to float. The frames are synchronous—they are sent one after the other. Data, however, may have to float because of jitter, a slight misalignment among two connecting paths.

A Switching Fabric

SONET includes extensive specification of how STS data streams can be combined together into bigger pipes. Three STS-1 signals, for example, are multiplexed into an STS-3 signal. Alternatively, instead of multiplexing the STS-1 signals, they can be concatenated together to form a single concatenated STS-3c pipe, used by services such as ATM.

SMDS

SMDS, the Switched Multi-megabit Data Service, is similar in some respects to Frame Relay in that they both offer an interface to high-speed, wide-area networks, based on a datagram service. SMDS, developed by the research arm of the telephone companies, Bell Communications Research (Bellcore), is meant to operate at speeds ranging from 1.544 Mbps (T1) up to 45 Mbps (T3).

SMDS provides three levels of interface to the network, each known as an SMDS Interface Protocol (SIP). At the top level, Level 3, SIP presents a datagram service. The user puts together a datagram of up to 9188 bytes and specifies an address for the destination.

The datagram service presented by Level 3 of the SMDS is a radical change for the primary developers of SMDS, the telephone companies. The RBOCs and PTTs have emphasized a circuit-switched service, not surprising given the voice-based origins of the telecommunications companies.

This datagram is then presented at Level 2 of the SIP. Level 2 takes the datagram and breaks it up into 53-byte chunks, known as cells. The ATM overhead is 5 bytes, leaving a payload of 48 bytes. SMDS then allocates another 4 bytes as part of the adaptation layer, leaving a payload to the user of 44 bytes per cell. These cells (along with cell headers) are then moved down to the physical layer.

The physical layer of SMDS is known as the Distributed Queue Dual Bus (DQDB), an interface based on dual fiber optic cables. Cells are transmitted over this DQDB to the central office. At the central office, the cells are received by a switch, known as a Metropolitan Switching System (MSS).

The MSS is a high-speed, cell-based switch. All incoming cells are routed to the appropriate output line, where they end up (in most cases) going back over a DQDB to the destination customer.

SMDS was designed to be compatible with the emerging B-ISDN standards. In particular, the switching technology is based on the ATM standards in B-ISDN. SMDS services can, at least in theory, provide a graceful upgrade path to a B-ISDN-based network.

SMDS is also based on some other key standards. The IEEE 802.6 committee has developed a standard for Metropolitan Area Networks (MANS). SMDS is closely aligned with the 802.6 standards.

Figure 4-3 shows more detail of the SMDS-based protocols. The Customer Premises Equipment (CPE) is usually a router and a CSU (the interface to the network). The router uses the DQDB bus to communicate across the Subscriber Network Interface (SNI) to the telephone company. There, an MSS—which is basically an ATM switch—switches cells. Notice that the SMDS network is within the confines of a telephone company. There are two switches in this sample network, and the switches communicate with an Inter-System Switching Interface (ISSI).

The basic service of SMDS is the transmission of datagrams of 9188 bytes or less. The MSS validates each incoming SMDS packet and makes sure that the source address matches one of the addresses that are assigned to that subscriber network interface. Address screening allows a user to restrict the source or destination addressees with which a particular CPE can communicate. This feature allows a logical private network to be formed over the broader SMDS network.

Address screening can be positive or negative depending on the subscriber preference. Positive screening allows a user to send to a certain group of people. Negative screening prohibits a user from sending to a designated group (the network equivalent of barring access to 900 phone numbers).

A Switching Fabric

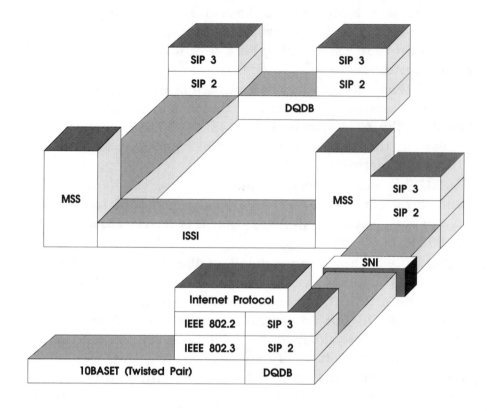

Figure 4-3 SMDS

An SMDS address is ten decimal digits in length, using the same format as telephone numbers as administered by the North American Numbering Plan (NANP). A single Subscriber Network Interface can be addressed by 16 or more different addresses.

Group addressing is used for multicasting. A multicast group can have several hundred to several thousand individual members in it. A particular individual address can participate in at least 48 different groups.

Figure 4-4 shows the SMDS packet at SIP Level 3. The SMDS address field is split into two pieces. The first four bits are the address type field which indicates if the address is an individual or group address. The next 60 bits are for

Reserved		1 byte
Begin/end tag		1 byte
Length indicator		2 bytes
Destination address		8 bytes
Source address		8 bytes
Higher layer protocol ID		6 bits
Pad length		2 bits
Quality of service		4 bits
CRC-32 Present Flag		1 bit
Header extension length		3 bits
Bridging Field		2 bytes
Header Extension		12 Bytes
Data		Up to 9188 Bytes
Pad		0-3 Bytes
CRC-32		4 Bytes (if present)
Reserved		1 byte
Begin/End Tag		1 byte
Length		2 Bytes

Figure 4-4 SMDS Level 3 Format

the ten digits used for the address. The 10 decimal digits are encoded with each decimal digit taking a nibble, 4 bits are used for the address type and the remaining 16 bits are left open. There is a provision to migrate towards 48-bit IEEE-style addresses in the future.

The header extension is used, among other things, for carrier selection. Normally, a carrier is selected as a default when the customer subscribes. In a world of highly-interconnected SMDS switches however, it may be necessary to select a carrier on a per-datagram basis.

The Level 3 Protocol Data Unit (PDU) of up to 9188 bytes of user data plus the header and trailer, is broken up into 44-byte segments and inserted into a series of Level 2 cells.

A Switching Fabric

Access Control		8 bits
Network Control Information		32 bits
Segment Type		2 bits
Message ID		10 Bits
Sequence Number		4 Bits
Segmentation Unit (Payload)		44 bytes
Payload Length		6 bits
Payload CRC		10 Bits

Figure 4-5 SMDS Level 2 Format

The Level 2 cells are basically ATM cells with an adaptation layer built in (see Fig. 4-5). The SMDS cell has a header and a footer, together with a 44-byte payload. Notice that the first two pieces of the header, the access control and network control information, are equivalent to the five-byte ATM header. The next two bytes of the SMDS cell conform to what is called the adaptation layer in the ATM cell.

The access control field has two relevant sets of bits in it. The busy bits indicate that the source is busy and should not be sent an immediate cell with data in it (empty cells are always sent). The other set of bits is used for request levels. A request level is a form of prioritization. If each cell is labelled with a priority level, the switch can control what form of data gets access to the bus during busy times. A relationship between a CPE and an MSS operates at a certain priority level.

When the CPE sets a request bit, this informs the switch that another cell needs to be sent at that priority or higher. The MSS will hold off sending lower-priority cells until it sees the request bit clear, but will send any higher-priority cells.

The network control information field is four bytes wide and has one of two values in SMDS. If the cell is empty, it contains all zeros. If the cell contains traffic for SMDS, it consists of 20 ones, six zeros, and the string 100010.

The segment type indicates the cell's contents. There are four segment type codes:

- 00: continuation of message (COM)
- 01: end of message (EOM)
- 10: beginning of message (BOM)
- 11: single segment message (SSM).

When SMDS receives a BOM cell, it checks the Level 3 address to decide how to route the rest of the message. The ATM cell header address is set to all ones.

SMDS also uses this information for two additional functions. The destination uses the segment type to decide if reassembly is necessary to form a Level 3 PDU. The switch also uses the flags as a basis for regulating the throughput of a link. If the switch sees a beginning of message or single segment message, it knows that it has seen a Level 3 PDU and can do appropriate accounting operations.

The adaptation layer has two pieces. Each Level 3 datagram is given a message identification. Each segment of the datagram has a sequence number. At the remote site, the Level 3 reassembly algorithm can detect if there are any missing cells using the sequence number.

The SMDS Physical Layer

The lowest level of SMDS is the physical layer. Until the widespread deployment of DQDB, the transmission system can be either a DS1 or DS3 line. A physical layer convergence protocol provides an insulating function, allowing future migration to other physical layers.

A DS3 signal has many similarities to the SONET physical interface (except that it is electrical and not optical). A DS3 signal is a series of frames. The DS3 frame is built as a set of seven subframes of 680 bits each. Each subframe is divided into eight blocks of 85 bits. The first bit is overhead, leaving 84 bits of payload. Out of a total of 4760 total bits, 4704 are available as the payload and 56 are devoted to overhead. The frame is sent at the rate of 44.736 Mbps. After the overhead, the DS3 yields a payload rate of 44.210 Mbps.

The DS1 signal is both slower and simpler. It has an information payload of 24 octets and a payload rate of 1.536 Mbps. The frame operates at 193 bits per frame with a gross rate of 1.544 Mbps.

On top of either of these two bit pipes is the physical layer convergence protocol. In the case of a DS3 signal, the physical layer convergence protocol constructs payloads of 12 rows of octets. These payloads are then inserted into the DS3 frame. The physical layer convergence protocol also includes path overhead and framing bytes, similar to SONET.

An example of an overhead function is the bit-interleaved parity bit, calculated on the basis of the previous frame and inserted into the overhead section of the current frame. The overhead also includes a yellow indicator, which is set after 2-3 seconds of consecutive problems have been detected. The yellow indicator is cleared after the line operates correctly for 10-20 seconds.

Access Classes

Use of the SMDS pipe is governed by a concept known as access classes. An access class is a guarantee by the SMDS network for a certain level of average throughput. A single datagram operates in a bursty fashion at the full capacity of the pipe (DS1 or DS3). The access class governs the sustained rate of throughput.

Access classes really only apply to the DS3 environment. A single access class pertains to DS1 lines, offering throughput at DS1 speeds. For DS3 lines, five sustained rates are offered:

• Access Class 1: 4 Mbps
• Access Class 2: 10 Mbps

- Access Class 3: 16 Mbps
- Access Class 4: 25 Mbps
- Access Class 5: 34 Mbps.

Access Classes 1–3 match the speeds of, respectively, the 4-Mbps token ring, Ethernet, and the 16-Mbps token ring. These matches are no surprise, of course, since one of the primary early applications of SMDS is bridging two LAN systems together.

To send a Level 3 datagram across the subscriber network interface, a node must have enough credits. The MSS monitors incoming traffic from a particular subscriber interface and discards data exceeding the credit limit. Credits are used up based on the number of bytes in the datagram. The sending node checks the length field of the PDU and determines if there are enough credits to send the datagram. If so, the datagram is sent down to the segmentation layer and the credit balance is appropriately decreased.

If there are not enough credits, the node is forced to wait. Periodically, more credits will accumulate. When enough credits accumulate, the node may send the datagram.

In the long run, credits are delivered at the rate agreed upon by a subscriber's access class. This means that the sustained throughput rate cannot be greater than the access class. In the short run, as long as credits have been accumulated, the node is able to send bursty data at the full rate of the pipe. These bursts can be fairly long, assuming enough credits are accumulated.

Is ATM the Answer?

ATM is widely accepted by the telephone companies as a way of providing simultaneous voice and data services. Not everybody sees ATM as the only answer, however. A notable exception is a research project at IBM's T.J. Watson Research Center in Yorktown, New York. PARIS is the Packetized Automatic Routing Integrated System. The assumption of

A Switching Fabric

this project is that packet switching is fine and that decomposition into cells is needless overhead for data.

The prototype PARIS switch consists of ten fiber lines, each operating at 100 Mbps. The network is virtual circuit-oriented like ATM, but uses a different approach for routing of traffic.

In ATM, each cell includes a virtual circuit and virtual path identifier. A switch looks at this information, looks up the routing in a routing table, plugs in the new VPI and VCI information, and sends the cell along the new path.

In ATM routing decisions are made for each cell by each switch. In PARIS, when a circuit is set up, the network control unit on the switch decides the appropriate path and returns that information to the user and the intermediate switches. Paths are thus preconfigured (as in SNA).

In addition to the use of packets instead of cells and paths determined by the network control unit, the PARIS switch has several other interesting features. The switch features an input throttle that prevents one user from overwhelming the switch. A user may only send a packet when it has a token. A token is sent to the user based on some average data rate. The user is able to accumulate tokens allowing for occasional bursts. If no tokens are waiting, the user must wait until the next token is delivered.

The PARIS group justifies the packet transfer mode approach by using studies on network traffic that were conducted at MIT, Berkeley, and the University of Delaware. Most of those studies showed that packets were either short (less than 50 bytes) or long (around 1000 bytes for an Ethernet).

In packet transfer mode, payloads can vary from 1 byte to 8 kbytes. The PARIS header is 12 bytes long. The PARIS team argues that, for very short packets, ATM cells have unused bandwidth, and for very long packets ATM has excessive fragmentation. The PARIS project thus argues that ATM switches have to work harder and use excessive bandwidth.

The big difference between the two projects is one of perspective. The ATM switch is based on an assumption that a network will carry many different kinds of traffic. PARIS rejects that assumption, and suggests that data traffic should use a data network.

For Further Reading

ANSI, "American National Standard–For Telecommunications–Digital Hierarchy–Electrical Interfaces." ANSI T1.102-1987.

————, "Broadband Aspects of ISDN, Draft of BISDN ATM aspects Standard" T1S1 Technical Subcommittee, T1S11.5/90-090R1 June 1990

————, "Digital Hierarchy—Optical Interface Rates and Formats Specifications". T1X1.5/90-025R3//T1X1/90-055R2, November 1990.

————, "DSS1–Signalling Specification for Frame Relay Bearer Service". T1S1/90-213R1, December 3, 1990.

Bellcore, "Generic System Requirements in Support of Switched Multi-megabit Data Service, Bellcore Technical Advisory." Bellcore Technical Advisory, TA-TSY-000772, Issue 3, October 1989.

————, "Local Access System Generic Requirements, Objectives, and Interface in Support of Switched Multi-megabit Data Service." Bellcore Technical Advisory, TA-TSY-000773, Issue 2, March 1990.

Dicenet, G., *Design and the Prospects for the ISDN*. Norwood, Mass.: Artech House, 1987.

Dix, F.R., et. al., "Access to a Public SMDS Offering" *Computer Communication Review*, Volume 20, Number 3, July 1990, p. 46.

Minzer, S., "Broadband ISDN and Asynchronous Transfer Mode (ATM)." *IEEE Communications Magazine*, vol. 27, no. 9, pp. 17-24, September 1989.

Piscitello, David M., and Kramer, Michael, "Internetworking Using SMDS in TCP/IP Environments" *Computer Communication Review*, Volume 20, Number 3, July 1990, p. 62.

– 5 –

Stacks

Different kinds of stacks—the network and transport layers—have become fungible modules. They use the same substrates. Look at a typical network cable with an analyzer and you will often see TCP/IP, DECnet, XNS, Novell, and various utility protocols (ARP, LAT, MOP) all sharing the same underlying substrate.

A given stack will support many different substrates (or go out of existence due to lack of flexibility). A given substrate will support many different stacks. This line between the substrate and the stack is one of the major opportunities for interoperability. Pick one from Column A, one from Column B, and you have a working network (or at least a working transport layer service).

The stack has several responsibilities in the network. First, the stack has the network layer and thus combines different substrates into a working internetwork. Second, the stack has the transport layer and thus provides end-to-end data transfer.

We will see that there is a bit more going on here than just the forwarding of packets and the sequencing of incoming data to form an end-to-end connection. To the user of the service, however, all stacks appear the same; the transport modules provide the interface to the network for upper-layer services.

This split between the stack and upper layer services that use the stack is not just a theoretical one. Just as vendors support many different substrates, they are beginning to support many different stacks. The substrates and stacks are then used with different applications in the computing environment provided by the vendor.

The way that stacks, substrates, and environments are combined is one of the subjects of this chapter. We will look at STREAMS and the Transport Level Interface from AT&T and the concept of towers used in DECnet/OSI Phase V, both mechanisms used to combine modules. We will also briefly examine the question of internetworking connection-oriented and connectionless networks—a method of transparently creating a path where none previously existed.

The second subject of this chapter is how stacks are being made to go bigger and faster. Very fast substrates like SMDS and ATM do no good if the transport layer refuses to submit data because of a limited ability to keep track of old, unacknowledged data still in transit. We will look at the venerable TCP transport protocol and some of the efforts that have made it go faster and faster.

For the time being, we will assume that all routers in the network have a complete, accurate routing database containing instructions on how to reach every possible destination in the network. There is no immaculate conception of routing databases, of course. We will examine this difficult issue in Chapter 6.

Towers and Streams

If the transport service is a fungible commodity, then it makes sense to hide the underlying network from the application. For example, if TCP and TP4 both provide reliable end-to-end communication, an application ought to be able to work over either one. The key to this interoperability is a transport level interface. We will look at one specific example of a transport level interface, AT&T's Transport Level Interface (TLI), part of the System V Interface Definition. TLI is built on top of STREAMS, a fundamental part of many versions of the UNIX operating system.

STACKS

STREAMS is an operating system mechanism meant to allow a process to access a device driver. The process might be a command line interface and the device driver a terminal controller, or the process might be a network stack and the device driver an Ethernet controller.

When a stream is first created, it consists of a device driver and stream head. User programs are able to send data to the stream head, which passes messages downstream. Modules can be pushed into the stream, as when an IP module is added onto a stream with an Ethernet device driver.

Because messages are passed downstream, any data from the user program would first hit the IP module. The IP module would decide what to do with the message. Usually, an IP module adds header information to the user data and then send the packet down to the Ethernet controller. There is no requirement, however, that the IP module send the same message downstream (or any message, for that matter).

STREAMS-based message passing offers quite a bit of flexibility. An encryption module, for example, might be pushed into the stream. The module takes all messages that normally would have gone from the network layer to the driver and intercepts them before passing the message on down to the driver.

What makes STREAMS so powerful is the combination of the ability to push and pop modules into the stream and the definition of standard messages. TLI is an example of a standard set of messages used by transport service providers. A user of TLI is able to specify a generic function such as "enable connection" which results in a TLI message going downstream. The TLI messages are intercepted by transport modules in the stream.

An example of a user program that uses the TLI interface is the Transport Independent RPC (TI-RPC) mechanism, part of the Open Network Computing environment. TI-RPC is a remote procedure call module that uses STREAMS and TLI to access different stacks.

Stacks

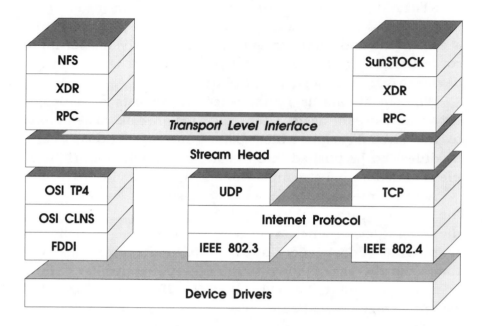

Figure 5-1 STREAMS and TI-RPC

Figure 5-1 shows a possible configuration for TI-RPC in a STREAMS environment. Notice that RPC, the user of the stream, is in turn a service provider to applications. These applications can be generic, like the Network File System, or custom programs as in the case of an RPC service on Sun's internal network that monitors the current price of Sun shares on the stock market.

User programs such as NFS are twice insulated from the underlying network. NFS communicates with RPC (using XDR to represent data), asking for services and procedures. RPC, in turn, picks whichever transport stack is available to communicate with the destination server.

These two levels of insulation do not prevent a program from exercising a high degree of control. A user program can specify the type of transport connection and other important parameters. A transactions program, for example, might specify a generic connectionless transport service, or might even specify the specific use of the User Datagram Protocol (UDP). Parameters such as the retry interval or window sizes can also be controlled if necessary.

One feature of STREAMS that makes it ideal for a networking environment is the multiplexing module which allows several different streams to be connected to make a river (to continue the water metaphor). TCP and UDP are two transport services that use the IP network layer service. The IP module would be a multiplexing module, accepting messages from both the TCP and UDP streams. A device driver, such as an Ethernet controller, can also be a multiplexing module, providing service to IP, ISO CLNS, and Novell IPX.

Notice that STREAMS is really an operating system feature which allows us to push and pop modules. Because it is part of AT&T's SVID, it plays an important role in many UNIX mutations. STREAMS has also been incorporated into other operating systems, notably Novell's NetWare Operating System.

TLI is not the only transport interface on the market. X/Open, a non-profit consortium of companies that has been remarkably successful in pushing standards out into the marketplace quickly, has defined the X/Open Transport Interface (XTI). XTI defines a standard interface between a UNIX process, the end point of the network (at least as far as the stack is concerned), and the transport service provider. The XTI interface includes provisions for connection establishment, data transfer, and connection release.

XTI, like STREAMS and TLI, is a local matter. It is simply the way for a program to request the services of a stack. In fact, it is possible to have different mechanisms on each side of a connection. An RPC user might have STREAMS and TLI as methods of using a TCP stack. On the other side, the TCP stack might use sockets as the method of operating over the operating system. Because the interface between the two systems is TCP, the fact that one uses sockets and the other uses STREAMS is immaterial.

Stacks

It should be noted that although STREAMS is an elegant architecture for providing operating system support to network modules, an elegant architecture does not always translate to ease of use in implementation. In particular, converting the large numbers of Sockets-based programs in the UNIX world to STREAMS is no trivial task. The ability to pop a new transport module onto a stream does one no good if no transport modules have been ported to STREAMS.

Towers

Another interesting example of multiprotocol support are towers, a concept used in DECnet/OSI Phase V. STREAMS is the method used in an operating system for moving data between modules. Choosing which module is left unspecified—should the application use TCP/IP or OSI to reach a destination? In DECnet, STREAMS-like functionality is provided by multithreading in the operating system. What is interesting in DECnet, however, is how it decides which combinations of protocols to use.

When an application wishes to communicate with a remote application, it contacts the session layer of DECnet, passing in the names of the application and the host. Every host in a network has a unique name, maintained by the DNA Naming Service.

The session layer sees the connection request and sends a packet to the naming service, including the name of the host. The naming service returns a set of towers. A tower is a set of addresses from the different layers. We have a data link layer address (e.g., Ethernet), a network layer address (an OSI address), and a transport layer ID. If two towers are identical, there is a path between the two applications. There may be several different paths. The application might be able to tolerate different kinds of transport protocols, for example. The tower can extend even higher, identifying presentation layer contexts, or other data that specify the nature of the connection.

STACKS

A tower set is the set of possible paths between two applications. Each application picks from this tower set. An application might prefer to use TP4, the OSI network layer, and an underlying Ethernet network. Another application, using large amounts of data, might pick the 100-Mbps FDDI data link instead, but be willing to live with the TP0 class of transport service because the underlying data link is virtually error-free.

The concept of towers is integrated into a DECnet environment through the naming service and session control layer. The session control layer maintains all local tower sets: the possible ways that a remote application might communicate with a local application. The session control layer then uses the naming service to make that information available to the rest of the network.

When an application requests a connection to some remote object, the local session control uses the DNA Naming Service (DNANS) to retrieve the remote objects tower set, then finds the intersection with local tower sets.

Often, there will be several possible paths between two applications. The path that is picked is not specified in DNA and is left up to each implementation. In DECnet/OSI Phase V, there are at least two transport service providers; the older Network Services Protocol (NSP) and ISO TP 4 (See Fig. 5-2).

A typical application in this environment is the Data Access Protocol (DAP). DAP is a service that provides a core of connectivity in a DECnet. It is used by older, Phase IV nodes as well as being a service used internally in a Phase V network.

If DAP is being used to communicate between Phase IV and Phase V nodes, then the result of the tower set is simple because only NSP can be used to communicate with Phase IV nodes. Between Phase V nodes, the tower set would include both NSP and TP4. Because TP4 appears to be a key protocol in DECnet/OSI Phase V, one would expect the application (or the session control layer on behalf of the application) to choose TP4, but there is no requirement that it do so.

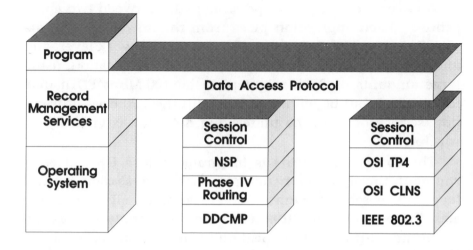

Figure 5-2 DNA Towers

Towers illustrate the problem of finding possible paths between two end points, and then choosing an appropriate one. The people who implement networks on operating systems must strike a difficult balance between making the network transparent and allowing control when it is desired.

For many applications, most characteristics of the network may be irrelevant. A messaging service, for example, may desire a reliable transport service, but not care about issues like the number of retries allowed. If the transport service breaks, the messaging service will simply retry at a later time. For a file service, however, a client module may wish to specify infinite retries, as in the case of remote mounting of the paging area for the operating system.

Transport Bridges

The DECnet/OSI Phase V towers assume that there is some path between two communicating end nodes. It uses a mechanism such as DNANS to find the tower set for each end node, then examine the intersection of the two sets. If there is some intersection, the node picks a viable one.

STACKS

What happens when the intersection of the two sets is empty? This issue if becoming real in the OSI world, where some nodes use the connection-oriented network service and others use the connectionless network service. Even though the two nodes share the same transport services and other parts of the stack, they do not have a network layer protocol in common. In effect, the two are nodes are not connected.

How this situation came to be illustrates the pitfalls of depending on OSI as a solution to all problems. OSI is broad enough to support many different computing paradigms. In many countries, at the network layer, the paradigm is a connection-oriented substrate based on X.25 protocols. If you have error-correcting, connection-oriented network protocols, the transport layer can be lightweight, based on TP0 instead of the more robust TP4.

The other half of the OSI world is not on an X.25 network, but uses connectionless services like Ethernet. For these users, TP0 would not be enough and the additional guarantees of TP4 are needed.

Note that the final service provided is the same in both cases. The combination of TP0 and X.25 is end-to-end reliable data delivery. The combination of a connectionless network service and TP4 provides the same end-to-end reliable data delivery. Upper-layer services such as X.500 do not particularly care which combination of stacks are used. The upper layers of the network will perform their tasks on either stack.

When the intersection between stacks is empty—the path does not exist—there are three possible solutions. First, you can give up, which is not usually an acceptable solution (at least without further analysis). Second, we could redo the end systems so that they support the other combination: adding an Ethernet controller to the X.25 network, for example.

The third solution is to bridge the two worlds together. This solution is known as transport-level bridging (in contrast to MAC-layer bridges). Much of the work on transport-level bridging comes from a group of Internet researchers

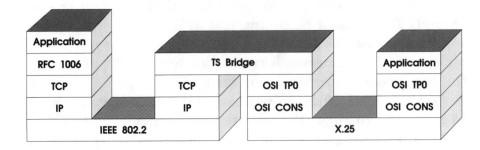

Figure 5-3 TS Bridges

that includes Marshall Rose, developer of ISODE, and Steve Kille from University College London.

A transport level bridge is a gateway between two stacks that offer the same transport service. The bridge accepts an incoming connection from one environment, starts a connection to the other environment, then simply relays data between them.

Transport-level bridges are not an elegant solution, but they solve operational problems in real networks like the Internet. The Internet will not only have connection-oriented and connectionless network services, it will also have different types of transport providers.

Figure 5-3 illustrates two concepts. First, there is a transport bridge that is used to connect two different transport stacks, in this case TCP-based and OSI-based modules. Second, there is RFC 1006, a mechanism used to graft OSI applications on top of the TCP transport layer.

The reasoning behind RFC 1006 is that TCP provides a similar functionality as ISO TP4 protocols. Because the TCP Internet has a large, stable basis, it makes sense to begin deploying ISO applications on the existing TCP infrastructure.

In addition to bridging the TCP and OSI stacks, transport bridges could also be used for bridging within the OSI environment. An application that used TP4 and the CLNS could communicate with a peer using TP0 and CONS.

The biggest issue in transport service bridging is deciding how to specify an address. When a destination gets a connection request, the source address will signify the transport service bridge, not the real source address. Likewise, when a source wishes to establish a connection, there needs to be a way to encode the real destination in a way that is transparent to the calling application.

Even if we have a convention for encoding addresses, there is still the issue of finding the bridge. This is a naming issue and can be addressed by name servers like DNANS, the Internet Domain Name System (DNS), or X.500. It can also be solved on a case-by-case basis by setting up configuration files on local systems.

How Fast Can They Go?

If you are in the business of making network protocols, it is tempting when faced with a new problem to try to come up with a new solution. This is the case with fast networks. Many researchers are proposing alternative network and transport protocols that offer features specifically designed for a world of high-speed networks.

It is interesting, however, to put this research in perspective by asking how well the current protocols perform. After all, compatibility with current protocols means that existing applications can be simply moved over to high-speed networks without any changes.

A series of studies were conducted at Cray Research, Inc. by David Borman and several others to see how fast TCP could go. Because a Cray computer can spit out data at very high speeds (the HSX channel operates at 800 or 1600 Mbps), it is important to make sure that the network does not become the bottleneck.

One Cray experiment, described in the Computer Communication Review, was a high-speed link (T3) between a Sun workstation in San Diego and a CRAY Y-MP/8 in Eagan, Minnesota. In this demonstration, two applications were run on the Cray computer and the results displayed on the Sun screen.

In such a wide-area environment, delay creates one of the biggest bottlenecks. Round-trip delay on the T3 link was 49 ms. With a small window size in TCP the window very quickly fills, and the limit on throughput becomes the amount of time it takes to get the acknowledgement back to the sender.

With the default four-kbyte TCP window, a 44.5 Mbps pipe ends up with a throughput of only 0.5 Mbps. UDP, however, had a throughput of 19.5 Mbps. Cray's calculations showed that to get 19.5 Mbps throughput of UDP with TCP, the window size would have to increase to 119 kbytes. An intermediate window size of 48 kbytes increased throughput to five Mbps.

Delay is the key in such a wide-area environment. Assume a round-trip, cross-country delay of 30 ms. The amount of data that can be outstanding is potentially the speed of the link operating for the time of the delay—the number of unacknowledged bytes that a node can send.

Cray calculated that for a DS3 line, the product was 164 kbytes. In other words, to allow any one TCP connection to use the entire 44.5-Mbps bandwidth, the TCP window must be at least 164 kbytes. For the 100-Mbps FDDI, the window size must reach 366 kbytes and for HIPPI, 2.929 Mbytes.

Even a relatively slow T1-speed satellite channel can easily have a bandwidth times delay product of 10^6 bits or more. This product is equivalent to 100 outstanding TCP segments of 1200 bytes each. Even terrestrial paths can have these problems. A 30-ms cross-country delay on a DS3 line (45 Mbps) also exceeds 10^6 bits.

Long-delay, high-speed links are known as long, fat pipes. If TCP is to work successfully over long, fat pipes, it must use the bandwidth effectively. There are really three limitations in the basic TCP protocol:

• A window size limitation

- Cumulative acknowledgements
- Round-trip timing.

To handle long, fat pipes, the transport connection must be able to handle larger windows. Larger windows mean that the node must have buffer space to keep all unacknowledged packets. The original 64-kbyte limit for TCP obviously won't work for higher-speed technologies.

The window limitation was changed with a simple extension to TCP proposed by Van Jacobson and Robert Braden which allows two nodes, at the time a connection is established, to define a window scaling factor. The factor agreed upon is used to scale the window that is actually sent.

The window scaling factor takes the actual window and shifts it over a number of bits. If a window of 00010 (binary) is sent, this normally indicates to the receiver that two bytes may be sent. However, if there is a scaling factor of three, the number is read as 10000 binary (notice that three 0s are added as we shift the window over). The window thus reads 16 (2^3) instead of 2.

Scale factors up to 2^{14} may be specified when a connection is established, meaning that the original 64-kbyte window limit for TCP is increased to 1.04 Gbytes, equivalent to a three-Gbps link to the moon.

The second problem is cumulative acknowledgements. In the default TCP specification, if a particular packet of data has a problem, the sender is forced to resend all packets after that point, even if the other packets had no problems.

A TCP option was added to handle the problem of selective acknowledgement. Negotiating selective acknowledgement (SACK) is handled in two phases. First, when the connection is set up, both sides must agree to use SACKs. Second, as an option in subsequent TCP packets, the receiver includes a SACK which specifies the length and the offset of the data being acknowledged.

The third basic problem in the default TCP specification is measuring the round trip timing (RTT). Most TCP implementations use the RTT as the basis for their retransmit timers, on the theory that if the round-trip delay is long the network is congested, and it thus takes longer to receive acknowledgments. To properly react to network congestion, we need an accurate RTT.

In most implementations, RTT is measured as the interval between the time when a packet leaves and the time it is acknowledged. Because there are cumulative acknowledgements in TCP, most RTT timers are based on a single measurement per window. While this convention is fine with small windows, it can cause problems when windows become very large.

One solution to measuring the RTT is an echo option. The data in the echo option are immediately sent back, allowing a measure of the round trip delay to be obtained at negligible cost.

How Fast?

Given all these enhancements—scaled windows and sequence numbers, selective ACKs, and echoes for timing round-trip delay—how fast can TCP/IP go? Cray tried to test the maximum speed.

First, two Cray Research computers located at NASA-Ames Research Center were connected by 800 Mbps HSX channels. Memory to memory throughput was able to reach speeds of 363 Mbps. In a software loopback mode on a CRAY Y-MP computer, speed went up to 631 Mbps. The results from this first round of testing were based on a window scaling factor of 1.

Several rounds of tuning and debugging ensued. First, the window scale was raised. Then, various changes were made to the TCP implementation, such as adding Van Jacobson's TCP header prediction algorithms. Header prediction is based on the fact that most of the time, we can predict what the values of the header fields will be (e.g., the next sequence number in the chain). If a packet meets these predictions, processing is minimal.

All these optimizations were able to increase software loopback throughput from 350 Mbps to 461 Mbps on a single processor CRAY-2 computer. The software loopback on a CRAY Y-MP computer showed memory-to-memory speeds of 795 Mbps. This experiment demonstrated that TCP and IP are not the bottleneck in limiting throughput. The limiting factors then become factors such as the memory bandwidth, interrupt processing overhead, and the amount of buffer space.

How Big Can They Get?

Before we turn to the question of how we navigate this interconnected mesh of networks, let's stop and look at how big an internetwork we may be facing. As we have seen, no single network will end up being used—the dream of a single architecture for all nodes is simply unrealistic.

Still, different architectures are being connected at different levels of functionality. Even if we have Digital's Easynet and some university on BITNET or the Internet, they can at least exchange messages.

So how many addresses will there be? This issue is intricately tied to the question of how addresses are assigned. In the TCP/IP world, for example, an address is a 32-bit integer that is split into a network address and a local host addresses.

Network addresses can be class A, B, or C. A Class A address uses seven bits for the network portion and 24 bits for the host portion. This allocation means that there can be only a few Class A networks, but each one can have many hosts.

Class B networks have 16 bits of network (actually 14 bits after you count the flags that indicate the address type) and 16 bits for the host address. This means that you can have up to 2^{16} hosts in a Class B network. A Class C network has only eight bits for the local portion, allowing up to 255 hosts.

The problem with IP addresses is that everybody wants to be a Class B network. The result is that available addresses are getting used up. As described in a presentation by Noel Chiappa, a consultant active in the Internet Engineering Task Force (IETF), the IP address space is not used efficiently.

A 32-bit address gives, in theory, four billion distinct addresses. In reality, the address space must be structured. There are 2^{21} Class C networks, or around 2 million possible networks. While most networks would be size adequately with 255 hosts, the size of the flat routing tables would kill routers.

With the Internet growing very quickly—the NSFnet routing tables had 2000 networks in October, 1990 and 2,600 networks just eight months later—it is obvious that the address space will run out at some point. Several possible solutions were advanced by Chiappa, such as rearranging the number of Class B networks, defining address extension mechanisms, or even redefining the format of the IP packet. If the format of the IP packet is revised, using the OSI packet format might be an alternative (although this solution presents some very serious conversion problems for the network).

OSI addresses present a different problem. In OSI networks, the address space supports several different addressing schemes and can be up to 20 bytes long. The address starts with an Authority and Format Indicator (AFI) that indicates the form of the following address. The AFI might signal an ISDN-style address, a telex address, or (more commonly) an ISO-administered address.

ISO addresses are assigned hierarchically based on geography. Countries are assigned certain prefixes and the country then doles out addresses. In the U.S., there are several places that will be administering ISO addresses, including the General Services Administration and ANSI. The delegation of the address space and the maintenance of address registries are two bureaucratic issues that are a long way from being solved.

How Big?

Assuming we can solve our problems of administering addresses, navigating through the web of the Internet, and solve related problems such as congestion control, how big might the networks get? Mike Roberts, vice president of networking for EDUCOM, a consortium of universities interested in computers and networking, has given this issue some thought.

Let's say there are 50 million PCs in the United States. That amount shows the potential size of a network based solely on pent-up demand. Do all of these nodes need to be part of a network? If we remember that networks have various levels of functionality, it is reasonable to say that every one of those 50 million PC systems will end up on a network, even if it is simply to pick up and drop off mail or faxes.

Can it get bigger? There are 90 million residences in the U.S. Computer literacy is currently limited to only 10 percent of households, or an initial population of nine million households, which will grow substantially. Currently, the population of college students is about eight million. If only 50 percent of young people graduating from colleges are computer literate, we can add one million new users per year.

Another way to think about the scope of this potential audience is to realize that there are over four million scientists and engineers that work in the U.S. There are already several million Internet users. Even counting a system for each Internet user and scientist (with a great deal of overlap between the two groups) would be low, as many people who are not computer literate may be using a computer embedded in a product, as in the case of a mapping system for a car that gets local topography information from the network.

Will everybody need their own network address? You bet. Simply using Kermit to upload files to a bulletin board is not going to keep anybody happy for very long. Distributed file systems, RPC-based applications, automated transactions processing and EDI, all require real network citizens, not just terminal emulators.

Look at telephone systems. There are over 90 million access lines for residents and 40 million business lines in the U.S. alone. Does each phone line require a host address? A network address?

In many cases, a single phone line will be a link to the network. Many businesses may connect one or two phone lines as the outside access path to a LAN of 50 or 100 users. Subject to access control and security, outsiders should be able to send data to any one of those individual users.

Even households will have LANs requiring many network addresses for a single access line (probably a 2B+D ISDN interface). After all, many will soon consider it absolutely essential to query the home refrigerator before leaving work to see if any shopping needs to be done.

The home network is not that farfetched. When the subject of the eventual size of the network was raised on an Internet mailing lists, several people responded with information about home networks and home control systems. One person controls her home lighting system with a PC-based controller. Her church uses a Honeywell system that controls heating and lighting functions. The next logical step is to make these functions available remotely.

Remote functions have real use. Your burglar alarm ought to be able to send a packet out over the network to your current location in times of trouble. You should be able to turn up the temperature in your ski cabin before you arrive. Of course, you would probably prefer that your ski cabin and burglar alarm are not available to others—security and access control become interesting issues in a global network.

Several interesting examples of such non-human users have shown up on the network have surfaced over the past few years. Some people at MIT hooked up their elevator on a network so they could summon the elevators while seated at their consoles, thus squeezing a few more seconds of work out of the day. John Romkey of Epilogue Technology put a toaster on the 1990 INTEROP show floor, allowing pop tarts to be warmed up before the arrival of hungry network managers. Simon Hackett in Australia was able to control a CD player located in Silicon Valley at TGV, turning on music remotely in the middle of a management meeting.

Needless to say, access control issues become a bit more important. As Vinton Cerf of the Internet Activities Board observed, this situation is a network administrator's nightmare. We can soon find ourselves coming home to find that the kids down the street turned off the water heater or the resident teenager has sent a 500 page message into the high-quality laser printer ("Does he think paper grows on trees?").

For Further Reading

Comer, Douglas, *Internetworking with TCP/IP* (vol. 1, 2nd ed.). Englewood Cliffs, N.J.: Prentice Hall, 1991. The standard text on TCP/IP.

Jacobson, V., *Compressing TCP/IP headers for low-speed serial links.* RFC 1144, February 1990, 43 pp. (Format: TXT=120959, PS=534729 bytes).

Jacobson, V., Braden, R.T., and Zhang, L., *TCP extension for high-speed paths.* RFC 1185, October 1990, 21 pp. (Format: TXT=49508 bytes).

Nicholson, Andy, et. al., "High Speed Networking at Cray" *Computer Communication Review*, Volume 21, Number 1, January 1991, p. 99.

Rose, Marshall, *The Open Book* Englewood Cliffs, N.J.: Prentice Hall, 1989. The best book available on OSI.

Sidhu, Gursharan S., et. al., *Inside AppleTalk*. Reading, Mass: Addison-Wesley, 1989.

Stevens, W. Richard, *UNIX Network Programming*. Englewood Cliffs, N.J.: Prentice Hall, 1990. A look at TCP/IP and UUCP from the point of view of the UNIX operating system. A valuable look at the internals.

X/Open, *X/Open Portability Guide, Networking Services*. Englewood Cliffs, NJ: Prentice Hall, 1988.

-6-

Glue

On a simple network, routing is simple. Workstations on an Ethernet can communicate with each other using the services of the substrate. When substrates are combined to form an internetwork, things get a bit tricky.

On a single Ethernet, there is one issue that must be resolved; mapping the network layer address to the Ethernet address. In the TCP/IP world, this mapping is performed using an Address Resolution Protocol (ARP). An ARP is a packet that contains the IP address of a desired destination. The ARP is submitted to the data link layer with instructions to broadcast (or multicast) the packet onto the substrate. The node with the target IP address (or in the case of proxy ARP, some node acting on its behalf) will respond with the mapping of the network layer to Ethernet addresses. ARPs have been defined for Ethernets, FDDI, SMDS, and most other multiaccess data links.

Address resolution is very different from routing. With address resolution, the target node is assumed to be present. When we route packets, there is a need to discover the path to the destination. Only after a path is discovered can the network layer move packets across an internetwork toward the packet's eventual destination.

In this chapter, we look at the question of how paths are discovered. By the time a data packet hits a router, the process of discovery will have been completed and a routing database constructed. The network layer module simply consults that routing database and forwards the packet.

There are several different ways of building routing databases. We will start with two extremes: manual configuration (SNA) and no configuration (extended Ethernets). Then, we will go on to look at how large internetworks can be built using dynamic routing protocols. We start with interior protocols, used within a tightly integrated routing domain. Next, we will look at how routing domains are connected to form internets (and the Internet). Finally, we will discuss policy routing.

Hardwired and Random Networks

We look first at two methods for configuring networks that can almost be considered networks without routing: IBM's System Network Architecture (SNA) and extended Ethernets. These two methods lie at opposite extremes of the routing spectrum in almost every respect, beginning with the computing philosophy behind the architectures.

SNA is a network architecture for networking an organization, as opposed to TCP/IP which is a network architecture for internetworking multiple organizations. SNA was designed to allow many terminals to talk to a few host systems in a hierarchical network architecture. While enhancements to SNA allow it to be used across organizations (and TCP can certainly be used within a single organization), SNA retains much of its original character.

An SNA network, even today, is limited to 255 nodes. A node is a host, such as a 3090 mainframe, or a communications controller, such as the 3745 or 3705. Very few SNA networks have more than 20 or 30 hosts, but these are hosts that may have several thousand simultaneous users.

Attached to the communications controller are peripheral devices. The typical device is the cluster controller, which in turn has IBM 3270 terminals attached to it. The resources attached to the communications controller are controlled by a Network Control Program (NCP) for that controller, just as the host resources are controlled through the Virtual Tele-communications Access Method (VTAM). It is this collection of NCP and VTAM instances that make up the SNA network.

Each NCP and VTAM has a routing table. The routing table is manually generated by the network manager and consists of a series of static routes. There may be alternative routes between two end points, but the alternatives are static.

When an SNA session is initialized, a path is assigned to the session. All data for that session will travel over the same path. If there is a disruption in the network, the session will terminate and a new one must be started. The disruption in service may be transparent to the user if the programmer has built in synchronization and restart facilities, but otherwise the user must start it again.

Static routing means that the process of building and managing a routing table can be quite complex. It is up to the network manager to figure out how data should cross the network. There are routing table generator tools which can automatically generate the tables, but many sites use the product of the tools as a starting point and hand-tune the tables before restarting the network.

One consequence of this approach to configuring routing tables is that when a new node gets added to the network, all the tables must be regenerated. Regeneration, of course, means that the network must stop operation. It is this type of feature that led to the old saw that if IBM ran the phone company, everybody would have to hang up when a new phone was added.

Static routing tables are not necessarily inappropriate. They won't work on large networks with thousands of nodes, but static routing tables do allow very close tuning of an SNA network with a few nodes but very large numbers of transactions.

Glue

Extended Ethernets

The opposite extreme of static routing tables is the extended Ethernet. On a single Ethernet, routing is simply the broadcasting of a packet onto the medium. If the destination node is on the network, the packet reaches its destination. If not, the packet goes into the ether.

In an extended Ethernet, a bridge operates at the Medium Access Control (MAC) layer to transparently forward traffic to another Ethernet. Forwarding of traffic is transparent to both the sender and the receiver.

To operate, a bridge must know which addresses are located on which side of the bridge. If two nodes are communicating on the same Ethernet, there is no need to forward traffic. Only when the destination address lies on the other Ethernet (or the destination address is unknown) does the bridge forward the data.

Extended Ethernets can be quite large, involving many different Ethernets. In fact, it is possible to have a single data packet cross eight bridges before reaching its true destination. Each bridge listens, recognizes the destination address, and forwards the packet.

Each bridge introduces delay. The process may be transparent to the end nodes, but the delay is not. Some time-sensitive protocols, such Digital's Local Area Transport (LAT), may timeout.

LAT is a timer driven protocol used to deliver terminal data to hosts (and host data to printers). A typical LAT terminal server will send a packet every 80 ms. Each time the terminal server sends a packet, it expects an immediate reply. A timer is set, and if a reply is not received before the timer expires, the packet is retransmitted and error recovery procedures are invoked.

If there are eight bridges in the path, 160 ms of delay can easily be added to the round-trip time, not counting propagation delay, overhead for collisions, and processing delay on the end nodes.

Timing becomes an important issue when a wide-area bridge is used, because WAN links, operating at slower rates and longer distances, may introduce even more delay. Most cases of LAT installations operating over WAN bridges to form an Ethernet limit themselves to two bridges in the path between source and destination.

Because the Ethernet service is defined as not duplicating packets, it is important for the bridge not to rebroadcast a packet back over a source Ethernet. This does not apply with only one bridge, but when there are several bridges it is possible that the topology will form a loop.

To avoid loops, an example of a routing problem in the extended Ethernet, bridges automatically organize themselves into a spanning tree, a hierarchical configuration with no loops. Between the spanning tree algorithm and automatic learning of destination addresses, the extended Ethernet is a way of automatically setting up the network.

Many network managers took the automatic configuration of bridges as a signal to build the whole network as a single extended Ethernet. While a few bridges to extend the reach of a few Ethernets makes a lot of sense, it does not make much sense to make a whole network that way (just as it does not make sense to manually configure every single route).

A big problem with an extended Ethernet is that multicasts and broadcasts can reach very large numbers of nodes or can have ambiguous semantics. If we broadcast a query for an available printer, for example, we might not want to get 500 replies.

A middle ground makes judicious use of extended Ethernets. Often, bridges will be used for certain classes of traffic, filtering out all other protocols. Because LAT does not have a routing layer, and thus cannot use routers or any resources not on a single logical Ethernet, it makes sense to use bridges to connect terminal servers on one Ethernet to hosts on another Ethernet. Bridges also make a lot of sense for work groups split over a WAN connection. The bridges isolate the services on each Ethernet, but make connectivity possible when necessary. For other services, however, many networks use the routing layer to forward traffic among different subnetworks instead of trying to make all subnetworks appear as one.

Dynamic Routing

Dynamic routing protocols are how routers discover the best path from one point to another. Before we can look at the question of dynamic routing, however, we need to organize the world of interconnected networks into a more simple topology.

This simplification is accomplished using the concept of a routing domain, known also as an autonomous system (AS). A routing domain is a network (or series of networks), the details of which are hidden from the outside world. If we present a packet to one of the routers on the border of this routing domain, that border router will figure out how to deliver a packet.

Once inside the confines of the routing domain, there may be a very complex topology, consisting of many different subnetworks and networks. This infrastructure is hidden from the outside world.

Given this hierarchy, we have two problems. First, if we are outside of the routing domain of the destination, how do we find a path to the border of the domain? This question is addressed in a subsequent section on exterior routing protocols.

The second question is how does a border router (or any router, for that matter) inside of a routing domain keep abreast of the inner topology of that domain. This question is the province of the interior routing protocol.

There are a wide variety of different routing protocols. Much of the TCP/IP world (and the XNS world) use a protocol known as the Routing Information Protocol, or RIP. Although there are differences between the XNS (e.g., true XNS as well as derivatives such as Novell's NetWare) and the TCP/IP version, the basic concepts are the same.

In RIP, every router must know the location of every node inside of the routing domain. This knowledge is gained using a periodic exchange of information. Each router sends out a packet which lists all nodes and networks that router is able to reach, along with a cost.

For instance, say that a border router knows it can reach Network 1. It sends a RIP packet to some router in the interior. Now, the interior router is able to reach Network 1. Likewise, the interior router is able to reach some interior node. By sending this information to the border router, the border router now knows how to reach that interior node by sending packets to the interior router which will know what to do with them.

In most networks, there will be many different routes to a given node. To handle the selection of the best route, RIP assigns costs to routes. The cost is some arbitrary number between 1 and 15. A cost of 16 means that a node is unreachable.

If a neighbor router sends out a RIP packet saying that Node X is available at a cost of 5, the router that receives that packet will do two things. First, the router's own routing database is updated, showing that to reach Node X, use the neighbor router.

Second, other routers must be told that we can reach Node X. The cost is no longer 5, however. The cost is 5 from the neighbor router to X, plus the cost it takes to reach the neighbor router. We thus broadcast a cost of 6 or higher (many implementations default to a cost of 1 for each hop).

RIP is known as a distance-vector routing algorithm. Distance-vector means that for each destination, there is the distance, the cost, and a vector, the name of a neighboring router. The vector just shows the beginning of the path to the destination, not the whole path.

RIP, in particular, does not scale well to very large networks. First, a cost metric of 1 to 15 limits the diameter of a network to at most 15 hops. If you want to differentiate links with different speeds by assigning higher costs to slower lines, the diameter is further limited.

A more serious problem with RIP is not the choice of metric but the basic assumption of the distance vector algorithm. A distance-vector algorithm has a router tell its neighbors about the world. Instead of passing along the status of the links in the network, the best path is pre-computed and a cost for this vector is sent to neighbors.

In times of stability, this scheme works fairly well. However, during times of network instability, RIP can take a long time to stabilize the routing database because every router is broadcasting the state of the world and it takes a while for those states to converge on a common view of the network topology.

Distance-vector algorithms may be sub-optimal, but the drawbacks should be taken in perspective. Inside of a particular routing domain, RIP works fine in small networks where RIP packets are small and the topology is simple. It is even possible to scale distance vector algorithms to medium size networks. DECnet Phase IV, for example, uses this type of routing exchange and has resulted in networks of 40,000 nodes.

To make the networks scale a bit better, however, the routing domain is split into two levels. Nodes and routers in DECnet Phase IV are organized into areas. An area can have up to 1023 nodes, but typically will have 500 or less. Most routers inside of the area are designated as area routers, which are responsible for knowing how to reach each node and router inside of the area.

A routing domain can have up to 63 areas in it. Routers on the border of an area are designated as level 2 routers. They are responsible for knowing how to reach any area in the routing domain.

If a node needs to send a packet, it hands the packet off to a Level 1 router. If the destination is in another area, the packet is handed off to a Level 2 router. The packet winds its way through the Level 2 topology until it reaches the destination area, where it is handed off to a Level 1 router for delivery.

In DECnet there are two levels of routing exchanges. First, there are packets exchanged between all Level 1 routers within a particular area. These packets allow routers to keep abreast of area topology. A similar set of packets are exchanged between Level 2 routers, allowing them to keep abreast of reachability information for areas.

Link State Algorithms

A distance-vector algorithm requires each router to inform every other router about every reachable node (or area or network). As the number of nodes increases, the amount of routing traffic can increase markedly. Another approach is the link state routing approach. In distance-vector, we tell our neighbors about the world. In a link state algorithm, we tell the world about our neighbors.

In the distance-vector approach we sends packets periodically to our neighbor with the whole state of the world. In the link state approach we send much shorter packets, containing a list of our neighbors, but we send the packets to the whole world.

Whole world, of course, is a bit of an exaggeration. Link state packets are sent to other routers. In DECnet Phase V and in the OSI protocols, the routing domain is split into areas. A link state packet would be sent to all routers inside an area for Level 1 routing, and among the Level 2 routers for inter-area routing information.

Link state algorithms have been adopted in most large networks. In the TCP/IP world, the Open Shortest Path First (OSPF) protocol is used. In the OSI and DECnet world, the protocol is the Intermediate System to Intermediate System (IS-IS) protocol. As we shall see, the two protocols are very similar.

Glue

The OSI Approach

In the OSI world, there are four sets of standards that govern the network layer. The actual deliver of the data is the responsibility of one of two different services:

- A Connectionless Network Service (CLNS)
- A Connection-Oriented Network Service (CONS).

Either the CLNS or CONS would be part of the protocol stack, used with one of the OSI TP classes. Together, they form the basic service of moving data from one node to another node.

The other two protocols are routing exchange protocols. The first is the End System to Intermediate System (ES-IS) protocol, defined in ISO Standard 9542. ES-IS allows two neighbors on a substrate to find out about each other by exchanging periodic "hello" messages.

ISO Standard 9542 is sometimes known as a neighbor acquisition protocol because it is the way that a router finds out about neighbors, both end and intermediate systems. Once neighbors are acquired, the IS-IS standard is used to exchange information between routers.

IS-IS defines the format for a Link State Packet (LSP). As with DECnet, the network is split into areas. At Level 1, the LSP contains the address of all of its neighbors. At Level 2, the LSP contains simply the prefixes that identify networks, instead of containing full host addresses. The two levels form a routing hierarchy.

Link state packets are sent periodically on a special multicast address. If a router receives a link state packet on one link, it will send that packet back out to all the other links so the packet is flooded within the area.

In addition to periodic link state multicasts, a router will send out a link state packet when the neighboring topology changes. These multicasts are sent when a new end node has joined the network, for example, or when a link goes down.

To ensure that an instable topology does not result in all available bandwidth being taken by the link state packets, there is a throttle that governs how often a particular router may send packets on the network. This throttle bounds the percentage of the total bandwidth that may be taken up by routing protocols (not an inconsequential issue on very large networks where routing protocols have, on occasion, taken up all available bandwidth).

The concept of keeping track of all neighbors is fine for point-to-point links, but may result in a very large list of neighbors on an Ethernet or other multi-access LAN. If there are several routers on an Ethernet, all the routers should have the same list of neighbors (at least on the Ethernet link). Having each router multicast this list wastes resources and leads to synchronization problems if the lists disagree. To attack the problem of the multi-access LAN, IS-IS uses the concept of a designated router. Only one of the routers on an Ethernet will send out link state packets which list the nodes on the LAN.

Selection of the designated router is part of the ES-IS protocol. ES-IS packets from routers have a priority indicator used to elect the designated router. The highest priority router wins, thus allowing an organization to have an optimized machine handle routing questions. If that optimized server crashes, however, the next election might allow another machine to become the designated router.

An end node will send packets by default to the designated router. This does not mean, however, that all other routers on the Ethernet are inactive. Occasionally, a packet will come in off the Ethernet to the designated router, then go right back out the same Ethernet to another router which has the appropriate link to move the packet one step closer to its destination.

In this case, using the designated router is a waste of processing power and bandwidth. To prevent this waste, the designated router will send out a redirect message to the end node. The original data packet is also sent out to the appropriate router.

The redirect message informs the sending node that if it wishes to send data to a particular destination, it should use a particular suggested router address. The end node will incorporate that information into the end node cache. When subsequent packets are sent, the end node cache is consulted to see if the destination is known. If not, the designated router gets the packet.

The OSPF Approach

As is often the case in the continuing wars between TCP/IP and OSI there are some pragmatists that want to make the worlds interconnect, and there are others that feel that the two worlds are incompatible. This latter view is particularly true in the area of routing protocols. For example, a t-shirt circulating in the Internet community reads:

IS – IS = 0

It turns out that there are few differences between OSPF and IS-IS, except for the fact that one works in TCP-based networks and the other works for OSI networks. OSPF takes a routing domain and splits it up into a set of network areas. The same basic algorithm as IS-IS is used to allow routers in an area, or backbone intra-area routers, to converge on a common view of the network.

There are a few minor differences, of course. For example, the OSPF specification includes provisions for a backup designated router on a multicast network such as an Ethernet. When the designated router fails the backup can immediately take over instead of having to hold a new election.

Both IS-IS and OSPF are working protocols. IS-IS forms the basis for Digital's DECnet/OSI Phase V. OSPF has several independent implementations and has been deployed in important operational networks such as the Bay Area Regional Research Network (BARRnet).

Exterior Protocols

In the TCP/IP world, networks are grouped together into collections of autonomous systems (AS). Each autonomous system is a group of hosts and routers. The routers are responsible for determining how to route traffic inside the system. The routers all share a common routing protocol (e.g., OSPF). This routing protocol is known as an interior routing protocol because it applies within the confines of the cloud that makes up the AS.

The autonomous systems are also connected to form the broader Internet. At the edge of each AS are border routers; routers that connect to another cloud. Neighboring autonomous systems may well use different interior routing protocols. To communicate reachability information among autonomous systems, an exterior routing protocol is used. An example of an exterior routing protocol is the Exterior Gateway Protocol (EGP) used to communicate between the NFSnet backbone and the regional networks connected to it.

This model is a bit simplified, as it is quite possible that, inside of the autonomous system cloud, there are multiple routing protocols. In the TCP/IP world, we often see RIP, OSPF, and a variety of other routing protocols being used, often simultaneously.

EGP is a way to exchange network reachability information among two neighbors on the border between two routing domains. This exchange can be within an autonomous system, but more often it is used to exchange routing information among different administrative domains.

EGP defines a set of basic messages that are exchanged between peers. There are three functions to the EGP protocol:

- Acquiring neighbors
- Monitoring neighbor reachability
- Exchanging network reachability information

The protocol is based on periodic polling using Hello and I-Heard-You (IHU) message exchanges. There are also commands to periodically poll a neighbor and to solicit updates.

All EGP commands and replies have a sequence number. An EGP node keeps track of the last sequence number received in a command from a particular neighbor. That sequence number is then used for all replies and indications to that neighbor until a different sequence number is received from that neighbor.

EGP divides an internet into a "core" AS and many "stub" ASs. The core AS acts as a hub for passing routing information between different stubs. Typically, a regional network would be the stub as far as the NSFnet core is concerned. A local network might then (if they are using EGP) be a stub and the regional a core.

Neighbor acquisition is based on a two-way handshake by which two nodes agree to exchange request and confirm messages. Acquisition is terminated by cease and cease-ack messages.

Neighbor reachability is determined with Hello and IHU responses. The gateway sending the Hello is in active mode, the gateway that responds is in passive mode. After neighbor reachability is determined, network reachability information is exchanged via both polls and updates. There is a minimum two-minute separation between messages to prevent flooding a network with EGP packets.

A typical router speaks some interior gateway routing protocol in addition to EGP. In a typical example, the Berkeley 4.2 EGP implementation, the router keeps two sets of tables. One has exterior routes learned via EGP exchanges. The second table keeps track of interior routes learned by some other protocol (e.g., RIP).

When a new EGP update is received, this information is put into the exterior routing table. The normal rules apply: we always update a packet in which the advertised gateway is the same as the one we have, and we also do an update if there is a different advertised gateway with a lower metric.

After some period of time, we delete an un-updated route. Generally, any route that is not updated within three times the maximum poll interval is deleted. There is one exception to this convention, the default route. Most routing protocols maintain a default route which is used whenever a network is totally unknown. The basic idea is that this router does not know, but some bigger, smarter router might have an answer.

The worst that can happen is that the neighbor router also does not know the destination and simply returns a "Destination Unreachable" message. Slightly better would be a redirect message from ICMP. Even better is that the neighbor does in fact know what to do and simply sends the packet on its way.

Policy Routing and BGP

In the original Internet, there was a simple model of a single core forming the top of a hierarchy. EGP assumes such a world. With multiple cores, the NFSnet people were forced to engineer a hierarchy by manually adjusting routes to form a spanning tree. EGP's core-centric approach is just one of its problems. The EGP protocol, like the distance-vector, requires each router to tell its neighbor about the world. As the NFSnet continued to grow, EGP messages got larger and larger.

To solve problems that result when an old protocol designed for a relatively small, slow network is used in a much faster and larger environment, EGP is being replaced with a newer protocol called the Border Gateway Protocol.

In EGP, reachability information is exchanged between neighbors. When a recipient sends the reachability information on, it makes no mention of the source. In BGP, reachability information is conveyed using what is known as an Autonomous System Path. As the information moves through the Internet, a list of the systems it traverses is accumulated. The use of paths is a straightforward way of solving problems of routing loops, and can even be used for policy based routing decisions.

The autonomous systems path is one of several different route attributes that may be attached to a route. This attribute is known as a well-known route attribute. Other route attributes (e.g., cost, restrictions, and traffic loading) can also be added on.

Routing information between systems is exchanged using an incremental fashion in BGP. In EGP, the entire database was periodically dumped. Using incremental updates greatly decreases the amount of bandwidth needed.

BGP is built on top of the TCP transport layer. Because TCP is a reliable, stream-oriented transport service, issues like retransmission, sequence numbers, acknowledgements, and fragmentation can be avoided by BGP.

BGP sessions are set up between all neighbors that are routers on the border of an AS. Normally, BGP sessions are kept between two routers located in two adjacent autonomous systems.

Because all border routers in an AS must present a common view of the world, there needs to be a way of making sure they all agree. One can use the interior protocol for moving this reachability information around. It is also possible to use BGP internally to an AS as a way of making sure border routers all agree with each other.

Policy Based Routing

BGP is based on exchanging reachability information with a neighbor. For the series of networks that our autonomous system can reach, we send a BGP message. That message has a series of path attributes. A path attribute might be list of ASs that this particular reachability information has gone through. Every autonomous system that receives the message adds itself to the path attribute.

Other path attributes can also be defined. For example, we might define the fact that a particular path is secure, cheap, or has some other attribute we like. Every time the reachability hits a new autonomous system, the BGP router examines the message. It is important for that router to indicate if this particular attribute is satisfied at this point on the path or if we have broken the chain.

Knowing that a chain has been broken is important,because eventually the message will be put to use in choosing a route. If security is an issue, for example, we may wish to know that all systems in the route between a node and its destination are able to handle that level of security.

BGP does not handle policy decisions, it only conveys the information necessary to make the policy decision. The basic information is reachability, but other policy information can easily be added on. How that information is used is up to a particular autonomous system. We might decide on an arbitrary policy that paths involving fewer autonomous systems are better than paths involving more. We might make a policy decision that we prefer going through one core instead of another.

For Further Reading

Callon, R.W., *Use of OSI IS-IS for routing in TCP/IP and dual environments.* RFC 1195, December, 1990, 65 pp. (Format: PS=381799, TXT=192628 bytes).

Clark, D. D., "Policy Routing in Internetworks" *Internetworking Research and Experience*, Volume 1, Number 1, September 1990, p. 35.

Distance-vector Multicast Routing Protocol, RFC 1075.

EGP and Policy Based Routing in the New NSFnet Backbone, RFC 1092.

Estrin, D., *Policy requirements for inter- Administrative Domain routing*, RFC 1125.ps, November, 1989, 18 pp. (Format: PS=282123 bytes).

Estrin, Deborah and Steenstrup, Martha, "Inter Domain Policy Routing" *Computer Communication Review*, Volume 21, Number 1, January 1991, p. 71.

Honig, J., Katz, D., Rekhter, Y., and Yu, J., *Application of the Border Gateway Protocol in the Internet.* RFC 1164, June 1990, 23 pp. (Format: TXT= 54988 bytes).

Jacobsen, ed., *Special Issue, Routing Protocols.* ConneXions, Vol. 3, No. 8, August 1989. Available from INTEROP, Inc.

———, *Special Issue, Routing Protocols.* ConneXions, Vol. 5, No. 1, January 1991.

Leiner, B.M., *Policy issues in interconnecting networks,* RFC 1124.ps, September, 1989, 54 pp.

Lougheed, K., and Rekhter, Y., *A Border Gateway Protocol (BGP).* RFC 1163, June 1990, 20 pp. (Format: TXT=69404 bytes).

Moy, J., *The Open Shortest Path First (OSPF) Internet routing protocol specification,* RFC 1131.ps, October, 1989, 103 pp. (857280 bytes).

Routing Information Protocol, RFC 1058.

Yu, J., and Braun, H-W., *Routing between the NSFnet and the DDN,* RFC 1133, November 1989, 10 pp. (22,607 bytes).

–7–

Environments

We are in the middle of the Open Wars. There is a pitched battle in the computer industry to control the upper layer protocols for a user's network. Particularly interesting are the "open" solutions, those standards that are presented as the solution to interoperability in heterogeneous networks:

- The Open Software Foundation
- Open Network Computing
- Open Systems Interconnection

The Open Software Foundation (OSF) is a consortium of computer companies that are attempting to define a common operating environment for workstations. The OSF effort is only a few years old, but with the backing of Digital, IBM, and Hewlett Packard it has a lot of muscle.

A very similar effort to that of OSF is a set of standards originally developed by Sun Microsystems consisting of the Network File System and related protocols, bundled under the marketing term Open Network Computing (ONC). ONC has been around for many years, and thus has a very large installed base—over a million nodes at last count.

A third environment is being presented as the solution to all problems of connectivity and communications functionality: the Open Systems Interconnection (OSI) network architecture developed under the auspices of the International Organization for Standardization (ISO). Governments in many

131

countries have adopted selected subsets of OSI, known as Government OSI Profiles (GOSIP) and have made them a requirement for interconnectivity (and, more importantly, for procurement activities).

An important difference between OSI and the other two solutions is that OSI attempts to provide the communications infrastructure instead of a complete environment. For example, OSI has a file transfer protocol instead of a distributed file system. OSI provides the protocols between systems, whereas ONC and OSF deal with the operating system and other aspects of the computing environment.

There are various other collections of protocols bundled together as operating environments that are also important. Microsoft's LAN Manager is certainly one area, as is IBM's System Application Architecture (SAA). Novell has a different environment (the NetWare Core Protocols), as do AppleTalk and Banyan.

In this chapter we will look at some of these environments and what they try to do. We concentrate on network services. These are fairly modern protocols, such as naming services, the X Window System, remote procedure calls, and similar services that form a computing platform suitable for highly functional distributed computing. We also discuss OSI and GOSIP in order to differentiate the OSI communications infrastructure from the complete computing environments found in ONC and OSF.

Rarely will an organization of any size want to settle on one of these bundles of services. OSF by itself may be appropriate for the engineering group, but the mainframe will use SAA and SNA, and finance may have DECnet, which is itself a collection of several different types of environments.

Open Network Computing

We start, for historical reasons, with the ONC platform. ONC was developed by Sun Microsystems, but is freely licensed. Over 290 organizations have licensed ONC and over 90 computer vendors have ports available. The idea behind ONC was fairly simple. A group of engineers at Sun got together and defined a protocol to build a Network File System (NFS). Thinking ahead, they took the remote procedure call and external data representation services, and defined them as general purpose protocols.

NFS is a fairly simple service. For the user, files on the network appear to be in some local virtual disk drive. Software, data, and even the operating system can be stored on one or more remote servers. The RPC service underlying NFS is also fairly simple. RPC allows a local program to communicate with a series of remote procedures. These remote procedures are accessed by the main program the same way as local procedures.

RPCs and the subsequent definition of an external data representation, are the keys to client-server computing. The program on the workstation is (usually) the client, accessing a set of services on various servers located throughout the network. An NFS server is certainly one kind of server, but we will see many other kinds of servers throughout this book.

Although ONC is best known for the NFS service, there are other services that play an equally important role in building the network environment. For example, the ONC naming service is the Network Information Service (NIS). NIS was originally known as the Yellow Pages, but Sun ran into some copyright difficulties for using a name that already had fairly definite meanings in the paper world of publishing.

NIS allows a user to present some name and get back an attribute of that name. The most basic application of this service is for naming hosts. If we have names for hosts on the network, then we do not have to refer to them by their 32-bit IP addresses (or worse, their 20-byte OSI addresses).

Giving names to computers also allows us to give a single computer multiple IP addresses, perhaps one for each network a server or gateway is on. We can also move a service to another computer. By updating the naming service with a new address the move remains transparent to the user.

There are many other uses of a naming service. Take groups, for example. When we send electronic mail, we often address groups of users. Keeping group definitions on a network-wide name service makes the groups accessible throughout the network. Names are used by many ONC protocols, including the underlying RPC mechanism and NFS. RPC uses the name service to find the location of RPC servers on the network. NFS uses the name service to find NFS servers on the network.

Figure 7-1 shows the ONC computing environment. Notice that the RPC mechanism, through STREAMS and the Transport Level Interface, can operate on both TCP/IP and OSI networks.

In addition to the ONC services, a typical Sun distributed network has another set of services, the windowing system. RPC is ideal for program-to-program communication, but the window system is better suited for program-to-display communication.

The heart of the windowing system, as with most workstations, is the X Window System developed at MIT and widely implemented. Version 11 of X, X11, is part of the Sun Open Windows environment. X is based around a workstation known as the X server. The server has a display, a mouse, and other devices. X controls how different applications can share the display with the proper events (such as a mouse click) being deployed to the appropriate program on the network that controls the window in which the event occurred.

The low-level specification of X is fine for machines, but requires a bit of work for the programmer. Toolkits are usually distributed with implementations of X that allow the programmer to easily put together a menu, window, or other common objects.

X is a bit-mapped display model. This imaging model is suitable for many tasks, but there are times when other im-

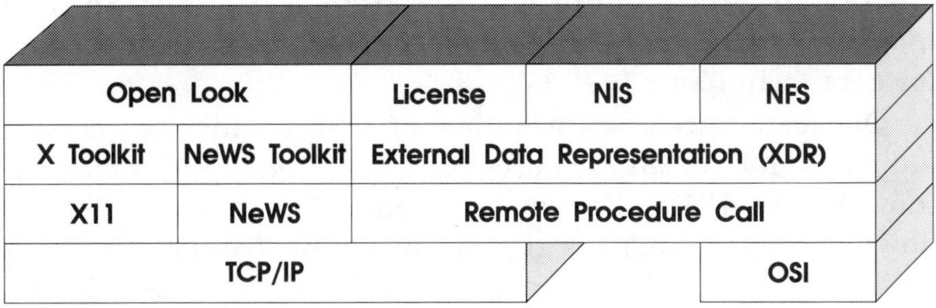

Open Look	License	NIS	NFS
X Toolkit	NeWS Toolkit	External Data Representation (XDR)	
X11	NeWS	Remote Procedure Call	
TCP/IP			OSI

Figure 7-1 ONC

aging models are useful. One such model is the Network Extensible Window System (NeWS), which is similar to Display PostScript. PostScript is a very powerful language for representing objects on two-dimensional surfaces. The extensions to the language for a windowing system include provisions for color, two-way communication, parameter driven procedures, and garbage collection.

Built on top of both X and NeWS, two alternate models for imaging and windowing, is a look and feel standard, Open Look. Open Look specifies what a menu will look like, how help functions work, what scroll bars do, and other aspects of the user interface. A common look and feel means that the user is able to very quickly access functions on new applications without extensive training.

As can be seen, the environment is a complex interaction between many different sets of protocols, operating system functions, and windowing systems. Before we delve a bit deeper into the functionality in the ONC environment, we should first look at the other two major contenders, OSF and OSI.

OSF

The Open Software Foundation (OSF) was formed as a result of companies like Digital, IBM, and Hewlett-Packard realizing

135

how important UNIX would be in the future. OSF was an attempt to wrest control of UNIX from AT&T (and Sun) so that OSF sponsors would not be dependent on competitors for core technology.

One can trace the formation of OSF to an unsuccessful bid by Digital for an Air Force contract. Digital bid their own mutation of UNIX, known as Ultrix. The bid was turned down because Digital's Ultrix was not compatible with AT&T's System V Interface Definition (SVID). When Digital was disqualified from the bidding process, they protested to the General Services Administration (GSA), arguing that to require SVID instead of any mutation of UNIX was unfair. GSA turned down the protest.

Companies like Digital and Hewlett-Packard saw the handwriting on the wall. They would need UNIX products to bid successfully on large government and corporate contracts. However, control over the UNIX interface definition was in the hands of AT&T.

The original purpose was thus to come up with a non-AT&T UNIX, based on standard interface definitions like the Portable Operating System Interface (POSIX) and other definitions for operating systems.

When the OSF group got together, however, they realized that providing an operating system definition would, by itself, not be enough. Distributed computing environments are based on more than UNIX kernels; they include window systems, RPCs, naming services, and a variety of other mechanisms.

The scope of OSF quickly expanded to include more than the standard definition of an operating system (known as OSF/1). OSF submitted Requests for Technology (RFTs) to the industry and a mad scramble ensued to turn vendors' proprietary solutions into OSF standards.

Figure 7-2 shows the OSF environmental stack. Notice that the core is OSF/1, a portable operating system. OSF/1 takes features from POSIX, SVID, and other operating system interfaces and blends them into the OSF/1 specification.

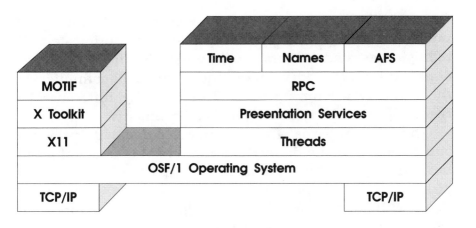

Figure 7-2 OSF

Built on top of that specification is a threads mechanism, which allows a process to start a task without waiting for it to complete before going on to other matters.

One of the main areas for standardization is the area known as the Distributed Computing Environment (OSF/DCE). DCE is the interface from the workstation to the network. DCE includes a naming service, a remote procedure call, and a distributed file system.

DCE has been one of OSF's biggest areas of controversy. The remote procedure call, taken from Hewlett-Packard's NCS architecture, is in direct competition with ONC's RPC. The file system, taken from the Andrew File System (AFS) at Carnegie-Mellon University and subsequently commercialized by Transarc Corporation, is in direct competition with NFS.

Another area that OSF has addressed is the question of window systems. Based on the X Window System, OSF added a standard set of tools and a "look and feel" toolkit for windows known as MOTIF. MOTIF defines what a standard component on a screen might look and act like: menu bars, window appearances, borders, backgrounds, and the like.

Environments

OSI and GOSIP

OSF and ONC are, to some extent, focused on the local computing environment where workstations communicate with tightly integrated servers. OSI protocols, in contrast, are aimed at a much wider environment where all computers in the world can communicate. This is a key difference between OSI and the OSF and ONC environments.

The OSI standards effort is a massive one, with protocols and standards being defined for an incredible range of activities, ranging from conferencing to transaction processing to distributed databases. The OSI agenda is extremely ambitious, with a large part of the effort going into network management, security, and applications.

Not everybody, indeed probably no single vendor, will ever implement all of OSI. Instead, a subset is picked. There are various subsets that have been defined, but the most popular ones are the Government OSI Profiles (GOSIPs).

Why should government standards be so influential? Government in most countries are also one of the largest customers for computer equipment. A GOSIP standard in Britain, Japan, the U.S., or any other country tends to get a vendor's attention.

The effect of government procurement standards can be dramatic. Many people credit the U.S. government's wholehearted support for TCP/IP with the introduction of so many products. The heterogeneous nature of the TCP/IP market in turn attracted research laboratories, corporations, and many others to the marketplace.

The GOSIP profile is fairly simple. In the U.S., for example, GOSIP requires FTAM for file access services, X.400 for messaging, and a simple subset of the OSI lower layers (See Fig. 7-3). GOSIP is not meant to take the place of environments like OSF or ONC, only to supplement standardized, UNIX-compatible computing enviornments witha general communications enviornment. The two are not incompatible.

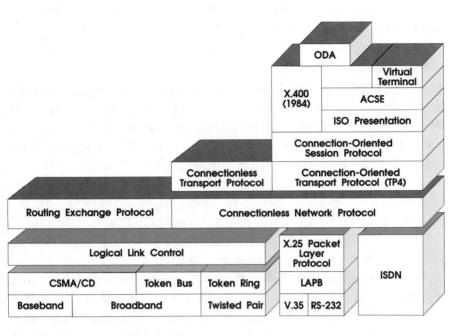

Figure 7-3 GOSIP Version 2

An important aspect of GOSIP is that it requires only that a collection of systems offer the GOSIP services, not that every one of those systems use GOSIP services as its native communications protocol stack. It does not matter if a workstation runs Novell NetWare on top of an ARCnet interface, so long as at least one server on the network supports GOSIP services. GOSIP defines a standard interface into a network and makes no requirements as to what happens on the other side of that interface.

GOSIP standards are not meant to be a single, static architecture. The groups that drive GOSIP—in the U.S., the National Institute of Standards and Technology—envision GOSIP profiles as representing waves of technology. Version 1 of U.S. GOSIP, for example, did not include the virtual terminal service or the ES-IS routing protocols, features added in Version 2. Version 3, assuming the profiles work as intended and continue to gain support with government agencies, will have even more functionality.

The O* Wars

Any one of the environments described in this chapter could be the subject of a complete book—Marshall Rose's *The Open Book* is devoted exclusively to OSI, for example. The subsets picked by a particular vendor (Digital's DECnet Phase V for example) can also easily fill a volume.

It is useful, however, to step back for a moment and look at which services are being offered. It is interesting to see how similar environments like OSF and ONC are. We saw in Chapter 5 that underlying transport stacks such as OSI or TCP/IP also deliver very similar functionality.

These similarities mean that gateways can begin connecting different environments together. In message handling, for example, UUCP, X.400, SMTP, and many other message handling domains have been connected together with minimal loss of functionality and transparency at the gateway.

Window Systems

The RPC paradigm is appropriate for clients and servers that are doing cooperative distributed computing to communicate with each other. There is another paradigm that is also used on the network, asynchronous events (e.g., interrrupts) from programs that are displayed on workstation screens. This is the domain of the window system.

Both OSF and ONC use windowing based on the X Window System, developed at MIT as part of the Athena project (Athena also brought us Kerberos, an important security mechanism discussed in Chapter 8).

The X Window System is a way for different programs on the network to share the real estate on a user's display screen. Note that the workstation now becomes the server—the windows server—and the program becomes the client. The workstation and the host computer have switched roles from their RPC relationship.

The X server on the workstation handles events from many different clients throughout the network. One client may wish to redraw a window, another may want to resize a window, a third may wish to display a menu. The X server takes these events and decides how to handle them: in which order, to which program on the workstation, and how to handle display issues like colors.

X by itself is thus an asynchronous protocol for the network allowing the transmission of events. The X server takes those events and gives them meaning, both within the context of the X protocol and for particular application programs.

X handles how windows are displayed, but is strictly a bit-mapped imaging model. Bitmaps are not very useful for 3-D imaging, or applications that can make better use of imaging models like PostScript. Many X implementations thus use X as the basic controller, but then add other imaging models inside the window. Digital's DECwindows is an example of such a hybrid. Application programs have at their disposal the basic X calls, but can also make use of models like PHIGS (for 3-D) and Display PostScript.

In addition to basic X functionality and alternate imaging systems, it is always helpful to provide a library of useful routines. The basic X release from MIT includes a series of widgets, things like menu buttons, or window creation routines, for example.

The OSF world has adopted X as the basic windowing system and then added a toolkit on top of it. The toolkit provides a standard look and feel to the window system. All windows look the same, all menus act the same. The hope is that software will be easier to use and learn because the procedural details, like getting help, are only learned once. This combination of X and a common look and feel is packaged as MOTIF by OSF.

ONC has no windowing system but this does not mean that one does not do windows on Sun workstations, only that marketing has created seperate packages. Sun has a windowing system called the Network Extensible Window System (NeWS), a windowing system that has a PostScript display model, and the X Window System. Sun also has a standard look and feel licensed from AT&T called Open Look.

OSF and ONC have a lot in common at this point. OSF has OSF/DCE, which is quite similar to the ONC RPC. OSF has MOTIF, Sun and AT&T have Open Look. Both use the X Window System, and OSF members like Digital have imaging models to Sun's NeWS.

Naming

ONC, OSI, and OSF all have a problem in common: finding applications. This problem is the province of the naming service. Naming services let us take some name and resolve it. Given the name of a host, we may wish to resolve it into a network address, an attribute of a host name. There may be many other attributes to a name in addition to network address.

In OSI, this service is provided by X.500. X.500 is a descriptive naming service. We identify a resource by describing a series of attributes. The resource might be an electronic mail address, which would be described by specifying the human name and organization of the person to whom the address belongs.

A descriptive name service can be thought of like the Yellow Pages. Given the name "Smith" at "General Motors" we might get back a whole list of people. X.500 is thus an ideal candidate for applications such as finding usernames in an X.400-based worldwide messaging system.

X.500 is an attempt to provide a global directory for use in OSI networks. It is based on a strict hierarchy and assumes each administrative domain provides information on its members (there are no provisions for caching). Much of the real X.500 work has been done at University College London and with PSI's White Pages implementation. A pilot project will begin deployment of X.500 in the Internet in 1991.

The distributed ONC and OSF environments have a very different type of problem. They are more interested in performance than generality. Instead of specifying a name by some combination of attributes, the ONC and OSF naming services work off of primitive names. A primitive name is a full, unique name. For example, a primitive name for a computer might be:

computer_name.engineering.GM.COM

Notice that the name is structured into a series of subdomains. The computer itself is in engineering which is part of a company called GM which is part of the domain of commercial organizations.

The ONC and OSF worlds assume that the user knows this name. The result of a lookup to a primitive naming service is some attribute, such as network address. A primitive naming service is thus equivalent to a white pages service, performing only lookups whereas X.500 performs both lookups and searches.

Think about an RPC-based application in ONC. A user wants to mount an NFS file system from some host, "NFS_Server," for example. Before the NFS client is able to set up a TCP connection or RPC binding to that remote destination, it needs to know a network address. The client would use the Network Information Service (NIS) to find an IP address for the named server. In the OSF world, instead of NIS, the client program uses the OSF/DCE Naming Service, which is adapted from Digital's DNA Naming Service.

X.500 and the primitive naming services are both needed. Primitive servers take their name from the type of names they handle—the services they offer, such as replication of data, coordination of updates, and good access control, are actually quite advanced. X.500, on the other hand, provides great flexibility.

Data Access

Built on top of the RPC mechanism are a series of applications. The basic application in the ONC environment is the Network File System. The Network File System is a file service which allows a remote file system to appear to be locally located, a process known as mounting the remote file system.

Making remote file systems accessible the same way as local file systems is one of the most important tools on a network. Tutorials and help information, for example, often take a very large amount of space. Distributing the documentation as books to each user has fallen out of favor with most—it is simply too expensive and bulky. On-line manuals, however, are also bulky, using expensive disk space. Giving each user a copy of on-line manuals does not make sense, so a single (or a few) sets are put onto specialized servers on the network, and NFS is used to make the manuals appear locally mounted on every workstation.

Saving disk space, however, is not the real purpose of a distributed file system. NFS is really meant for data sharing so that data on the network can be structured as a single, large file system. No matter which computer you sit down at, you should always see the same view of your data; your home files will always be in the same place.

Saving on disk space is just a specific example of data sharing. Moving files to remote servers allows the workstation to be smaller. Shared data like applications, the operating system, or help pages, can be moved to large, well-managed servers. A workstation can be dataless, holding a small disk drive used for local paging and swapping, or even diskless with all activity going over the network using NFS protocols. Servers can backup workstations by mounting their file systems and spooling them to a tape drive.

There are a whole host of applications available in all the different environments for data access. After all, this function is one of the core applications on any network. Whereas

ONC has NFS, the OSF/DCE includes the functionally equivalent Andrew File System (AFS).

AFS and NFS are distributed file system protocols that make collections of remote files appear to be locally attached. There are also other file access protocols that work in a less transparent fashion. In the OSI world, such access comes from the File Transfer, Access, and Management (FTAM) protocols. FTAM is a way to request whole files, records within files, or file attributes (e.g., the creation date or owner of a file). Somewhat equivalent services to FTAM are the old TCP/IP File Transfer Protocol (FTP) and Digital's Data Access Protocol (although it should be noted that FTP operates on bulk files instead of individual records).

Messaging

For many users electronic mail is the single most-used network application. Here the differences between environments goes away quickly.

X.400, a CCITT and ISO protocol for message handling systems, is quickly being accepted as a standard for store-and-forward message delivery. Neither OSF nor ONC address this area, leaving messaging systems to be addressed by other groups. Most network stacks have their own messaging systems. In the UNIX world, message transport is often handled by UUCP, in the TCP/IP world by the Simple Mail Transfer Protocol (SMTP).

Many vendors also have their own protocols. Digital has the MAILbus architecture, IBM has the SNA Distribution Services (SNADS) for MVS and the Professional Office System (PROFS) for the VM/CMS operating system. MCI has its MCI-Mail EMS architecture. Novell uses Action Technologies's MHS product.

X.400 is the glue that connects all these proprietary systems together into a general message-handling system. Most vendors have X.400 gateways for their proprietary systems, translating addresses and message formats into the appropriate format for the target system. Gateway systems are becoming widespread, especially between the X.400 and the SMTP-based Internet. Many of these Internet gateways come from work done at University College London (UCL) and the University of Wisconsin at Madison.

This is not to say, however, that X.400 is simply an interface to proprietary systems. Several vendors are making native X.400 implementations. Retix, for example, specializes in native X.400 (and other OSI) applications in various platforms.

Combining Environments

Vendors, despite marketing literature to the contrary, rarely limit themselves to a single environment. Granted, some exceptions exist. Retix, for example, has built a nice business out of OSI-compliant networking software. Most of the large vendors, however, have a more heterogeneous architecture, mixing pieces from the O* environments with their own proprietary protocols.

This combination of protocols defines the vendor's network architecture. We will look briefly at IBM, Digital, Sun, and Novell to see how they mix and match different services. Other vendors have their own mixes of protocols.

The vendor's network architecture is the starting point for a user's network architecture. It is a rare user that uses a single vendor's architecture in its entirety. IBM and Digital, for example, have offerings so vast in scope that it would be a strange organization indeed that needed the entire product line.

Instead, a user picks pieces. Some users choose to pick pieces from a single vendor. Large corporations, for example, often limit their choices to the IBM or Digital catalog, going so far as to buy commodity items like cable or tapes from their primary vendor.

Increasingly, however, users will pick pieces from many different vendors. Workstations from Sun, Digital, and Silicon Graphics, X Terminals, terminal servers, printers, routers, and back-end minicomputers can all combine to make a network tailored for an organization.

To make this heterogeneous mix of systems (and users) work together requires more than simple solutions. Standardizing on X.25, OSI, and FTAM, for example, will provide a common solution but will fail to meet the needs of users that need distributed file systems.

We will return to this question of diversity of protocols and coexistence of different environments later. For now, however, let us look at how four major vendors have combined the different architectures into their own network architectures.

OSF and IBM

The strong participation of IBM in OSF may seem a bit perplexing at first glance. After all, IBM has its own all-encompassing architecture, the System Applications Architecture (SAA).

IBM is big enough, however, that they can have multiple all-encompasing architectures. SAA is how mainframes and other computers communicate. SAA has a common user interface (look and feel), a common communications interface (à la DCE) and other standard interfaces, all based on compatibility with the SNA architecture and the needs of large mainframe systems.

SAA is thus the native networking architecture for the upper end of the IBM environment. SAA does not, however, provide an adequate solution for workstations like the RS/6000. IBM supports OSF for a workstation environment, with the RS/6000 acting as the gateway into SNA and SAA.

IBM mainframes can do more than just speak SNA, however. IBM supports TCP/IP and NFS, as well as OSI on their mainframes. The strategy at IBM is to make the IBM fit into multiple environments.

The strategy is really quite simple. IBM wants to be able to sell hardware into any environment. If the user community is specifying OSI, IBM is not so committed to SNA that it

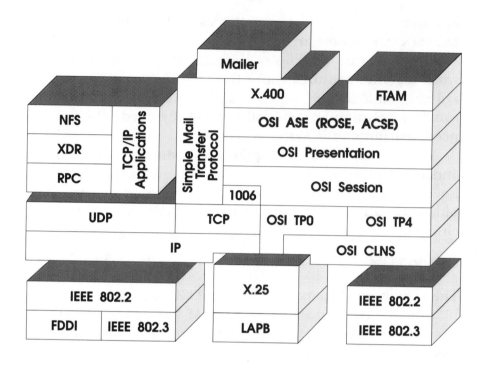

Figure 7-4 Sun TCP and OSI Support

would neglect a large market. In fact, IBM has played a key leadership role in the development of OSI, devoting considerable staff to chair ANSI and ISO committees.

Sun Networks

Sun networks, naturally enough, make heavy use of the UNIX operating system, TCP/IP networks, and the ONC family of protocols. Just providing TCP/IP and ONC, however, is not enough to sell into some companies. The government, for example, wants to see both TCP/IP and OSI compatibility. Other customers have DECnet, or large SNA installations.

Connectivity to other environments is provided with gateways. SunLink MHS, for example, is the gateway that links the TCP/IP-based messaging system to any X.400 message handling system. Figure 7-4 shows how Sun's overall architecture blends elements of OSI and TCP/IP. The addition of

SunLink products can also provide gateways to SNA or DEC-net environments.

The important questions with gateways are their level of transparency and functionality for the user. Some gateways, for example, require the user to log onto some intermediate gateway system and then use a specialized protocol to access remote services. Other gateways may only support a subset of the functionality in a remote system.

Other gateways are totally transparent. For example, there is a Sun NFS gateway, built on top of a channel-attached SNA gateway, that allows the workstation user to treat an MVS mainframe as just another file system. Granted, it is a very large, fairly cumbersome file system, but nevertheless a network-based file system. The Sun SNA Gateway acts as a proxy for the mainframe, accepting requests from workstations and forwarding them.

Other gateways provide connectivity to OSI, translating messages between applications, such as SMTP and X.400, or FTP and FTAM.

Notice that the workstation uses a native environment, such as TCP/IP. Just because a Sun workstation usually runs TCP/IP, however, doesn't mean that the network is not GO-SIP compliant. GOSIP requires a point of entry into the network, not an all-encompassing implementation.

Novell

Novell's Netware has several components. First, there is the underlying network, which consists of a modified version of the Xerox XNS protocols. This modified XNS, called IPX by Novell, supports a variety of substrates including token ring, Ethernet, ARCnet, and X.25.

Built on top of IPX is a proprietary environment known as NetWare. NetWare has one component for the server, which is a proprietary network operating system developed by Novell. The second component goes on a PC client running OS/2 or DOS.

Environments

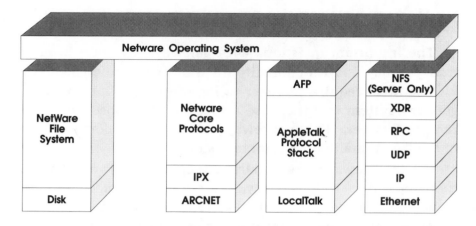

Figure 7-5 NetWare

To integrate a NetWare network into other environments, there are two strategies. The first is to make remote servers look like a proprietary Novell system. To do so, a piece of software called Portable NetWare is put on the remote system (e.g., a VAX running the VMS operating system).

Portable NetWare allows users to store files on the VAX (or other host), access VAX-based printers, and log on as a virtual VT100 terminal to the VAX. Notice that Portable NetWare does not give direct access to network environments such as OSF or ONC, it simply makes the remote system look like a NetWare server.

The other strategy is to allow the client workstation to access multiple environments. In this configuration, the client workstation supports two types of services; NFS and NetWare. When speaking to a NetWare server, the workstation uses NetWare protocols. When speaking to a Sun or other NFS server, the workstation uses the NFS and RPC protocols. Both operations are transparent, masked under a common interface, such as the DOS data access commands.

There is a potential problem with running dual environments on a PC—DOS is somewhat limited in its memory-management capabilities. Running two environments simultaneously works fine as long as the user doesn't need to run an application.

Instead of running multiple environments, Novell networks tend to keep the clients running NetWare and provide gateways on the servers. For example, there is an implementation of NFS for the NetWare server. However, this server is strictly a client implementation, allowing NFS clients to access server files (see Fig. 7-5). A Sun workstation, or any other NFS client, can access files on the Novell server using NFS protocols. Notice that the NetWare client, the PC, is not participating in this exchange since it does not have NFS support.

NFS support by Novell means that the NetWare server is also an NFS server. The same underlying files can be accessed by the two different file access protocols. The NetWare server can also serve an AppleTalk environment (where Macintosh systems use the AppleTalk Filing Protocol) or a LAN Manager environment.

Novell's reason for pursuing interoperability is clear. In a single departmental solution, proprietary environments like NetWare are fine. When the NetWare network is connected to a broader environment, however, support for standards becomes crucial for survival. If Novell doesn't allow the user to access the TCP/IP-based laser printer down the hall, the user will find a solution that does.

DECnet/OSI Phase V

DECnet Phase IV is a proprietary network architecture that was first introduced in 1980. DECnet Phase IV has a variety of different proprietary protocols, such as the Data Access Protocol (DAP). DAP is a file access mechanism, somewhat similar to FTAM or FTP. Unlike FTAM or FTP, however, DAP is able to operate only within a fairly constrained environment. The protocol has its origins in the RSX-11 operating system for the PDP-11, and is used mostly on Digital operating systems (although implementations of DAP do exist for

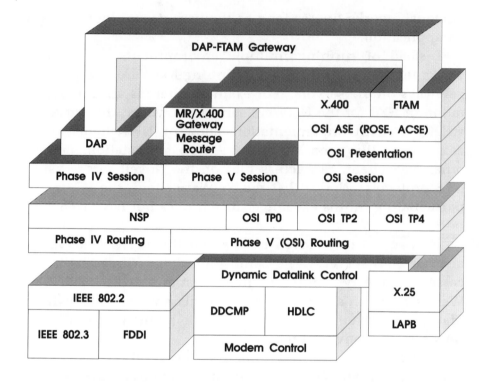

Figure 7-6 DNA Application-Level Gateways

generic UNIX platforms and even for systems such as IBM's MVS/TSO).

DAP's focus on the RSX, and later VMS, operating systems means that it can have less limited functionality. DAP protocols, unlike FTP, allow access to specific blocks of data in a file. DAP supports multiple access methods to files, such as indexed or hash data organizations.

DAP is not the only protocol in DECnet. CTERM protocols are for virtual terminal emulation and there are a host of other services ranging from remote booting to name servers to network management and videotext.

This proprietary environment of Phase IV has been used in many organizations and is even used for at least three major networks. The High Energy Physics Network (HEPnet) and the Space Physics Analysis Network (SPAN) are two world-wide networks based on DECnet. Digital's own internal Easynet is also based on DECnet.

These networks are very large: SPAN has over 17,000 hosts, HEPnet has over 2500 hosts, and Easynet reached 40,000 nodes in 1991. However, more and more of these environments have needed to add support for other networking environments.

It is not unusual for a network to run both DECnet and TCP/IP at the same time. Increasingly, OSI implementations are being required. To support all three major environments, DECnet, TCP/IP (and ONC), and OSI, a major change in the DECnet architecture was needed.

The result was DECnet/OSI Phase V, announced in 1988 and just beginning to be deployed in 1991. DECnet/OSI Phase V is really an architecture that accommodates multiple architectures (see Fig. 7-6).

Let's stop for a second and look at the challenge faced by Digital. Any improvements to the venerable Phase IV of DECnet must be backwards compatible—you do not sell more VAXs by obsoleting your current customer base.

A large part of the workstations being sold by Digital have ended up in TCP/IP-based networks. Supercomputer centers and national laboratories, for example, buy many different kinds of workstations. TCP/IP works on all the machines, so sites are often reluctant to add DECnet.

The third requirement for Digital network architects is moving towards OSI. Digital has repeatedly learned the lesson that while proprietary architectures may be better, open ones sell better; witness, for example, the demise of the Rainbow and the rise of Ultrix at Digital.

Putting all these conflicting requirements together, Digital decided to create a many-headed monster (not the term used by Digital, of course). For strictly Digital implementations, the new network architecture uses OSI for the lower layers and the current Digital applications for the environment.

Environments

The Digital environment is a mix of the OSF Distributed Computing Environment and proprietary Digital applications. From DCE, we see the naming service (originally developed by Digital) and the remote procedure call mechanism (developed by Apollo). In addition, we see Digital products such as the DAP protocols, virtual terminals, Digital's distributed file system, and many other services.

This is the native architecture, meant to run on workstations and servers on the DECnet. In addition, those same nodes are also able to participate in the more general OSI environment. Here, instead of using the DECnet session layer and related upper layer protocols, the nodes use OSI protocols. These services are fairly basic: FTAM, the virtual terminal service, and a gateway to X.400.

How can Digital support multiple environments on one node? The trick is insulation at two levels. Programmers see high-level interfaces, such as the Record Management Services (RMS), the interface to the VMS file system. RMS insulates the underlying protocol that is used to obtain a file from the higher-level language.

Another example of insulation is the Digital Command Language (DCL), the command shell seen by interactive or batch users. The user does not use the FTAM or DAP protocols to request data—users see the DCL "copy" command, which submits requests to RMS, and only then to the particular service used to access data.

The second level of insulation is below the environment. Mechanisms like transport interfaces, towers, and a naming service (itself a layer of insulation), different combinations of protocols and services can be used, providing interoperability at many levels.

For Further Reading

Boland, Tim, *Government Open System Interconnection Profile Users' Guide*. NIST Special Publication 500-163, August 1989. Order from Superintendent of Documents, U.S. Government Printing Office, Washington, D.C., 20402.

Corbin, J., *The Art of Distributed Applications—Programming Techniques for Remote Procedure Calls.* New York: Springer Verlag, 1991. The definitive look at the ONC RPC mechanism by one of Sun's senior engineers.

Linnell, Dennis, *The SAA Handbook.* Reading, Mass: Addison Wesley, 1990. A good look at IBM's SAA by a prominent SNA expert.

Malamud, Carl, *Analyzing DECnet/OSI Phase V.* New York: Van Nostrand Reinhold, 1991. A look at Digital's combination of OSF, OSI, DECnet, and TCP/IP (includes a discussion of towers).

———, *Analyzing Sun Networks.* New York: Van Nostrand Reinhold, 1991). ONC protocols, including NFS, RPC, and services such as the automounter and license server.

NIST, "Government Open Systems Interconnection Profile (GOSIP), Version 2." Federal Information Processing Standard (FIPS) 146-1, April 1991.

Open Software Foundation, *The OSF/Motif Series.* Englewood Cliffs, N.J.: Prentice Hall. A series of books giving detailed information on Motif. OSF also publishes technical information directly, as in the case of the official OSF coffee cup which lists their guiding principles.

Rose, Marshall, *The Little Black Book: Mail Bonding with OSI Directory Services.* Englewood Cliffs, N.J.: Prentice Hall, 1991.

———, *The Open Book.* Englewood Cliffs, N.J.: Prentice Hall, 1989. The best book available on OSI, especially valuable in the upper layers of the protocol stack.

Sidhu Gursharan S., et. al., *Inside Appletalk.* Reading, Mass: Addison Wesley, 1989. Excellent description of the protocols by the Apple technical staff.

Sun Microsystems, *NFS: Network File System Protocol Specification*, RFC 1094.

———, *RPC: Remote Procedure Call Protocol* (ver. 2). RFC 1057.

———, *XDR: External Data Representation Standard.* RFC 1014.

Environments

X Window Manual Set. San Jose, Calif: ASP, Inc., 1989. Three-volume compilation of the MIT X Window System documentation.   A   similar   compilation   is   available   from O'Reilly and Associates as part of their Nutshell series.
X Window System Protocol (ver. 11).   RFC 1013.

– 8 –

Securing Open Systems

"We are at risk."

So begins a report of the National Research Council, a research arm of the National Academy of Sciences, on the subject of computer security. The report is the result of a year-long effort chaired by Dr. David D. Clark of MIT. The committee included such notables as Butler Lampson, architect of Digital's security framework, and Peter Neumann of SRI International, noted for his catalogues of security problems. The committee also included Stephen Kent of BBN, an author of the RFCs for the Internet Privacy Enhanced Mail (PEM) prototype.

In contrast with most treatments of the subject of computer security, this report is extremely well-written. The Clark committee pursued a broad mandate from DARPA, the originator of the study, to look at a "national research, engineering and policy agenda to help the United States achieve a more trustworthy computing technology base by the end of the century."

With such a mandate you have to go beyond just recommending longer passwords and the committee did in fact come up with an extremely comprehensive policy. Security is more than just protecting your own assets. It is a fundamental aspect of being a good corporate citizen. Members of the Internet should protect their own system out of self-interest, but also out of a broader mandate to protect their neighbors.

Securing Open Systems

Network architectures work at many levels. Security at one level may be bypassed by going to a lower level—a process known as tunnelling. In networks, most people see security at the application level. Telnet and FTP, for example, require that the user type a password. The password is an authentication measure.

A password is an appropriate means of authentication in some situations, but it is certainly not the only way to secure networks. As an authentication measure, it is fairly weak, subject to attacks from many quarters. The encrypted passwords can be stolen and then attacked methodically, particularly easy to do when users pick short passwords. Passwords are also extremely vulnerable to social engineering. If we look under the keyboards of many terminals, or try the names of a user's friends and relatives (and dogs and cars), or even if we simply call the user up and ask them, we stand a very good chance of finding out the password.

A password is weak means of authentication. Even if passwords were a better authentication mechanism they would not suffice as security goes far beyond simple authentication. Guarding against replays and eavesdropping, access control for resources, alerts to management, and the verification of the integrity of programs and data are all important aspects of security.

A network needs a security infrastructure. Within the confines of a work groups, the structure may be fairly loose, but will guard against unauthorized intrusions from other work groups. Even in the broad confines of the Internet, security is becoming increasingly important. Episodes like the Morris worm not only show the vulnerability of networks, but draw the attention of policymakers to the limitations of networks (see the book by Peter Denning at the end of this chapter for more details on the Morris worm). As Dr. Clark observed, the fact that the Morris worm may attack his computer bothers him not nearly as much as reading about it in *The New York Times*.

In this chapter, we will look at the issue of securing open systems. Several efforts are underway that allow secure communication among groups within the confines of the broader Internet. These efforts are based on public key cryptography, in particular the version of public key cryptography developed by Rivest, Shamir, and Adleman at MIT and subsequently commercialized by their firm, RSA Data Security, Inc. (RSADSI).

We will look at the basis for public key cryptography and the RSA version. RSA is the underlying technology not only for Internet pilots, but is also built into commercial offerings from Lotus, Novell, Digital, Motorola, and many others.

After a general review of public key cryptography, we will look at the Privacy Enhanced Mail prototype on the Internet. PEM applies RSA technology to electronic mail, allowing services such as authentication, nonrepudiation, and encryption of body text to be offered on top of existing message-handling systems.

Next, we will look at the concept of a certification hierarchy, the infrastructure used not only in the Internet but as part of the X.509 CCITT standards for security. Certification hierarchies are more significant than any of the specific pilots like PEM because they enable a broad-based use of security over many different applications.

Securing open systems is part of an even broader problem, managing open systems. We will look briefly at the question of network management. Protocols like SNMP and CMIP are combined with standard database definitions, known as Management Information Bases (MIBs). SNMP provides a standard definition of how to get remote management data, while MIBs defines the data. Many vendors are building higher-level architectures on top of these protocols. We will look at one, SunNet Manager, to illustrate the issues that these management architectures are attempting to address.

Kerberos

A password is short and easy to remember, a trait that endears them to human beings, entities with low tolerance and limited RAM. Short and easy to remember, however, kind of defeats the purpose of a security system.

The length and complexity of the password illustrates a standard tradeoff on security: security consumes resources and thus costs money. Longer passwords cost resources (irritation among the user base), but make systems harder to break into. Changing passwords frequently and prohibiting repeats likewise make passwords more secure but more bothersome.

On computer networks, a user will typically have many different accounts. Because the security perimeter is the remote node or application, you need a password to access these remote services. The password goes over the network in clear text (unless you have data link level encryption facilities), making it liable to eavesdropping.

Even more dangerous, however, is the fact that many systems allow a user on one system to access another without a password. The first system is the security perimeter, as in the case of a user being required to logon to the first VAX in a DECnet. Other systems, for the purpose of convenience use mechanisms like the DECnet proxy login or the UNIX "rhosts" database to allow a user to quickly move around the network without relogging in. While proxy logins are convenient, they do allow one penetration of a security perimeter to reach multiple systems.

This type of problem was faced by Project Athena, the ambitious MIT effort to computerize its entire campus. As the reader might guess, the MIT campus is a challenging environment in which to administer networks. If the network manager leaves a security hole, you can be sure that some undergraduate will make a project out of finding it.

The goal of Project Athena was to allow all students to work on all workstations on campus. Any user should be able to go up to any workstation and login, seeing the same view of files and other resources anywhere on campus. Distributed file systems, name servers, multimedia messaging, the X Window System, and a variety of other services made up Project Athena, a research effort that had a dramatic effect not only on the MIT campus but in the entire computer industry.

An important part of Project Athena is the Kerberos distributed security system. Kerberos is a system where a client and server share a key used to encrypt data over the network. Because the cryptography is based on shared keys, Kerberos is known as a symmetric security system (in contrast to public key cryptographic systems).

The central issue in Kerberos is the manner by which those symmetric keys are distributed over the network to the client and server so they may begin communicating with each other. This is a classic bootstrap problem—how do you distribute sensitive information over an insecure network to allow secure communications to begin?

One solution to key distribution is to do so offline. Out-of-band distribution is how passwords usually work. Your initial password is written on a slip of paper and mailed to you (with the intention that it be committed to memory and destroyed rather than taped next to your terminal).

When a user walks up to a workstation on the network, she types in a password. On a normal UNIX system the user would be prompted for a password, the password would be encrypted, and then compared against the value stored in the /etc/passwd file.

In Kerberos, the workstation takes the username and sends it off to Kerberos. Kerberos checks that the client is known to it. If so, it will send a ticket to the ticket-granting service, letting the server know that it should expect a client to contact it soon.

Kerberos next sends back a packet to the workstation that is encrypted with the user's password. Inside of that packet are the same ticket that was sent to the ticket-granting service, plus a session key. The workstation will prompt the

161

user for a password and use it to decrypt the packet from Kerberos. At this point, the workstation is ready to contact the ticket-granting server, which will, in turn, give the client access to resources on the network, such as remote file systems or messaging services. Notice that the password has never entered the network, and in fact isn't even stored on the workstation—it was used solely to decrypt the first packet.

Armed with a ticket, the client is able to approach the ticket-granting service. The ticket is only good for a limited duration, and must be periodically renewed, preventing somebody from capturing an old ticket and masquerading as the user.

Any session between a client and a server has a session ticket, which includes the name of the client, the server, the client IP address, the current time and lifetime of the ticket, and a random session key.

The whole ticket is encrypted with the server's key password. The server can thus decrypt the ticket, but the client is unable to modify the ticket. A ticket is an example of an authenticator, a set of credentials that proves that this client is a known entity. When the ticket-granting server sends a session ticket back to the workstation, there is one more piece of information that is needed—a copy of the session key (the workstation can't use the copy inside the session ticket because it is encrypted with the server's key).

All the information that the workstation receives: the ticket for a server and the key for a session, are encrypted with the key that is shared between the client and the ticket-granting server.

How tickets and authentication are used is beyond the scope of Kerberos—Kerberos simply delivers credentials. A server might ignore authentication, allowing any user in. Or, the authentication might be used only at the beginning of a session. It is possible for truly paranoid applications to check each packet coming in.

Public Key Cryptography

Kerberos has the same problem as all symmetric key systems, distribution of the shared secret to the client and server. It does not scale to very large networks, such as the Internet, because there needs to be a way to pass keys across Kerberos domains.

Another way to handle authentication is public key cryptography. Symmetric key systems like Kerberos depend on a single key used to encrypt and decrypt data. In a public key system there are two keys, one to encrypt data and the other to decrypt data.

The two keys are known as public and private keys. The private key is a secret, known only to the user. The public key is known by the whole world. If the public key is used to encrypt data, then only the private key can decrypt them. Likewise, if the private key is used to encrypt data, the public key is used to decrypt them.

The reader might wonder what the sense is of encrypting data with a private key when the whole world can decrypt the data. Encryption with a private key (and the subsequent decryption by the public key) is a way of verifying the identity of the sender. Data encrypted with a public key are not secure from decryption, but the recipient is assured of the identity of the sender.

Public key systems are based on the fact that certain mathematical operations are much easier to perform in one direction than another. The Diffie-Hellman method, used in Sun's Secure RPC and Secure NFS, is based on the fact that it is much easier to raise a number to a power than it is to find the root. Sun takes a well-known constant, and raises it to the power of a key, a 192-bit number.

While public key cryptography is ideal for the initial authentication of data, Sun uses a shared symmetric key (distributed using a public key) for encryption of user data. Symmetric systems are significantly faster than public key systems. The public key is used to distribute the symmetric key which is used to encrypt session data.

The RSA method is even more powerful than the Diffie-Hellman method, relying on the fact that it is much easier to multiply two large prime numbers together than it is to factor the product. This computational difficulty is expressed in MIPS-years, or how many years of CPU time would a 1-MIP machine take to break a key.

A recent example of breaking a number was the 155-digit number broken by a team of researchers led by A. Lenstra. The team used an ingenious algorithm to break up one of the simplest possible 155 digit numbers: two 1s with 153 zeros sandwiched in the middle. Even this extremely simple number took over 250 MIPS-years to factor. More complex 155-digit numbers can easily result in millions or tens of millions of MIPS-years. Massively parallel processors like the Connection Machine have provided improvements of 100 to 1000 times over traditional processors, but the problem is still several orders of magnitude beyond today's computational capabilities.

In the RSA system, keys typically range from 512 to 1001 bits long (150 to 301 decimal digits) and can be significantly harder to break. For example, one of the public keys used by people communicating with RSA is 301 digits long and would take over 1 trillion MIPS-years to break given the current state of research in number theory (or at least according to the research in number theory that has been published openly).

The reader may wonder why, in a book on open systems, the proprietary technology developed by one team of researchers and commercialized by RSA Data Security, Inc. is being discussed instead of some open standard. The reason is, for the time being at least, the RSA system is widely accepted as the most secure. In fact, the RSA technology is patented. The RSA system is specifically mentioned in Internet RFCs and in an appendix to X.509 as the basis for public key cryptosystems. For the time being at least, the only system that has promise of providing a truly secure, scalable security infrastructure is the RSA technology. Of course, if RSA proves unreasonable in its demands, an alternative will soon surface.

The fact that RSA technology is patented is subject to some limitations. First, the original research was done with government money, so the federal government is able to use the technology royalty-free. Second, not all the patents apply overseas, so RSADSI only enjoys full protection within the U.S. RSADSI thus needs to figure out how to take its limited monopoly on the best technology currently available and turn it into money for stockholders before the patents run out or alternatives are developed.

One strategy by the company has been to license the technology (or software based on the technology) to computer vendors. RSA technology forms the basis for security in Lotus Notes, an example of so-called "groupware" conferencing software. Novell uses RSA in NetWare as part of the bindery, their naming service and security system; Tektronix uses it to protect fonts on its printers; Motorola uses the same technology to provide secure voice communications; and even Smart Cards use public key cryptography to authenticate a card to the device that is reading it (and vice versa).

In addition to licensing software based on the technology to vendors, RSA has taken a more nontraditional tack, allowing free use of its algorithms in the Privacy Enhanced Mail (PEM) for non-commercial users (there will be a small cost for certificates). The federal government funded the development of PEM software by Trusted Information Systems. PEM is free to all users of a valid certificate. Why would RSA give away vital technology? The key is support—even non-commercial users may wish to pay money for commercial PEM software, which would presumably have better support, documentation, or features than the free version.

Privacy Enhanced Mail

Privacy Enhanced Mail (PEM) offers three basic services to the user:

- Confidentiality
- Authentication
- Message integrity assurance.

Confidentiality is the first service many people think of, based on encrypting the message contents. However, the other two services may ultimately prove the most useful.

Authentication is how we can make sure that a message from a user is in fact from that user. If a customer submits a mail message that is formatted for electronic data interchange (EDI), it would be nice to know that the order does in fact come from a real customer. If a message is authenticated, the sender is unable to later repudiate the message.

Message integrity assurance is an equally important service. Message Integrity Checks (MICs) are a way of insuring that a message has not been tampered with.

Fig. 8-1 shows a message that has been sent with PEM, over both SMTP and UUCP message transport mechanisms. The message uses all three services, integrity, authentication, and confidentiality. Because confidentiality is used, we are unable to read the text of the message. Message integrity is provided by the MIC-Info field, which in this case is using the Message Digest 4 algorithm developed by RSA.

The rest of the fields in the message are support fields for PEM or are used for authentication purposes. We will examine the structure of some of these fields, in particular certificates in a few moments.

Fig. 8-2 shows another PEM message, this time using only two of the services. The text of the message is sent in the clear, but we can be assured that the sender is in fact David Balenson of Trusted Information Systems, one of the developers of PEM.

While PEM performs many services, there are several services that are not addressed:

- Access control
- Traffic flow confidentiality
- Routing control

STACKS

Delivery-Date: Wed, 17 Oct 90 11:16:56 -0400
>From balenson@TIS.COM Wed Oct 17 11:16:55 1990
Return-Path: <balenson@TIS.COM>
Received: from TIS.COM by TIS.COM (4.1/SUN-5.64)
id AA09188; Wed, 17 Oct 90 11:16:55 EDT
Message-Id: <9010171516.AA09188@TIS.COM>
To: galvin@TIS.COM
Subject: Sample Privacy Enhanced Message (Integrity, Authentication and
    Confidentiality)
Date: Wed, 17 Oct 90 11:16:47 -0400
From: balenson@TIS.COM

——PRIVACY-ENHANCED MESSAGE BOUNDARY——
Proc-Type: 3,ENCRYPTED
DEK-Info: DES-CBC,a954db29e0f919eb
Sender-ID: balenson@tis.com:/C=US/O=Trusted Information Systems/O
    U=Glenwood/:39
Certificate:
    MIAwgKADAgEAAgEnMAkGBFUIAwMCASAwQjFAMAkGA1UEBhMCVVMwIgYDVQQKExtU
    cnVzdGVkIEluZm9ybWF0aW9uIFN5c3RlbXMwDwYDVQQLEwhHbGVud29vZDAeFw05
    MDA4MjExOTM2MzNaFw05MjA4MjAxOTM2MzNaMEsxSTAJBgNVBAYTAIVTMCIGA1UE%0
    ChMbVHJ1c3RlZCBJbmZvcm1hdGlvbiBTeXN0ZW1zMBgGA1UEAxMRRGF2aWQgTS4g0
    QmFsZW5zb24wNjAJBgRVCAEBAgEgBCkwJwQg2FRrHgGi7WpiGgwvbbyBUqW3oKFP0
    I2jVCEYEh2t+FK8EAwEAAQAAMAkGBFUIAwMCASAEIHBiEqkhQvcYD71dhOxtxIZ3
    DsT0HXraxVCp7TEegu+VAAA=
Issuer-Certificate:
    MIAwgKADAgEAAgEBMAkGBFUIAwMCASAwQjFAMAkGA1UEBhMCVVMwIgYDVQQKExtU
    cnVzdGVkIEluZm9ybWF0aW9uIFN5c3RlbXMwDwYDVQQLEwhHbGVud29vZDAeFw05
    MDA3MTkxOTM5MDhaFw05MjA3MTgxOTM5MDhaMElxQDAJBgNVBAYTAIVTMCIGA1UE
    ChMbVHJ1c3RlZCBJbmZvcm1hdGlvbiBTeXN0ZW1zMA8GA1UECxMIR2xlbndvb2Qw
    NjAJBgRVCAEBAgEgBCkwJwQgyneM2/2WyiSZQmixzcRk8i+92Vfu03InR/oiJOSH
    YG8EAwEAAQAAMAkGBFUIAwMCASAEIHSBPC8uADcdm/2TLdYjjPdLt9c5zmVccGJ/
    Z89gEtCsAAA=
MIC-Info: MD4,RSA,
    a+HSzLgJlYEsotKTmm9BpJvcoeFoqL2UqV+RXeeJr70=
Recipient-ID: balenson:/C=US/O=Trusted Information Systems/OU=Gle
    nwood PEM-1/OU=Glenwood/:39
Key-Info: RSA,Y18R5F6VhOiiC3NvT1QW6wTjjqMkex0vozvraDLVw8c=
Recipient-ID: galvin:/C=US/O=Trusted Information Systems/OU=Glenw
    ood PEM-1/OU=Glenwood/:1
Key-Info: RSA,NsTA+l0CqBBY8YSDnXSwtLnGmQ6aQFEaB2+2Iqi6ZbI=
    J4GgvfKxxnkwfs6yP+AHVUOPjUQdHLd6GbVY1J9btImfB601DWdKCFfRvdt39GmZ
    /6sJHq9UkMpDD0MZDf+pVWZO/UzWwx1FP8GF2fm4unNTl0aEFR8/2v5zEqhEQJ3U
    odf2zSW7A20=
——PRIVACY-ENHANCED MESSAGE BOUNDARY——

Fig. 8-1 A PEM Message

Securing Open Systems

Delivery-Date: Wed, 17 Oct 90 11:16:56 -0400
>From balenson@TIS.COM Wed Oct 17 11:16:55 1990
Return-Path: <balenson@TIS.COM>
Received: from TIS.COM by TIS.COM (4.1/SUN-5.64)
id AA09188; Wed, 17 Oct 90 11:16:55 EDT
Message-Id: <9010171516.AA09188@TIS.COM>
To: galvin@TIS.COM
Subject: Sample Privacy Enhanced Message (Integrity and Authentication Only)
      Date: Wed, 17 Oct 90 11:16:47 -0400
From: balenson@TIS.COM

——PRIVACY-ENHANCED MESSAGE BOUNDARY——
Proc-Type: 3,MIC-CLEAR
Sender-ID: balenson@tis.com:/C=US/O=Trusted Information Systems/O
 U=Glenwood/:39
Certificate:

MIAwgKADAgEAAgEnMAkGBFUIAwMCASAwQjFAMAkGA1UEBhMCVVMwIgYDVQQKExtU
cnVzdGVkIEluZm9ybWF0aW9uIFN5c3RlbXMwDwYDVQQLEwhHbGVud29vZDAeFw05
MDA4MjExMjMzNTJaFw05MjA4MjAxOTM2MzNaMEsxSTAJBgNVBAYTAIVTMCIGA1UE
ChMbVHJ1c3RlZCBJbmZvcm1hdGlvbiBTeXN0ZW1zMBgGA1UEAxMRRGF2aWQgTS4g
QmFsZW5zb24wNjAJBgRVCAEBAgEgBCkwJwQg2FRrHgGi7WpiGgwvbbyBUqW3oKFP
I2jVCEYEh2t+FK8EAwEAAQAAMAkGBFUIAwMCASAEIHBiEqkhQvcYD71dhOxtxlZ3
DsT0HXraxVCp7TEegu+VAAA=
Issuer-Certificate:

MIAwgKADAgEAAgEBMAkGBFUIAwMCASAwQjFAMAkGA1UEBhMCVVMwIgYDVQQKExtU
cnVzdGVkIEluZm9ybWF0aW9uIFN5c3RlbXMwDwYDVQQLEwhHbGVud29vZDAeFw05
MDA3MTkxOTM5MDhaFw05MjA3MTgxOTM5MDhaMEIxQDAJBgNVBAYTAIVTMCIGA1UE
ChMbVHJ1c3RlZCBJbmZvcm1hdGlvbiBTeXN0ZW1zMA8GA1UECxMIR2xlbndvb2Qw
NjAJBgRVCAEBAgEBBCkwJwQgyneM2/2WyiSZQmixzcRk8i+92Vfu03InR/oiJOSH
YG8EAwEAAQAAMAkGBFUIAwMCASAEIHSBPC8uADcdm/2TLdYjjPdLt9c5zmVccGJ/
Z89gEtCsAAA=
MIC-Info: MD4,RSA,
jcEHmk46h6x+x6rKeAYAp1oFGiQE2VODfYJedWGZawU=

This is a sample privacy enhanced message with integrity and
authentication only.
——PRIVACY-ENHANCED MESSAGE BOUNDARY——

Fig. 8-2 A PEM Message

- Assurance of receipt
- Replay prevention or other stream-oriented services
- Serial re-use of a PC by multiple users.

Traffic flow confidentiality is not assured because the header
of a privacy enhanced message goes in clear text. An eaves-

dropper can tell that you are exchanging mail with a correspondent, but cannot read what is in the message (assuming the contents are encrypted).

Routing control, access control, and other areas are meant to be addressed by other portions of the computing environment. Access control is handled by individual applications (e.g., NSF) or by the operating system. Assurance of receipt is an issue for the message-handling system (e.g., SMTP), and some problems are the province of the purchasing department (the only reliable way to prevent serial re-use of a PC is to buy a different operating system or hardware platform).

PEM is built on top of the existing Internet transport mechanism, the Simple Mail Transfer Protocol. Messages that use PEM consist of the standard headers for a message, such as the address and source. In addition, a variety of other header information is defined.

PEM is based on two levels of encryption keys. First, there is the Data Encryption Key (DEK) used to encrypt text and to generate the message integrity check. The DEK is unique for each message and is generated based on DES, a family of methods for symmetric cryptography adopted by the U.S. government as a standard, and thus supported in software and hardware by a wide number of vendors.

The second key is the Interchange Key (IK), used to encrypt the DEK. If a mail message goes to multiple users, each recipient of the message gets a separate DEK, each encrypted with a different IK. Given an interchange key, we are able to decrypt the data encryption key, which can then be used to decrypt the message or message integrity check.

PEM standards are drawn in a general fashion allowing different kinds of cryptographic methods to be used. The initial implementation is based on RSA public key cryptography, but there is no reason that Kerberos or some other method cannot be used for the generation of interchange keys.

An outgoing message goes through four representations, starting with the a local message in some internal format.

Next, the message must be put into a representation that supports SMTP transport, based on 7-bit ASCII and carriage return/line feed for delimiters.

Next, the process of authentication and encipherment is applied to the message. A message integrity check is generated for the text. Then, any padding is added to the message so that it is an integral number of 8-byte quantities, necessary for encipherment.

It is not necessary to encrypt an entire message. Portions of the message may be excluded from encryption. Authentication, however, is always applied to the whole message. A region can be excluded from encipherment by delimiting it with an asterisk.

After a message has been enciphered, it needs to be put back into a printable encoding so that it can be sent over SMTP. The PEM standards take the bit string that is the message and converts it to a printable representation by taking each group of six bits and representing it as a printable character. The encoding thus takes every six bits and represents them as an 8-bit octet. The message thus expands by 33 percent. The result of the encoding is a series of lines that have 64 characters each.

Next, the entire PEM message is put inside of a regular message by adding the standard "to" and "from" headers. The PEM software can be thought of as a pre-processor. Once a PEM message is prepared, it is handed off to the underlying messaging system, in this case SMTP.

A PEM message consists of the "regular" headers that apply to all mail messages, plus PEM-specific information. As far as the SMTP transport mechanism is concerned, the remainder of the message is all text. Inside this body, PEM breaks the text down into a message body (possibly encrypted) and PEM headers.

Encrypted text might include information normally in a header line but considered to be sensitive. An obvious example is the "subject:" line of a mail message which should probably be encrypted if the message body is encrypted. Another reason for putting headers into the body of the message is so that they are part of the message integrity check calculation.

Certification Hierarchies

PEM defines the structure of a mail message. For PEM to work, there needs to be a way of distributing interchange keys. To communicate with a remote user, we must obtain a certificate. A certificate contains the following fields:

- Version number
- Serial number
- Certificate signature (and associated algorithm identifier)
- Issuer name
- Validity name
- Subject's public component (and associated algorithm identifier).

The subject's name, at least in the Privacy Enhanced Mail prototype, is an X.400 Originator/Recipient (O/R) name as specified in GOSIP Version 2. This distinguished name (distinguished denoting uniqueness as opposed to necessarily deserving of any respect) is less than or equal to 259 characters long. An example of an O/R name, this one for the Finnish computer expert Vesa Parkkari, is:

c=fi/a=elisa/p=mikrokonsultit/pn=vesa parkkari

This name includes a country, a message-handling administration (the Finnish Elisa network), an organization name (Mikroconsultit), and a personal name. A distinguished name must contain at least three pieces of information: the country, organization, and personal names. A name may also include zero to four organizational units.

Inside a certificate, the issuer is vouching for several things about the user. Normally, the issuer vouches for the person's name. Typically, the issuer will also identify a user with the organization and the role within that organization. Affiliation and role are quite important. A university, for example, issues certificates for students and staff. It is important that the roles of student and "purchasing agent" not be confused. A vendor would treat a message from a student asking for the purchase of 20 computers quite differently from a similar message from the university's purchasing agent.

The public key component of a subject includes an algorithm identification. For purposes of the Privacy Enhanced Mail prototype, this algorithm is the RSA software, but there is no reason why this couldn't be expanded to include other algorithms in the future. The key itself varies between 320 and 632 bits long.

The certificate signature is how we verify that a certificate has not been compromised (e.g., by changing the individual's organizational role from secretary to president). The signature is an encrypted, one-way hash function computed on the certificate's contents. The signature field is decrypted using the issuer's public key component. The decrypted quantity is compared to the hash quantity generated at the time the certificate is checked.

Normally, certificates are checked by software and not by users. However, good software ought to signal to the user when abnormal conditions occur, including when the software detects a valid, but unusual occurrence. For example, if GM verifies for a user's role within the Ford Motor Company, the software ought to bring this fact to a person's attention. The certificate may be valid but requires human interpretation.

To vouch that a certificate is real, it is signed using the public key of the issuing organization. To verify that the issuing organization is in fact real, we need the issuer's certificate. Eventually, the buck has to stop someplace. This is the root of the certification hierarchy. There are multiple certification trees, each one administered by a top-level certification authority.

The U.S. government is an example of a top-level certification authority, handling the certification of governmental organizations and employees (and probably contractors and national laboratories).

Another certification authority is RSA Data Security, Inc. (RSADSI), which has agreed to act as the root for other users of the Internet PEM software. For a fee ranging from $2 to $25, RSA will issue a certificate good for two years. It is possible for an organization to issue its own certificates, or to have RSA act as a co-issuer.

With RSADSI as a co-issuer or issuer of a certificate, there are three components to a certification hierarchy:

- the user
- an organizational notary
- a certification authority

The user is a person with a user agent, or possibly even a machine. After all, before trusting our secrets to a machine, we might want to certify that this is not some form of spoof by another host.

An individual user is able to obtain a certificate through the organization or directly through RSADSI. In either case, RSADSI ends up getting a piece of paper with four pieces of information on it:

- A name
- A postal address
- An Internet mail address
- A message hash

The message hash is a way of making sure that this certification request is coming from some known entity. The notary takes its own public key and generates this shorter hash function (writing down a public key is prone to error as it has more than 100 digits). If the user is applying directly as an end user, the paper is signed by a notary public.

The paper is used to provide a paper trail. The same information is then sent by electronic mail to RSADSI, along with the public key for the user. Needless to say, the user keeps his or her own private key private.

The organizational notary is an official representative of some organizational unit. Only an organizational notary can order certificates for an organization. Using organizational notaries is a bit more complex than the previously described method of ordering certificates.

The complexity is introduced because an organization may choose to vouch for different levels of information. In a university, we might just vouch that the person is a student. In a corporation, we might vouch for both the job title and the amount of purchasing authority of a person.

The organizational notary gets the relevant information from a user and packages it up into a PEM message and sends it to RSADSI. Protecting the message allows RSADSI to vouch that the message is in fact from a known notary.

After RSADSI generates a certificate, it sends two types of messages. First, a paper message goes back to the user containing the original hash function as well as the hash function based on the RSADSI public key.

Then, RSADSI sends electronic mail to the user that includes:

- The new certificate for the user
- The certificate for the issuing organization
- The RSADSI public key.

The public key is used to verify the certificate of the issuing organization. That certificate contains the public key for the organization, which is then used to verify the certificate for the user and make sure everything is in order.

Cross-Certification

Certification hierarchies are fine as long as you operate within a single hierarchy. As we have seen however, there may be multiple roots. In the U.S., the government and RSADSI administer separate trees. These tree roots cross-certify each other: the U.S. government vouches for RSADSI and vice versa, thus allowing a user from one tree to verify a user on another tree.

Certificates are carried in the x-issuer-certificate field. There may be several of those fields in a message. For example, say that Joe, part of the RSA tree, wishes to send to Bob, part of the U.S. government tree. Joe includes his own certificate. Joe also includes his organization's certificate, which is in turn vouched for by RSADSI. That means we need a certificate for RSA, which is signed by the United States government. For Bob, the United States government is a trusted source and Bob thus believes that RSA is real, which thus implies that Joe's organization and, in turn, Joe are real.

Certificate Revocation

Certificates by RSADSI are issued for a two-year period. Organizations may choose to have a shorter (or longer) period of time. What happens when we fire a user? That user will still have an apparently valid certificate as far as the rest of the world is concerned, and is thus a legitimate representative of the company.

To handle situations where a certificate has been compromised or revoked, a certification authority keeps a Certificate Revocation List (CRL). Each certification authority (CA) has a time-stamped list of its own revoked certificates, as well as a list of revoked certificates from other CAs.

These lists are stamped with two timestamps. First, they are stamped with the date of issue. More important, they are stamped with the time that the next list will be issued. If a CA advertises that it will publish a new list on a certain date, it must publish a list on that date. While it is possible to issue a list ahead of the publication date, there is no guarantee that other CAs will consult (or receive) that list.

A CRL contains a list of serial numbers for certificates. Every incoming certificate must be checked against this list to make sure that the certificate has not been revoked. A special revocation list is the list of revoked organizations. We hope, of course, that this list is fairly small.

Managing Open Systems

Securing networks is part of a broader problem, managing networks. If one reads the trade press, we can quickly come to the conclusion that network management is about the war between the TCP/IP-based Simple Network Management Protocol (SNMP) and OSI's Common Management Information Protocol (CMIP).

Network management is about much more than the protocol we use to ask a remote managed object for information. CMIP and SNMP provide the means for moving information across the network. Neither CMIP nor SNMP do any good unless there is some object at the remote end that has some information in which we are interested. Both TCP/IP and OSI worlds have defined architectures that let us define information of interest to managers.

Before we delve into these details, it is important to realize that network management is a pervasive issue in the network. Management is not just the configuration of routers—management includes accounting, security, planning, and all the other tasks needed to make a network work properly.

In this light, OSI subcommittees have been attempting to develop an architecture for network management. This architecture, like many other OSI architectures, is extremely broad. While OSI committees were battling the problem of managing future OSI networks, the people who help run the Internet, the Internet Engineering Task Force (IETF), had the problem of making today's networks work properly. The IETF, in one of its more dramatic success stories, decided that they had a problem that must be solved. There were a few false starts, but eventually a strategy was developed. The strategy has two pieces.

First, there is a way to define variables made accessible by managed objects, known as the Structure of Management Information (SMI). The SMI is an architecture for defining variables and assigning each a unique identifier. Variables can also have various attributes associated with them.

Actual definition of the objects, as opposed to the assignment of a unique identifier, is the province of many different groups. When an IETF task force develops a new network protocol, they also define a Management Information Base (MIB) which explains which attributes the new object shall keep.

There are a wide variety of different MIBs. To start things off, the IETF developed a core MIB, known as MIB-II because it is in the second iteration. This is supplemented by MIBs for different subnetworks (ARCnet, Ethernet, token ring), physical devices (T1 lines), services (OSPF and BGP routing protocols) or even arbitrary objects (John Romkey's toaster MIB for the SNMP-compatible toaster at INTEROP '90 comes to mind).

Notice the decentralized approach to network management. Each group defines the objects that are relevant to a particular module. This decentralized approach does not mean that a group is free to go off and invent nonsense—the IETF assists groups in making MIB definitions and helps to maintain uniform definitional syntax and quality.

The second part of the IETF effort has been defining protocols to access the MIB. Here, the Internet Activities Board decided that diversity should be encouraged since, at the time, no clear solution was in sight. Both the CMIP and SNMP camps were encouraged to continue their work.

The results of the competing efforts were dramatic. The SNMP effort quickly bore fruit, resulting in a fully-defined protocol, many implementations, and quick progress towards standardization. The CMOT effort never quite got off the ground and appears moribund.

SNMP defines standard data types for moving information over the network, defines primitive operations for getting those objects, and has additional features such as the ability to move multiple objects in a single request. Work continues on SNMP, adding features such as authentication.

SNMP and MIBs are merely the first step for network management. No user would want to type in SNMP PDUs

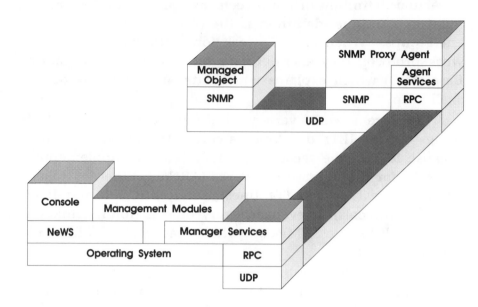

Figure 8-3 SunNet Manager

and submit them to the TCP/IP stack. A user interface, a database, and other aspects of the network management workstation all need to be defined.

There is another problem. No matter how good SNMP is, there will always be multiple network management protocols. SNMP usually uses the TCP/IP protocol stack. There are some devices that do not have TCP/IP. There are also instances where SNMP is not the appropriate paradigm for getting information. Other protocols, such as RPC, might be more appropriate.

Several vendors, including Digital, Hewlett-Packard, Silicon Graphics, Sun, and IBM have defined architectures for network management that build on primitive network protocols like SNMP. An example is SunNet Manager (see Fig. 8-1). SunNet Manager is an architecture for the network management workstation, using the services of the UNIX operating system and the NeWS windowing environment. Also on the

178

network management workstation are modules that process information, such as graphing data, plus a database for keeping track of historical information.

Throughout the network are a series of agents. Agents communicate with the network management workstation using the RPC and XDR protocols which are part of the ONC computing environment.

A typical agent would be one which is able to access information in the kernel of the remote node being managed. We can find out current memory utilization, for example. The returned information can be graphed, put into a form for display, or used to trigger an alert to the network manager.

A special agent is the proxy agent. The proxy agent serves two purposes. First, it provides translation to other network protocols such as SNMP. The proxy agent receives RPC-based requests from the network manager and turns them into SNMP requests. The results of the request are gathered by the proxy agent and then moved back to the network manager using RPC calls.

The second function of the proxy agent is insulation. For example, we might define a request to poll a particular station every five seconds to see if it is operational. If the poll fails, we want to be notified. If there are many managed nodes being polled on multiple subnetworks, it makes sense to isolate the traffic. After all, in this instance the manager is really only concerned when a poll fails. The proxy agent on remote subnetworks can take care of the polling, freeing the corporate backbone from being inundated with periodic keep alive requests and responses. Only when something is significant does the traffic go across the backbone and back to the network manager.

SunNet Manager is just one example of such an upper-level network management architecture. In fact, there are so many of these manager architectures being defined that people are beginning to toss around the idea of manager-to-manager protocols. (When the idea was broached at a recent IETF meeting, one wag in the audience suggested that the protocols include functions such as "Here's my card" and "Let's do lunch.")

Network management, particularly the subbranches of accounting and security, are the biggest challenges facing us. As networks get more pervasive—larger, faster, busier—we need to be able to control them. While no clear answers are available to such a complex cluster of problems, work in SNMP and MIBs is beginning to provide the answer and many of the best minds in the computer business are working on the problems.

For Further Reading

Denning, Peter J., ed., *Computers Under Attack: Intruders, Worms, and Viruses.* Reading, Mass: Addison Wesley, 1990. An interesting look at security threats including descriptions of several well-known worms and viruses.

Kent, S. *Privacy enhancement for Internet electronic mail: Part I—Message encipherment and authentication procedures [Draft]*, RFC 1113, 1989 Aug; 34 pp.

————, *Privacy enhancement for Internet electronic mail: Part II—Certificate-based key management [Draft]*, RFC 1114, 1989 Aug; 25 pp.

————, *Privacy enhancement for Internet electronic mail: Part III—Algorithms, modes, and identifiers*, RFC 1115, 1989 Aug; 8 pp.

Rivest, R.L., *MD4 message digest algorithm.* RFC 1186, October 1990, 18 pp. (Format: TXT=35391 bytes).

Rose, Marshall, *The Simple Book.* Englewood Cliffs, N.J.: Prentice-Hall, 1990. A good introduction to SNMP and SMI.

Security Study Committee (David D. Clark, Chairman), National Research Council, *Computers at Risk: Safe Computing in the Information Age.* Washington, D.C.: National Academy Press, 1991. ISBN 0-309-04388-3, 320 pp. Available in bookstores or by calling (800) 624-6242.

-9-

Long, Fat Pipes

"But why would I want a gigabit to my desktop?"

I had been enthusiastically describing the Gigabit Testbed projects coordinated by the Corporation for National Research Initiatives to a prominent member of the industry. Gigabits of network bandwidth, petabytes of secondary storage, and teraflop computers had all been bandied about in a description of tomorrow's high-speed networks when this question stopped me dead in my tracks.

"Why would I want a gigabit?" is similar to a question that was common a few years ago, "Why would a PC ever need a full 640 kbytes of memory?" Needless to say, as soon as people discovered spreadsheets, 640 kbytes was not only reasonable, it became the minimal acceptable amount. When we learn to make do with what we have, we sometimes forget that the driving force is not our ability to make do with the existing technological base but the demand by users to get work done.

To see why we might want gigabit networks, let's start again with the lowly PC. If you want to do computer-generated real-time graphics, think of the VGA interface on the PC. A VGA screen has 640 x 480 bits with 256 simultaneous colors. To support 256 simultaneous colors, you need one byte per pixel. If you are operating at 30 screens per second, generally accepted as the minimum acceptable rate for real-time video, you are generating a data rate of 73.728 Mbps.

Long, Fat Pipes

Now extend this analysis to workstations. Consider screens with 1000 x 1000 pixels and at least 2 bytes per pixel (yielding 64,000 simultaneous colors). All of a sudden we have increased our data rate from 73.728 Mbps to 480 Mbps.

Not every user needs 480 megabits per second on a transcontinental basis. Not every user is going to need all this bandwidth at all times. However, a few users will need this bandwidth at a time, and there are many, many users on real networks. We need both the capacity to deliver this bandwidth to the individual as well as the aggregate bandwidth to handle large numbers of users.

Another way to see the demand for high-speed networks is to examine how other portions of the computing environment are growing. A high-level (but not unusual) personal workstation has 100 Mbytes of storage, operates at 1-20 MIPS, and has 4-8 Mbytes of main memory. A rule that has held true for many years is that the shared computer of today ends up being the personal computer of tomorrow. A 1-20 MIPS machine with 8 Megabytes of Memory a few years ago would have been a large, shared VAX, but is now a personal workstation.

To see what the personal computer of tomorrow will look like, look at today's larger systems. It is not at all unusual to see 1 Gbyte of secondary storage, 20-50 MIPS systems, and 32-128 Mbytes of main memory. In fact, it is now possible (though fairly expensive) to buy personal workstations in this range. Over time, workstations will start to reach these levels for large numbers of people.

Let us look at even larger systems. Supercomputer centers and research laboratories are already working with terabytes of data. Groups like NASA are beginning to think in terms of petabytes (thousands of terabytes) of secondary and tertiary storage and some people are beginning to think in terms of exabytes (millions of terabytes).

Current large scale processors operate in the billion operations per second range. The High Performance Computing and Communications initiative will pour serious money into the development of a computer that will operate at a trillion operations per second.

Finally, look at main memory. Large supercomputer installations like the NASA-Ames Research Center have systems with main memories in the gigabyte range. In addition to a gigabyte of main memory, these systems often have another gigabyte or two allocated as a RAM disk. Systems with a terabyte or more of main memory are not that far off.

Balance is the key to any computer configuration. If the machines are faster and the disk drives larger, the networks also need to grow. If you need to load data into a terabyte of main memory, you are going to need more than an Ethernet.

The rationale for high-speed networks is particularly compelling if you realize that certain computer facilities will not be able to be duplicated. Computers are expensive, particularly supercomputers. In many cases, it won't make sense to buy one of each for each site. Instead, we need to put different computers in different locations.

Users will need to put these disparate computing locations together to form solutions to problems. Many efforts are now underway that try to see how different computing environments can be joined together to solve specific problems. In this chapter, we will look at two of these efforts.

Both the networks examined in this chapter, VISTAnet and CASA, are part of the National Gigabit Testbed program, coordinated by CNRI, the Corporation for National Research Initiatives. There are three other testbeds as part of the project. Funding of $15.8 million for this program comes from DARPA and NSF, with another $100 million in facilities, equipment, and personnel thrown in by a list of industrial participants that includes almost every major computer and telecommunications company in the country.

VISTAnet

The VISTAnet project is coordinated by the MCNC, a nonprofit corporation that runs the North Carolina Supercomputing Center. The group also runs another network called

Long, Fat Pipes

CONCERT which is a statewide private network built strictly on microwave towers. The network consists of three video networks that deliver NTSC signals to classrooms for classes and teleconferencing, plus a data network.

The VISTAnet project brings together three types of computers. First (of course) there is a large Cray computer. In this case the Cray computer is a CRAY Y-MP 8/432 with four processors, 64 megawords of main memory and another 128 megawords in a solid state disk. The machine has a peak performance of 1.2 Gflops. The Cray computer is located in a supercomputer center in the Research Triangle Park in North Carolina.

The second computer is a Pixel-Planes 5, an experimental machine developed at the Computer Science Department at the University of North Carolina. This machine does high-speed rendering of graphics. This autistic computer has the ability to do this one type of operation, and only this one type of operation, very fast. The Pixel-Planes is ideal for rendering polygonal images with lighting, shadows, and textures. The third machine is a MasPar, a commercial parallel processor, used for performing statistical manipulations.

All three of these machines are combined to help feed a workstation used by the Department of Radiation Oncology at UNC. The machine uses a joy stick to allow the physician to control a 1280 x 512 pixel color display that shows a three-dimensional representation of radiation doses.

The VISTAnet project links machines in three locations: the North Carolina Supercomputing Center (NCSC) in Research Triangle Park, and two departments at the University of North Carolina, the Department of Radiation Oncology and the Computer Sciences Department.

The three customer locations are near two different central offices, each operated by a different telephone company. University of North Carolina links up to a Southern Bell office. Research Triangle Park is served by GTE.

The two central offices are linked together with a 2.4 Gbps OC-48 SONET line. A Fujitsu FETEX-150B-ISDN ATM switch is placed in the Southern Bell office and provides OC-12C links to the two UNC departments, each link operating at 622 Mbps.

The Fujitsu switch is the primary switch for the network. The link to the OC-48 line moves data over to the GTE office. There, a broadband circuit switch moves data on toward the Cray computer. The circuit switch (also known as a digital cross connect) can also be used for other applications such as video teleconferencing.

Because computers do not have a raw SONET link, another standard is used to move the data onto the computer systems. A HIPPI to ATM Network Terminal Adaptor (NTA) provides this function. The computers have a simple HIPPI interface to the NTA.

The role of the NTA is to take incoming ATM cells and present them to the HIPPI interface at 800 Mbps. The NTA has to perform rate adaption between the ATM rate of 622 Mbps and HIPPI's 800 Mbps. The NTA also provides the connection management function. Remember that the HIPPI interface allows communication with one device at once, even though the ATM interface allows multiplexing of traffic. The NTA blocks calls until a virtual circuit is available to a remote HIPPI interface.

Why VISTAnet?

VISTAnet is in place mainly to do networking research. It sure helps, however, when you have a user. The user for VISTAnet is a fascinating experiment that applies high-speed networking to an area of medical practice known as radiation oncology.

When a person gets cancer, there are three ways to treat the cancer. Surgery and chemotherapy are often used, but suffer from many drawbacks. A third approach is to use radiation therapy. Radiation therapy takes a cancer and kills it with a beam of radiation. The problem is that both normal and diseased cells get killed when exposed to radiation.

Since the beam must pass through healthy tissue, a beam strong enough to kill the cancer will also kill healthy cells.

Luckily, the effect of radiation on cells is dependent on the dose. Small exposures do not hurt cells. If we split a radiation dose up into several beams that intersect at the diseased area, we can kill the diseased cells because they receive exposure to all beams. Healthy cells only receive exposure to a single beam and thus are able to survive.

Planning radiation treatment strategies starts with a CT scan of the diseased and surrounding areas. Because each cancer is unique—each has its own location, shape, and size—a doctor must develop an individual treatment plan for each situation that kills the diseased area without killing healthy cells.

Developing treatment plans operates in a very large parameter space with an infinite number of possible solutions. CT scans allow a two-dimensional view of the area. Analysis of a treatment plan shows the distribution of the dose over diseased and healthy areas within a single plane, but does not show the effect of the beams above and below the plane.

We thus have two problems. First, the number of possible solutions is very large. The number of beams, the locations of the beams, the position of the patient, and the type of shielding are just a few of the parameters. The complexity of the problem means only a few possible plans are tried.

The second problem is that the two-dimensional nature of the analysis means that only a portion of the effect can be seen. The result is that it is not uncommon for a treatment to get most of a diseased area, but not all, known as a local failure.

Estimates are that over 390,000 patients are treated per year with radiation therapy. Of those, 38,000 of the treatments are subject to local failures. While better diagnosis and treatment plans would not save all of those patients, it is likely that several thousand lives could be saved with better treatment.

Radiation oncology is thus a great application for high speed networking. When the VISTAnet project was trying to find an application for a gigabit testbed, they approached Dr. Julian Rosenman at the University of North Carolina.

Rosenman explained his problem in radiation oncology and explained his large computational requirements. To calculate a radiation dose distribution, a model consists of a system of 256^3 points. Each of these data points occupies 16 bits per point, resulting in a data rate of 256 megabits, clearly the province of a Cray computer.

The information coming out at this rate is not very useful as raw data. It needs to be graphically represented to be useful to a physician looking at alternative treatment plans. This data stream then goes into the Pixel-Planes 5 machine, 18 miles away from the Cray computer. This system is able to render the incoming data stream in near real time, at which point it needs to be displayed on a workstation, resulting in another very large data stream going over to the workstation.

VISTAnet is an example of how a single user can easily use a gigabit network. Visualization of radiation doses is an application that could not work in one site. It requires scarce facilities in multiple locations.

Note that in the medical field, it is not just the supercomputers that are scarce resources. Medical equipment is often very expensive and cannot be duplicated. Networks allow this scarce medical equipment to be used along with other scarce resources in other locations to form a more complete picture of diagnosis or treatment.

CASA

A second gigabit testbed project is CASA. CASA involves four of the most highly developed computing centers in the country:

- San Diego Supercomputer Center (SDSC)
- California Institute of Technology (Caltech)

- Jet Propulsion Laboratory (JPL)
- Los Alamos National Laboratory (LANL).

All four of these sites are known for providing the latest in supercomputer facilities. Caltech and LANL are both leaders in applying parallel processors such as the Connection Machine to real-world problems.

With all these large facilities, however, there are a series of problems that can overwhelm any one of these computer centers. CASA will tie all four of the sites together with an 800 Mbps computer network, spanning up to 1300 kilometers.

The three applications picked are, like in VISTAnet, applications requiring very high-speed networks. Like the VISTAnet radiation oncology example, they are real-world problems that require solutions unavailable on any one large computer system, or even in any one large computer center.

Predicting the Weather

Weather modeling is one of the applications that helps to spur larger and larger computers. Our weather system is so complex that most models concentrate on either the ocean or the atmosphere. Even dividing the problem into two leads to immense amounts of data.

Take atmospheric models, for example. If we take the world and divide it into grids of five degrees longitude by four degrees latitude, we have a fairly coarse grid of the world. If we model nine altitude layers, we have a grid of 72 x 44 x 9.

Even this coarse model of the atmosphere requires ten CPU seconds on a CRAY X-MP/48 to advance the model one hour. If we want to study a particular weather phenomenon, such as the Greenhouse Effect, it is not unusual to run a model through 50 years of space, requiring about 35 CPU days on the Cray computer.

Remember, this simplified model represents only one-half of the weather system, the atmosphere. The ocean model, at a coarse approximation, is a grid of 360 x 180, 27 levels deep. To advance this model a single hour, takes 20 CPU seconds on the CRAY X-MP/48, twice as long as the atmospheric model.

Although the atmosphere and the ocean have been separated, the weather should really be treated as a closed system. The output from the ocean model, especially sea surface temperature, is a key input to the atmospheric model. Outputs from the atmospheric model, such as winds and heat flux, are key inputs to the ocean model.

Under the direction of R. Mechoso of UCLA, CASA will combine two standard models to form a single closed system, the input from one model driving the other. Two machines will be used, one for each model.

The oceanic model will be put on a Connection Machines CM-2, which speeds the ocean model up by a factor of 50-100 times. The speedup is due to the superior programming model, for this particular application, of the massively parallel architecture.

The atmospheric model will be put on a CRAY Y-MP8/864, located at the San Diego Supercomputer Center. This particular configuration of the CRAY Y-MP yields speedup of twelve times over the CRAY X-MP. Notice that the ocean model will be running fifty times faster, whereas the atmospheric model will run only a dozen times faster.

To handle the mismatch, the hydrodynamic part of the atmospheric model will be moved over to the CM-2, leaving the Cray computer with atmospheric problems like cumulus cloud convection and radiation calculations. Of course, a tremendous amount of data needs to move between the Cray computer and the CM-2, including data such as temperature and humidity for each grid for each cycle. Estimates are that approximately 750 Mbps per second of data will be transferred between the two machines.

Why bother with all this? A unified model is a way of tuning individual components so they reflect reality much more closely. If valid inputs yield valid outputs, we can start

189

looking more accurately at questions like the Greenhouse Effect, forecasts of trade winds, and other global phenomena.

Quantum Chemical Reaction Dynamics

A second CASA application is the study of chemical reactions at the molecular level. This type of study is important not only in chemistry, but in molecular biology, materials science, and applied physics.

Studying chemical reactions is ideal for a high-speed networking project. Chemical reactions involve large numbers of matrix operations including inversions, multiplication, and Eigen analysis. Decomposing large problems on large machines thus requires a fairly constant flow of portions of matrices between the machines.

The particular reaction picked for the CASA testbed is the reaction of fluorine atoms with a hydrogen molecule. This reaction is the basis for today's most powerful chemical laser, the hydrogen-fluorine chemical laser.

Chemical reactions in general are not easy to simulate. Take a very simple reaction:

$$H + H_2 \rightarrow H_2 + H$$

At higher energies, this symmetric, simple reaction takes 200 hours of a CRAY X-MP and 128 Megabytes of main memory. The fluorine/hydrogen reaction ($F + H_2$) takes two more orders of magnitude: 12,800 CPU hours (1.5 CPU years) of the CRAY X-MP and two gigawords of main memory.

Why the increase in computational needs? As the reaction increases in complexity, the number of possible energy states between the atoms increases. The number of possible energy states, in turn, influences the order of magnitude of the matrices to be manipulated. The fluorine problem involves 5 to 10 thousand possible states.

Instead of using 12,800 hours of a CRAY X-MP, CASA will devote three machines to the problem:

- The SDSC CRAY Y-MP8/864, twelve times as fast as the X-MP
- A Mark IIIfp with 128 processors at Caltech, three times the speed of the X-MP.
- The CM-2 at LANL, 30 times the speed.

This combination of three machines is thus 45 times the power of a CRAY X-MP, assuming you can keep the machines busy. The problem takes only 300 hours on the combined system. The challenge in this problem is how to keep the machines busy.

3-D Seismic Profiling

Before we look at the CASA network itself, we examine one more CASA application, involving three-dimensional rendering of data from multiple earth-science data sets. This project is run at the Jet Propulsion Laboratory, but takes advantage of data and computers in different CASA locations.

Data in the earth sciences is increasing at fairly astonishing rates. There are a variety of different sources of this information: LANDSAT, topographic databases, and seismic databases, for example. One of the real challenging sources of information will be the space station, known as the NASA Earth Orbiting System (EOS). The EOS will be sending data down at the rate of 300 Mbps, equivalent to ten Gbytes every six minutes. And this is just one of many sources.

Combining information from different sources allows a variety of very important applications, including the modeling of earthquake faults, which allows prediction of an estimate of the order of magnitude of a coming earthquake (but not the exact time).

Earth sciences databases can be used for a variety of other tasks. Combined data sets have allowed researchers to discover that the Sahara desert was once a large river basin and even to find long-hidden roadways in Mongolia and Arabia, buried for several thousand years.

The point of the CASA application is to try and learn how to handle these very large datasets coming from different locations. For the JPL, this project is preparation for the flood of data expected from the space station. JPL is trying to learn how to handle data streams of three Gbytes/second and up which could require 90 Gigaflops or more to process.

Being able to handle data quickly is often crucial. An example is when the Voyager-2 was approaching Neptune. When the Voyager was 3-4 days out from the closest approach, an interesting feature was found on Neptune. Normally, it would take VAX systems weeks to analyze the data and provide positioning instructions for the on-board cameras. Instead, an eight-node Mark IIIfp was used to make the calculation quickly enough to send up repositioning instructions.

The particular application chosen will merge data from three sources to provide 3-D cutaways of the earth's surface, allowing the identification of fault zones and major plate thrusts. Interactive 3-D graphics are essential for this application, because researchers cannot tell ahead of time the level of detail and particular view they need when examining specific places in the earth.

The three sources of information include the LANDSAT thematic mapper, CALCRUST seismic reflection data, and elevation data from the Space Shuttle's imaging radar. The amount of data involved for each image produced is fairly amazing.

The LANDSAT thematic mapper, for example, involves a typical image of 90 x 90 kilometers. The image is broken up into 3000 by 3000 pixels with seven bands at ten bits, yielding 82 megabytes per data image. The shuttle elevation data form a 200-Mbyte raw data set that needs to be filtered each time to yield a 6000 by 6000 point image. The seismic database is 1–2 Gbytes, taking tens of hours on a VAX to reduce to the pertinent information needed for a single image.

Once the three databases have been filtered, it takes yet more computer power to combine them to yield a rendered

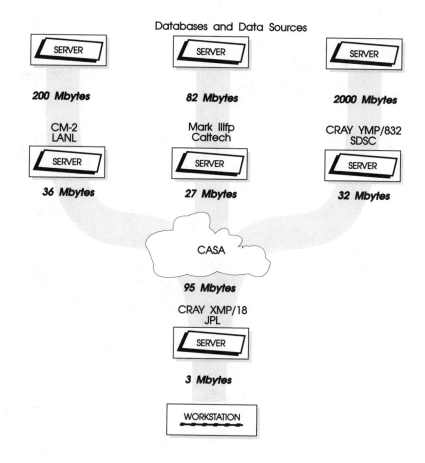

Figure 9-1 Data Filtering In CASA

image. On a VAX, for example, it takes 14-17 minutes per frame for rendering. A minimal animation would be 1400 frames, requiring over 16 days of computing time.

The strategy to solve this problem is to break the problem down. Rendering of the data is performed on JPL's CRAY X-MP/18. The actual data filtering is done at Caltech, SDSC, and LANL. Figure 9-1 shows the extent of the data filtering. Even with the processing done at remote sites, there is still,

193

Long, Fat Pipes

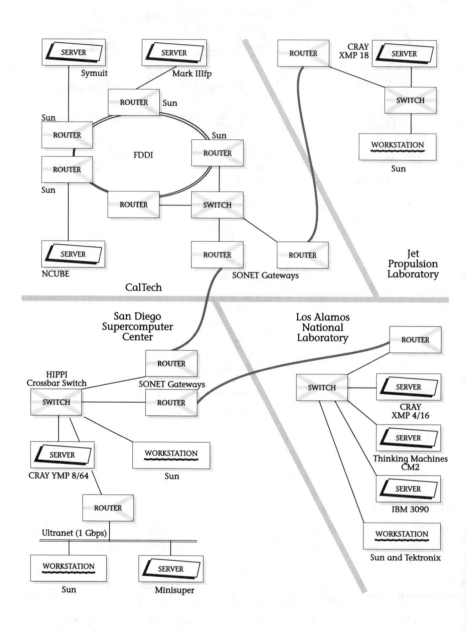

Figure 9-2 The CASA Network

if you have only one frame per minute, roughly 800 Mbps of data flow to the JPL.

If you wanted to do real animation, it would take a minimum of 30 frames per second, yielding a data rate of 23.5 Gbps. The amount of processing power to do this animation would be 63 Gigaflops (the four machines involved in the application deliver around two Gigaflops of processing power).

The CASA Network

The CASA network is a wide-area network. Each of the participating sites has a high-speed LAN, based on HIPPI. The host computers are all connected to the HIPPI switch. A HIPPI-SONET gateway is connected to the HIPPI switch (See Fig. 9-2).

The HIPPI-SONET gateway hooks up to long-haul optical fiber running the SONET protocols at STS-24 speeds (1.244 Gbps). Notice that SONET is being used directly instead of using an intervening ATM-based data link.

Linking HIPPI to SONET poses at least two problems. First, there is a difference in speed, with HIPPI running at 800 Mbps. Aside from rate adaptation, there is the more crucial problem of hiding latency. HIPPI won't let a source send data unless it has a ready signal. With a host required to store 64 ready HIPPI signals, and the propagation speed of HIPPI, we have a maximum HIPPI limit of 64 kilometers. CASA, however, needs 1500 to 2000 kilometers to function.

For HIPPI switches, CASA uses a switch developed at LANL in collaboration with DEC. The switch is a physical cross-bar switch; the switch actually moves to make the connection. This is a very fast physical switch, however, allowing a connection to be made in five microseconds if there is no contention.

The fiber for CASA is furnished by three telephone companies: MCI for the long-haul portion and the relevant Bell Operating Companies for the local loops. Built on top of this substrate is, to begin with, straight TCP/IP. If TCP proves inadequate as a transport layer, other candidates such as VMTP and NETBLT might be tried.

None of this, however, will be seen by the application programmer. The programmer would see, at the very lowest level, the UNIX sockets interface to TCP. Most programmers would work at even higher levels, using a collection of library routines such as Express. Express was designed for embedding information in C or FORTRAN programs that run on massively parallel processors. Express handles the questions of moving data and messages around and includes a symbolic parallel debugger and performance monitor for testing applications.

Is the project serious? In addition to tremendous manpower, it is interesting to look at how much CPU time has been allocated on the big machines:

- SDSC has allocated 1900 CPU hours on the Y-MP8/864.
- LANL has allocated 1100 hours on their Cray computer and 1100 hours on the CM-2.

The Cray computer CPU hours are supplemented by numerous other computers, not to mention a 1.2-Gbps, 1300-km fiber line.

Terabit Networks

If people are fielding large-scale field experiments for gigabit networks, others must be working on speeds an order of magnitude higher. This is indeed the case. The ACORN project, based at Columbia University's Center for Telecommunications Research is an attempt to field an experimental network delivering one or more gigabits of bandwidth to each workstation.

To achieve such speeds, ACORN taps the 50-100 Thz capacity of the optical spectrum. By contrast, the entire radio spectrum has a capacity of 20-30 Ghz. If you can successfully address the terahertz capacity of fiber, then networks with thousands of gigabit pipes can be constructed.

196

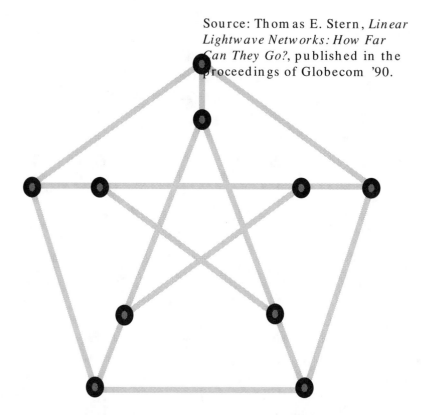

Source: Thomas E. Stern, *Linear Lightwave Networks: How Far Can They Go?*, published in the Proceedings of Globecom '90.

Figure 9-3 The Linear Lightware Network

ACORN aims more at the network than at the computers that use the network as was the case in the CNRI testbeds. The aim of the project is to field an experimental architecture that might form the basis of a fiber-based, wide-area public network.

A prototype of this network is up and running in a laboratory. The laboratory model consists of an entirely passive optical fiber network along with two (with future expansion to four) network interface units that provide ATM-like, gigabit-per-second ports to the user.

During 1992, ACORN will deploy the network in lower Manhattan with applications such as multi-media communications between workstations. The applications will test the network and begin examining how it will scale to large num-

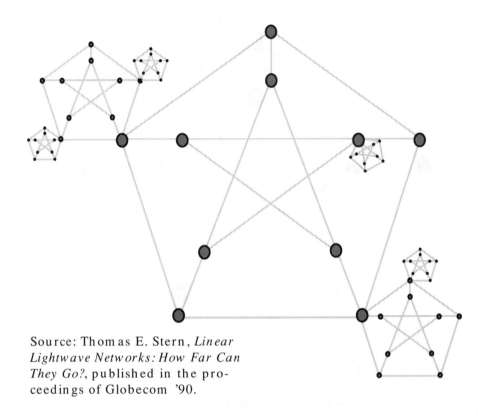

Source: Thomas E. Stern, *Linear Lightwave Networks: How Far Can They Go?*, published in the proceedings of Globecom '90.

Figure 9-4 An Extended LLN Topology

bers. The goal is a network expandable to millions of nodes with multi-gigabit universal service ports.

The network itself is based on dark fiber - fiber not limited by existing switching or transmission approaches. The network uses an architecture developed by Thomas Stern of Columbia, known as the Linear Lightwave Network (See Fig. 9-3).

A Linear Lightwave Network has several potential paths between any two hosts. By allocating different gigabit bands of the fiber to different circuits and by using different routes, any two users can communicate.

The nodes of this network are simple optical switches that can perform linear operations on optical signals: combining two signals together or splitting them based on their wave lengths. These interior nodes are built out of arrays of electro-optic directional couplers. The couplers use an electric signal to control the optical connections from input ports to output ports.

The ACORN project believes that this Linear Lightwave Network topology can scale to very large networks. The basic topology can be combined as a series of modules, forming a hierarchical system. Certain bandwidths would be used for long-haul connections, others would be used inside a module. Figure 9-4 shows such a potential topology.

ACORN is a research project, but illustrates current frontiers in high-speed network research. While the CASA projects aim at how large systems can use large networks, the ACORN TeraNet is aimed at a huge public network with aggregate capacities in the terabits per second.

CASA aims at a few users, but has firm applications in mind. ACORN has a few vague applications and applies them to large-capacity networks. In the next chapter, we will bring these two strands together and look at what a network with many people and large capacity might do. While CASA and ACORN are real, the next chapter enters the land of knowbots and shows a vision of why CASA and ACORN are so vital.

For Further Reading

Gigabit networks are new enough that few books and articles are available on the topic. There are, however, several excellent seminars on the subject. Van Jacobson teaches a seminar on fast transport protocols, Craig Partridge has a frequently held seminar on gigabit networks which is taught at INTEROP. For information on the Gigabit Testbed programs, write to the Corporation for National Research Initiatives in Reston, Virginia which coordinates the project.

Long, Fat Pipes

There are also frequent conferences on the subject. An annual event is sponsored by UMIACS, a research institute affiliated with the University of Maryland at Baltimore County. Information on other conferences can be found SIG-COMM's Computer Communication Review (CCR). For more information on CCR, send electronic mail to craig@bbn.com.

– 10 –

Digital Libraries

Throughout this book, we have looked at protocols that help form a very large, very fast network. Too often, we forget what these networks are being used for.

In this chapter, we will look at a vision of what the network of the somewhat near future might do. This vision, termed the Digital Library System, was developed by Bob Kahn and Vinton Cerf, both important contributors to the original ARPANET and its successor, the Internet.

Kahn and Cerf are not just dreamers; they are actively involved in the management of the Internet. Cerf is chairman of the Internet Activities Board and plays a key role in the development of the TCP/IP standards. Kahn has been one of the most active voices pushing for a gigabit National Research and Education Network.

The Digital Library System (DLS) is just one of many applications we can expect to see on the new and improved Internet. We picked the DLS as the end of this book for two important reasons. First, it is a fascinating vision of the future, and is thus intrinsically interesting.

A more important reason, however, is to show how even such an apparently grandiose vision as the DLS is not as farfetched as one might think at first glance. A variety of the pieces of the Digital Library System are beginning to emerge, ranging from library automation projects to resource discovery.

The DLS is thus just one vision of what an automated, digital library might look like—the DLS is thus not "the" but one of many possible worlds. Many different research efforts are working on the same problems and there is much work to be done.

A World of Knowbots

Perhaps the most futuristic-sounding component of the Digital Library System is the knowbot, an intelligent program that is launched onto the network. The knowbot visits different nodes looking for information of use to the knowbot's master. The knowbot performs tasks, perhaps rooting through databases or negotiating purchase terms for information, and sends messages back to its master. The master may be a person, but could well be another knowbot. Knowbots are not an idea unique to Cerf and Kahn. Marvin Minsky, for example, postulated a world of agents, intelligent programs that go around the network doing things for people (or for other agents).

According to Dr. Kahn, a knowbot is any program that causes actions to occur on another system. That action may be caused by some form of network protocol, or the knowbot might actually move itself over to the other system and execute the instructions, a process known as teleportation.

Teleportation? Shades of Star Trek! We will see that teleportation protocols already exist. Before looking at these futuristic-sounding mechanisms, however, let's step back and look at what a Digital Library System (DLS) is.

Think of a paper library system. There is a stack of paper, perhaps the contents of a file drawer or perhaps a bigger stack like the Library of Congress. Using a variety of mechanisms, you filter that stack and find the piece you are interested in, a letter or a book, for example.

Searching can be quite simple, as in the case of rifling through a file cabinet. Filtering can also be complex, as in the case of using the Library of Congress catalog to retrieve a reference book which then points to some other book.

The Digital Library System

Before we can describe what a digital library system is, you need to make a leap of faith and think of what the world is quickly coming to. Think of computers with real-time speech recognition, easy capture of images via scanning and telemetry and multimedia documents consisting of sound, voice, and high-definition television (in addition, of course, to more familiar forms of data representations).

It's tough enough today keeping track of the flow of information. Imagine what it will be like when these technologies allow people to produce information at even faster rates. Basically, technology will allow us to have larger and larger shovels. If we are not careful, we will soon bury ourselves.

The DLS is a way to keep track of this information explosion. First, there is an explicit recognition that information goes on-line. Once the information, ranging from on-line journals to simple message traffic, is on-line, there needs to be a way of registering, storing, and retrieving the information.

Information can be as simple as electronic mail or it can be as sophisticated as on-line registries of information. Take the medical profession, for instance. Kahn and Cerf paint the example of a system that allows one to capture and store a wide variety of information: x-rays, sonograms, and other images.

This information can be used at the atomic level by the medical profession to do tasks like biochemical simulation or patient-specific biochemical therapy. Futuristic? We saw in the last chapter how radiological oncology is beginning to do just that.

Massive amounts of detailed, on-line information mean that epidemiological studies, tissue mapping, or even computer simulation of therapies all become possibilities. Evaluation of surgical techniques or drug effectiveness are just two of the many such applications that come to mind.

Or, take the more mundane world of commerce. On-line blueprints of buildings mean that we have a library of parts to choose from for new buildings. On-line court decisions, corporate charters, and intellectual property claims allow us to find prior work and use it effectively.

The possibilities, as the saying goes, are endless. The problem is, with that much raw information, there needs to be a way to handle it effectively, both in the aggregate and for individual uses.

Enter the knowbot. Kahn and Cerf talk about vast arrays of information "sorted, analyzed and mined by tireless knowbots making their endless journey through information space." Knowbots are the agents that troll The Matrix looking for new resources that can be used. One of the problems in today's Internet is that new services and information are added, but it is hard to make the link between the service and the subset of users that are interested in the service.

A broadcast of the availability of a service quickly fails because there are so many new services that you have to ignore the broadcasts. This approach was tried on the Usenet by posting the availability of new FTP archives on a bulletin board. The bulletin board got so big so quickly that few except the most hardened use it.

Infrastructure

The proposal for a digital library system is really a proposal for a new infrastructure. Infrastructures are planned, of course, they do not happen by accident.

It is fair to say that today most text starts on a computer. Most often, however, the text ends up being delivered on paper. Finding relevant information is the key challenge. The aim of the Digital Library System is to keep that information digital. Keeping it digital is tough enough (imagine the challenge of petabytes of still images and exabytes of video libraries), but the real challenge is the question of intellectual property.

Take books, for example. Today, intellectual property for books is based on the ownership of pieces of paper. When you buy a book, you have a right to use a piece of information. You can give the book away, but you are not legally allowed to create a new copy using a photocopy machine.

In a digital library, however, paper does not exist. Copies are needed to share the information. Merely reading the information is making a copy. Mailing that information to somebody else is making another copy.

The challenge becomes more complex when we think of intelligent information sources. Imagine a "document" that is really an intelligent spreadsheet. You read the document as a way of making some sort of forecast. By reading the spreadsheet, you've agreed to perform some compensation to the owner.

If you mail the spreadsheet to somebody, or incorporate the results into a newer, fancier, superspreadsheet, there needs to be a way of making sure the original author is compensated. Of course, not every author will want compensation—a large amount of information is today in the public domain, as in the case of the RFC series where copyright is claimed but all copying is allowed.

Compensation for intellectual property is really the key obstacle that must be overcome to make the system work properly. Imagine a CD-ROM that has 1000 computer books on it. If you pay by the disk, when you read my book, James Martin gets a free ride on my writing. Likewise, James Martin might make a strong case that there is no reason for him to subsidize my work.

A better system is the model used by ASCAP for records. For records you buy, you pay by the physical copy. However, radio stations pay every time they use data by playing a record. Revenue for commercial radio use of records is based on actual play instead of the number of pieces of vinyl exchanged.

In the DLS, documents are intelligent entities. When you make a copy of a document, your document includes the active entity. The entity can be very simple, reporting back every time you make a new copy. Or, the entity can be intelligent, charging based on actual use.

The initial DLS architecture is focused on the domain of printed documents, which can be a tremendous amount of information. The key issue in this environment is simple document location. Intelligent knowbots and more structured documents have to wait—simple search agents ("KnowNots?") are the first step.

DLS Components

A digital library system consists of many different servers on a network, chief among them database servers. One database server might be an on-line card catalog, another might be an FTD Flower Server, accepting orders for flowers and sending them out via alternate media (trucks and delivery vans).

The user has a personal library system (PLS). The PLS is responsible for launching knowbots out to other servers to get the information you need. The PLS needs to keep track of what information you are interested in, not necessarily an easy task.

The DLS has a variety of utility servers to supplement the database servers. An accounting and statistics server helps make sure that the users are paying for things they use. A registration server takes incoming information and decides where it should go. An import/export server provides links to other worlds; a fax server, for example, would take incoming fax documents and process them for the DLS by either storing the image or using filters like optical character recognition. A transform server modifies the representation of information, as in the case of shifting from fax encoding to the Office Document Architecture (ODA), or even a simple transform to a Tagged Image Format File (TIFF).

A PLS includes a personal library, which might grow quite large. The library would include strictly personal documents, copies of frequently consulted information, the results of queries, and probably a cache of all recently accessed documents. In order to find the information you are interested in, the PLS may exchange tens of thousands of messages with the rest of the DLS.

These message exchanges are mediated by knowbots. Knowbots can be stationary and communicate using network protocols. Alternatively, knowbots can move over to another system where they dock into a port. The remote host provides a knowbot operating environment that gives the knowbot the resources it needs: file creation, memory allocation, CPU cycles, and any other resources needed to do work.

When a knowbot moves to another system, it may bring work documents along with it. These documents might be intermediate results, search plans and criteria, relevant output format templates, or information used for accounting or security purposes.

Knowbots are one kind of object. The actual documents stored in the DLS are also objects. The object could be a multi-media message, a videotape, or an intelligent entity such as a data-driven forecasting module. Every object has a special component called a courier. The courier is a special class of trusted knowbot that is the point of access to the object.

Not all objects need couriers. Those with no access controls can be simple objects with no functionality. For example, international standards documents could be provided at no cost on a public database server. These standards would not need couriers to mediate access; indeed such a database server would be almost trivial to implement (the TCP/IP standards are currently available on various Internet-based servers).

In some cases, the courier may be a passive courier, equivalent to a read-me file on a software distribution. In other cases, couriers report on usage, prevent copying the whole object or certain portions of the object, and perform any other functions that the object supports.

Registering a Document

An import server is where information enters the DLS. The import server accepts submissions as they arrive. The submissions may be part of an email message, an incoming fax, or a PC with a database of files to be added to the DLS.

Before an object can be added to the system, it needs to be classified. At the very least, we need to know the owner and origin of the object. In addition, we probably want to know any terms and conditions for its use, any descriptive information that will help in searches, the relationship to existing information, and some clue as to what format the information may be in.

The import server thus takes an incoming object and structures the information in a way that the DLS can interpret. Then, a knowbot is launched to a registration server. The knowbot has a copy of the object and its descriptive information and asks the registration server what to do with the information.

The registration server will, after examining the object, consult an index, cataloging, and reference server. The object is then moved over to a database server where it is incorporated into a database.

The job of the registration server is to make sure that every new object has a unique ID. The registration server will then report the existence of this new object to any relevant component of the DLS. For example, the accounting server will want to know that a new object exists so that it can charge for disk space. In addition, the accounting server will need to know if there are any charging policies for the object, so that the owner may be properly remunerated when the object is accessed by others.

Just because accounting servers exist does not mean that every user will be charged for disk space (or any other metric of system use) for every object. As with electronic mail systems, there is a question of who should pay; the object owner, the object user, or a third-party storage provider are all potential targets. There will be many times when information in a database will not be in a form that a given PLS will be able to accept. For example, take the case of storing documents in revisable form. A particular database server may choose to use the format advocated by the Association of American Publishers, the Standard Generalized Markup Language (SGML).

Your PLS, however, may be an ISOphilic PLS and thus use the Office Document Architecture (ODA). When your knowbot grabs an SGML document, it needs to stop off at a transform server to move the document into ODA format. Transform servers are essential in this environment. Images, for example, might be in Group III or Group IV fax. Or, they might be in TIFF, PCX, PICT, or any of the other wide variety of standards.

Building the DLS

The underlying architecture for a DLS is an object management system. In addition, there needs to be some form of knowbot operating environment, that allows incoming queries to be satisfied by giving a knowbot sufficient resources. Finally, there needs to be a teleportation protocol; a means of moving the knowbot around the network.

The assumption behind the DLS is that scope is not unlimited. There will probably be multiple digital library systems each confined to some region, corporation, organization, or other institution. Communication between different library systems is at a lower level of functionality than inside of a given DLS.

The PLS is primarily a visual means of interacting. Kahn and Cerf envision a personal library system with a wide variety of searching, cataloging, and retrieval knowbots. Those knowbots are represented visually.

Most important, this visual representation of information space is shared across multiple personal library systems, a concept known as a shared icon geography. In their vision, users can travel from place to place in this space. You select objects to examine, organize the objects into your own personal space, or share information with other users by copying icons.

The real challenge to building a DLS is not the software, but operational considerations. A digital library should, by definition, be broad in scope. A small DLS for a work group is nice (see the success of Lotus Notes for evidence of the need for these facilities). What makes the DLS useful, like any other form of communications, is the ability to scale.

Fax machines are an example of scaling. Only after they reached a certain level of market penetration did they truly become a useful part of the business toolset. The Internet is another example where fast growth has spurred even faster growth. Getting digital libraries established means that we need to take a hard look at the question of intellectual property and the revenues coming from them.

Do Knowbots Exist?

A description of Knowbots is certainly interesting, but also serves a more important purpose in a book on computer networks and interoperability. By showing just one vision—and there are many others—we begin to see why large-scale, high-capacity, ubiquitous networks are necessary.

In a way, the vision of a knowbot helps validate the work we have seen for B-ISDN, high-speed ATM switches, and multi-gigabit SONET pipes. More importantly, we can use the vision of knowbots and compare it to the current state of technology. Knowbots and the DLS appear at first glance to be an impossible dream, but a strong argument can be made that many of the pieces are beginning to be put into place.

Take the work of librarians, for example. Many of the largest libraries in the world, including the Library of Congress and the libraries of the University of California have their entire library catalogs on-line. In the case of UC Melvyl system, on-line means on the Internet and no access control; anybody can Telnet to the UC system and search the catalog.

Putting card catalogs on the Internet has been extremely successful. There are some more ambitious efforts also underway.

For several years, commercial service providers for databases have used custom interfaces to their data based on the model of a terminal calling up via a modem. Sometimes, the terminal can be located across an X.25 network on an X.3 PAD.

Of course, users are rarely on terminals these days. Usually, the user is on a PC using a terminal emulation program. Increasingly, the user is on a workstation and a network protocol is used to get to a modem on a communications server at the edge of the local network, which then places calls to information providers.

There is no reason why the Internet cannot substitute for X.25 or a dialup telephone line. After all, Telnet performs the same function of emulating a terminal. The catch has been the question of accounting and charging.

Most databases that are available on networks use a two-stage approach. First, users have a network service such as Telnet to get to the edge of the commercial provider's network. There, access control (account numbers and passwords) are used to let users access the system in question.

Finding Things

Getting database systems on line and handling the details of access control and accounting are fairly minor problems that are being solved today. There are no insurmountable technical obstacles—groups like the Internet Engineering Task Force have put an infrastructure into place that makes on-line databases feasible and practical.

Many groups are looking at the question of access control and accounting. Workshops are being held at Harvard, reports are being generated from Washington, and many commercial systems are up and running.

Digital Libraries

The big problem is finding resources. Even within the confines of the current Internet, just finding a resource can be a major challenge. Often, a user needs to procure the services of a local guru who can navigate the maze and find nuggets of information.

A few people are beginning to tackle this problem. The Corporation for National Research Initiatives has sponsored some work into knowbots. The result of this work has been some utilities for finding people on the Internet. To find a person, you send a message which contains all you know about a person to the Knowbot Information Service (KIS), a service developed by Ralph Droms as a CNRI research project.

For example, KIS could receive a query looking for Mike at Colorado. KIS will take the query and try to figure where that information might be. For example, KIS might use the TCP finger utility on a machine at the University of Colorado or the SRI International Network Information Center's WHOIS service.

Chances are that this particular query would return the name of Mike Schwartz, an active person in the area of resource discovery. Schwartz has constructed a similar device to KIS, known as Netfind. Netfind scans the Usenet newsfeed periodically looking for useful seeds of information. Netfind might learn, for example, that an organization "University of Colorado" exists in Boulder. Finding out about the existence of organizations and locales forms the seed database for Netfind.

When a user is looking for somebody, Netfind starts with the seed database. Then, Netfind accesses a wide variety of existing networks to find information. It might query the Domain Name Service (DNS), the finger utility, or anything else it can find. Netfind will even contact the Simple Mail Transfer Protocol (SMTP) on machines to see if it is handling mail for a particular username.

The result of services like Netfind and KIS is a decentralized directory service that can find over 1.5 million people.

The term directory service is a bit of a misnomer because most directory services are based on some form of centralized database. Netfind and KIS exploit existing sources of information. By using semantic knowledge of existing sources (such as the fact that a username appears in a certain line of the response from an information server like finger), multiple sources of information are marshalled to answer a query.

Schwartz has used this property of exploiting the semantic content of information sources to do a wide variety of other forms of resource discovery. For example, research projects are underway that are attempting to find useful database resources available on file systems like the Network File System or anonymous FTP.

Resource discovery without centralized administration is crucial. The Internet is too diverse to rely on a single directory service. There will always be many sources of information that can be queried.

The hope of people like Schwartz is a truly usable network. They envision a network where a user can plug a laptop in and see a visual representation of the network. The map would have useful resources: nearby printers, relevant databases, and useful utilities.

Erdös Analysis

Finding a particular person is one aspect of resource discovery. Given a few clues, utilities like KIS and Netfind can track down an address and username for that person.

What if you do not know the person? Instead of knowing the person by name, you might just know that you are looking for people interested in or knowledgeable on certain subjects. For instance, "Are there any biologists that specialize in the leg muscles of invertebrates like cockroaches?" It turns out that what we want are invertebrate pathologists and physiologists interested in the topics of work and motion.

One way to find this information is through a directory service like X.500. There is a problem, however. Somebody must put this information into a directory like X.500. It is doubtful that invertebrate physiologists would take the time out from their busy research to register themselves to some computer directory.

Schwartz at Colorado took the same reliance on the existing network protocols to come up with another approach. Before we describe this approach, however, we must stop briefly to describe a Hungarian mathematician named Erdös.

Erdös is an extremely prolific mathematician, constantly coauthoring papers with colleagues. It seems that everyone has coauthored a paper with Erdös—his total output is around 1000 papers.

To test the theory that everyone had coauthored papers with Erdös, another mathematician developed a metric called an Erdös number. If you coauthored a paper with Erdös, you had an Erdös number of 1. If you coauthored a paper with somebody who had coauthored a paper with Erdös, you had an Erdös number of 2, and so on.

It turned out that no living mathematician had an Erdös number greater than 6. Therefore, to reach all mathematicians, we could start with Erdös. Six hops later, we would have reached the edge of the network, a much more effective distribution mechanism than mass delivery to all mathematicians from some central list.

Schwartz decided to test this small world theory with the Internet. He put filters in 15 sites on the network that kept track of "To" and "From" lines on mail messages. The data were carefully protected to make sure that individual traffic had full privacy and only aggregate information was disclosed.

It turns out that the Internet, based on this sample of data, has a diameter of 12 or 13. Schwartz estimates that a more complete sample, by more accurately reflecting true traffic patterns, would show a diameter of 6 to 8. In other words, the small world phenomenon applies to more than mathematicians.

Schwartz applied the analysis to himself to see what types of people frequently exchanged messages with him. Not surprisingly, most of the people had a strong interest in resource discovery.

In other words, if we want to distribute information on resource discovery, the best way we could post that information would be to "people who are like Mike Schwartz." Even more powerful would be to find "people who are interested in things that Mike Schwartz and Vinton Cerf have in common." Distribution based on actual communication patterns is far more effective than posting the message on Usenet (where most people ignore it) or on mailing lists (where many relevant people might be missing).

Erdös analysis, Netfind, KIS, and other similar projects are all attempts to use the existing network in a more powerful manner. These efforts are succeeding—enough people are using the networks that the growth of the Internet is greater than 4% per month.

For Further Reading

Kahn and Cerf, *The Digital Library System.* Available from the Corporation for National Research Initiatives. Send electronic mail to vcerf@nri.reston.va.us or to the SNAILmail address in the back of this book (See "For Further Information").

Schwartz, M. F., "Resource Discovery and Related Research at the University of Colorado." *ConneXions*, Vol. 5, No. 5, May 1991, pp. 12-20.

Schwartz, M. F., and Tsirigotis, P. G., "Experience with a Semantically Cognizant Internet White Pages Directory Tool." *Journal of Internetworking: Research and Experience,* 2(1), pp. 23-50, March 1991. Available for anonymous FTP from latour.colorado.edu in the file pub/RD.Papers/White.Pages.ps.Z.

Schwartz, M. F., and Wood, D. C. M., "A Measurement Study of Organizational Properties in the Global Electronic Mail Community." Technical Report CU-CS-482-90, Department of Computer Science, University of Colorado, Boulder, Colorado, August 1990. Submitted for publication. Available for anonymous FTP from latour.colorado.edu in the file pub/RD.Papers/RD.For.Anon.FTP.ps.Z.

Schwartz, M. F., et al., "Supporting Resource Discovery Among Public Internet Archives Using a Spectrum of Information Quality." *Proceedings of the Eleventh IEEE International Conference on Distributed Computing Systems*, pp. 82-89, Arlington, Texas, May 1991. Available for anonymous FTP from latour.colorado.edu in the directory pub/RD.Papers/Email.Study.

– 11 –

Who Owns Standards?

Cost is real. In the long run, as technology becomes well understood and the resulting commodities are easily produced, the market begins to wield its invisible hand. Making technology a commodity is the whole basis for the push towards open systems. We want well-understood pieces to plug and play, allowing us to concentrate our efforts on the difficult problems; how to use systems, not how to make them.

Open systems allow many different vendors to sell commodity items. Just as importantly, open systems allow new, innovative products to easily hook on to the existing set of technologies.

Standards is the key to open systems. The accessibility of the standards are the key to making open systems widespread—open systems do no good if people do not know about them. This key point seems to have been forgotten in the rush to capitalize on the standards process.

What Is a Standard?

There are many definitions of a standard, but I will use a very simple definition. A standard is any useful convention that people know about.

Remember the old VAX 11/780 running the VMS operating system? That was a standard. Early versions of VMS were well-documented and one could easily build on it, add-

217

ing third-party compilers, applications programs, databases, and many other add-ons.

The VAX hardware was also a standard because it used a peripheral bus known as the Unibus. The specifications for the Unibus were published, allowing a wide variety of third-party products: array processors, disk controllers, network interface cards, and WAN communications controllers, to name just a few.

Notice that the Unibus is proprietary, but public knowledge about the nature of the interface to the proprietary Unibus makes it a standard. The BI-Bus, a successor to the Unibus, is not a standard. The interface is not well-documented because DEC considers the interface proprietary and information is limited to licensees.

Making information public is the key to being a standard. This is not to say that there is not room in the marketplace for proprietary solutions. There is room for both standards and non-standards in a user network. The pieces can work together. However, the major interfaces in many modern computer networks are based on standards. We use Ethernet, FDDI, HIPPI, or a raft of other interfaces to the substrate. We use sockets, TLI, or XDI as the interface to the protocol stack.

One should not confuse the origin of a technology with its status as a standard. Sun's Network File System was developed independently by Sun—there were no committee meetings, no consortia, no votes—just a few engineers in a room.

Yet, NFS is certainly a standard. This is because, once the product was developed, Sun announced the specifications along with a simple licensing policy. This strategy resulted in over 290 licenses for NFS and 90 implementations.

By making NFS a standard, Sun basically gave it away. Giving technology away did not, however, result in a loss for Sun. You can bet that a whole bunch more Sun workstations were sold because NFS existed and because of its wide acceptance. After all, wide implementations meant that Sun sales staff could sell their equipment into any network.

Giving something away is not enough to make something a standard. There are constant announcements by vendors of giveaways, often just as a mask to give legitimacy to some technical approach used in a product. A standard must be widely accepted, based on the suitability of the technology and the high quality of the engineering.

The first requirement, however, is that people know about a standard. Does the information have to be free and easily available on the Internet? Not necessarily, but that certainly makes it easier for people to find out about it.

Another key for a standard to become real is stability. One of the Sun network engineers has a saying up on his wall that reads: "Implementing standards is like walking on water—both work best when frozen." NFS became a standard partly because Sun did not immediately abandon the specification for something different. Of course, the amount of time that a standard should remain frozen is tricky—old technology quickly acquires all the stability of a petrified forest.

The Public Standards Cartel

When we think of standards, we often think of the public bodies: the International Organization for Standardization (ISO), the International Telegraph and Telephone Consultative Committee (CCITT), and the American National Standards Institute (ANSI). We occasionally think of standards makers, such as the Institute of Electrical and Electronic Engineers (IEEE), or the Electronics Industry Association (EIA), which has recently metamorphosed into the Telecommunications Industry Association (TIA).

Let's look at some of these groups and their roles. The clearest role is played by the standards makers. The IEEE, for example, makes standards in the area of local area networks—just one of the many activities of this professional society. They coordinated the work on the 802.2 Logical Link

Who Owns Standards?

Control, 802.3 Ethernet, and standard definitions for other types of LANs (token bus, token ring, MAC-level bridging, and metropolitan area networks).

The IEEE, in the parlance of the standards world, is a standards development organization. These standards developers are accredited, in the U.S., by ANSI, which is the standards czar. IEEE formally recommends a standard which then goes through the ANSI process to become an American National Standard. Of course, because ANSI has no official government recognition, it is important to recognize that an American National Standard is only an American national standard to the extent that it enjoys broad, consensual acceptance.

The TIA is another standards developer. They are best known for physical standards like the RS-232-C interface used on PC systems and terminals for serial interfaces. ANSI acts as a secretariat for bodies like the TIA and IEEE, helping coordinate the process by which a document becomes an ANSI standard.

ANSI also serves another very important role. It is the U.S. national representative to the International Organization for Standardization (ISO). ISO is made up of member bodies, one from almost each country in the world. ISO deems standards to be international standards, whereas ANSI just grants national status. Through a long process, member countries submit proposals to ISO to have them become international standards.

It is interesting that ISO is a private group, just as ANSI is. ISO (unlike the International Telecommunications Union which is a part of the United Nations) is not founded on an international treaty. ISO defines a member body as the "national body most representative of standardization in its country." In the U.S., ANSI is the sole official route into the ISO process.

The actual work of making standards is doled out by ISO to secretariats. The secretariat for Open Systems Interconnection (OSI) work is ANSI. ANSI thus plays an additional role; it coordinates the OSI standardization process for ISO. Technically, OSI work is sponsored by the Joint Technical Committee on Information Technology (JTC1), which is in turn made up of ISO and another standards group, the IEC.

After all this coordination, after several stages of draft proposals and draft international standards, we finally get a blessed document, an International Standard. ISO asserts a copyright interest in the document, carefully marking each with a fairly vague copyright assertion. Claiming a copyright interest is how ISO is able to maintain control over the distribution and pricing of the standard.

Neither ANSI nor the ISO has exclusive purview over standards. ANSI makes American National Standards, but there are also Federal Information Processing Standards (FIPS), standards coordinated by NIST and used by the Federal government. FIPS may or may not be the same as an ANSI standard.

At the international level, ISO faces competition from other international groups (the CCITT for example), regional groups (the European Computer Manufacturers Association and the European Telecommunications Standards Institute), and from national groups that may not agree with a particular international effort.

As the old saw goes, the nice thing about standards is that there are so many to choose from.

There are two issues of relevance here. First is how standards are made. Second is how the standards are distributed. We will return to both of these issues. First, however, it is interesting to look at three additional models for the standards process.

The IAB Model

The Internet Activities Board is a very different beast. This group shepherds the body of TCP/IP-based standards for the Internet community. As we saw in Chapter 2, the Internet is a very loose conglomeration of autonomous systems. The

221

Who Owns Standards?

IAB exercises a management role for the evolution of Internet technology.

One role of the IAB is to decide if certain conventions should be considered as standards in the Internet community. To assist in that process, the IAB formed the Internet Engineering Task Force (IETF). The IETF is a group of about 500 engineers and computer scientists that meet 3-4 times per year in person and communicate frequently over the Internet the rest of the time. The engineers come from large user groups, computer vendors, regional networks, telephone companies, and include any others who wish to participate. Openness is the key to participation—anybody can participate who wishes to.

The IETF is organized into a series of working groups, addressing a wide variety of issues. Some groups look at routing protocols, for example, or the structure of SNMP management information bases. Other working groups look at the mail system, examining extensions like X.400 pilots, gateways between SMTP and X.400, fax gateways, and the like. A typical IETF meeting will have over 45 different working groups.

The product of a working group is typically a draft document. Some documents are meant to become standards, other are optional conventions for a subset of systems, still others are purely informational. The draft documents are kept in various public servers and are accessible by anybody who has anonymous FTP or electronic mail capabilities.

At some point, a consensus is reached among people in the community that develop the document. The document often then becomes a Request For Comment (RFC), the official documents of the Internet. The RFC series are kept on-line and are maintained by Jon Postel, the official RFC Editor and a member of the Internet Activities Board.

RFCs that are on the standards track go through several stages, advancing from proposed standard to draft standard to standard. A standards-track RFC has an applicability of required, recommended, or elective (others are strictly informational and need no such classification).

Making an RFC a standard, or even putting it on the standards track, is the purview of the IAB. Containing international representatives from academia, industry, and the non-profit R&D community, the IAB works on a consensus basis.

Before the IAB moves a protocol to standards status, it uses two novel mechanisms (at least by comparison to other standards-making bodies). First, the IAB insists on seeing the protocol in action, as a working implementation.

Not only must the standard work, there must be two to three independent and interoperable implementations before the IAB will bless a standard. Requiring independent implementations ensures that interoperability bugs have been worked out and the standard can be implemented simply by reading the standards document and following the instructions.

Second, the IAB looks to the IETF for development of technical recommendations for new protocol standards. The IETF is a fairly raucous, but very effective organization. The emphasis is on making standards that work, since the engineers at the IETF have to go home and make the products or run the networks based on the products.

The OSF Model

The open nature of the IETF and the TCP/IP standards process are in sharp contrast to the approach taken by another standards-making body, the Open Software Foundation. Technically OSF doesn't make standards, it incorporates existing technology into its computing environment. However, by blessing technology, such as the AFS file system or the Hewlett-Packard RPC mechanism, OSF gives proprietary technology a standards-like veneer.

The main goal of the IETF is to define protocols that make the Internet operate properly. Granted, there are financial considerations and competition among vendors, but the focus is making networks, not money. OSF, by contrast, is a foundation with a board comprised of computer vendors who have decided that by making equipment interoperable through standards they will sell more equipment.

OSF is thus a members-only club. OSF members—vendors, users, Independent Software Vendors (ISVs) and any others that wish to join—get early access to technology to begin integration. Once the platforms are stable, anyone can license the OSF technology and the OSF has committed to putting specifications in the public domain.

OSF standards are made by having the foundation issue a Request for Technology (RFT). The request for technology results in several proposals from the industry for a standard. For example, OSF issued an RFT for the Distributed Computing Environment (DCE). Proposals were submitted from many places, but two strong proposals emerged. First, DEC, Hewlett-Packard, and IBM produced what became the winning proposal. DEC threw in its naming service, Hewlett-Packard added the Apollo RPC mechanism, and IBM helped finance a company called Transarc which commercialized the Andrew File System developed at Carnegie-Mellon University.

Another proposal was submitted from Sun Microsystems and its allies. They proposed the Network File System instead of AFS, the Sun ONC Remote Procedure Call, and the Netwise RPC Compiler. Remember, the consortium had been formed in response to Sun and many in the industry expressed some doubt that Sun would be able to win this competition.

A winning proposal means that the vendor has the opportunity to have its technology be part of OSF. The vendor agrees to a licensing arrangement, whereby OSF has a license from the vendor to incorporate the technology in an OSF product. OSF products, such as the OSF/1 operating system or the DCE networking environment, are then licensed out to OSF members such as Digital and IBM. The companies then use OSF and their own hardware to license systems to end users.

Here's the problem. If you are a small software vendor, it is a bit hard to submit your technology. The eventual revenue from OSF licensing would be very small. As a result, the technology that gets incorporated into OSF is typically the technology pushed by the large members of the consortium.

An OSF standard is very different from those produced by the IAB. The OSF wants plug-and-play workstations based on the same operating system to form work-area networks. The IETF is much more focused on how these work-area groups can have wider connectivity in a wide-area network.

Access to OSF information is more difficult than with IETF-developed documents, which are all kept on the Internet in various document servers. OSF carefully guards its process, trying to manage the release of information.

OSF information is carefully released to non-members, whereas the IETF puts draft documents on-line. The difference is one of philosophy—OSF draws a sharp division between members and non-members. This point was brought home forcefully when this book was in manuscript form. As is the case with all my books, I offer interested parties an opportunity to review the manuscript for technical accuracy, perspective, and completeness. The vast majority of reviewers provide a review. Those that decide not to do a review simply toss the manuscript away and forget about it.

OSF, however, rather then review or not review the manuscript, sent me a letter from their General Counsel, Ronald J. Paglierani. The letter, dated May 28, 1991, reads in part:

> "Because of our desire to maintain vendor neutrality, OSF cannot make a practice of reviewing, editing, and/or endorsing materials submitted by outside parties, nor do we wish to become involved in a debate

about the appropriateness of certain statements therein.

In any event, OSF must insist that you do not represent, either in the text of the book itself or in any other manner, that OSF in any way endorses or approves the contents of your book. I am returning the draft that you had forwarded to us, and I have verified that no copies of this draft have been retained by any OSF personnel."

The lack of an endorsement by OSF is no great loss since one was not requested in the first place. Indeed, one can argue that non-endorsement by OSF will provide a sort of Salman Rushdie effect ("Buy this book, OSF didn't endorse it").

The Instant Standard Model

There is another way of making a standard: declaring it to be so. The federal government, in its role as a very large purchaser, for example, can make anything it wants a standard just by requiring it for procurement. IBM can declare portions of SAA to be a standard—it sells enough equipment that third-party vendors are apt to listen. You can also take the Sun route—give it away and hope that it is good enough that people jump on the bandwagon.

Instant standards serve an important purpose. In many cases, it takes one smart engineer to figure out how to do something. Publishing the interface means that everybody else learns how to do it, creating a market where there was not one before.

Many of the most successful network standards started out as instant standards. The Ethernet, for example, was published jointly by Digital, Intel, and Xerox. It then moved toward IEEE standards status, and then finally became an international standard.

NFS is another successful example. NFS was simply announced. Vendors implemented it and it gained quick acceptance. It has now found its way into various portions of standards. The Internet Activities Board has NFS and RPC as optional protocols for TCP/IP. Even OSF, archrivals of the Sun NFS community, incorporated NFS as its "PC" distributed file mechanism (AFS is used for the larger systems).

The Importance of Public Standards

To many, standards are simply another competitive tool. If some key technology becomes a standard and a company is the first to make a product, it will make more money. This view of the standards process as just one more input into the financial equation shifts the focus from a long-term to a short-term basis. A prominent participant in the standards process from Digital Equipment Corporation, for example, refers to a "return on investment" for his company's participation in the standards process.

A return on investment is certainly a desirable goal. Members of the OSF are certainly expecting a strong return on their investment in the Foundation. The products of OSF should mean more equipment sold. Likewise, Sun certainly didn't give away NFS out of altruism—the rapid growth of the company is evidence of that.

There is a big difference between the results of the OSF and the Sun approach. With the OSF, there is a standard, but you need a license to use it. With NFS, you can go strictly off the public domain reference documents and produce your own implementation.

The same is true of any documents published by the IETF. For example, the Open Shortest Path First (OSPF) dynamic routing protocol came out of the IETF. Several vendors of routers took the specification and came out with products.

Wide dissemination of information has played a key role in the rapid and strong acceptance of many IETF standards efforts: SNMP, OSPF, the Border Gateway Protocol, and Privacy Enhanced Mail are just a few examples.

Who Owns Standards?

When anyone can use a standard, we see innovation. College students start using standards in projects. Public domain implementations are used by computer vendors for many of their network products. For example, at least 6 vendors use the University of Maryland implementation of the Border Gateway Protocol as the basis for their commercial products.

The X Window System is another example of public standards fueling innovation. X is sold by most workstation vendors as part of their products. Built on top of X are various look and feel standards and toolkits. X-only terminals are built by several companies, and form the basis for a very high-growth market niche. There is no doubt that X has helped fuel strong growth for the workstation market.

Notice that neither IETF standards nor X are public standards in the sense of coming from official standards bodies. In fact, in many cases standards coming from the more informal groups are adopted much more quickly—they are more relevant and are easier to get.

Making documents easier to get means that more people will look at them and the standards solidify much more rapidly. The public standards process, by sharp contrast, has many instances of specifications being moved through the process only to discover later that essential components are missing.

The standards process in the public sense has a very different focus than groups like the IETF. It is much harder to participate, requiring frequent trips to committee meetings in expensive locations. Very little work is done on-line.

To participate in the public standards process takes a large investment of time and money. The result is a very different type of participation. Access is expensive so participation is limited to big players (or small players with an awful lot at stake in a particular standard).

It is possible to track this standards process and not participate, but even that route is fairly expensive. There is no public mailing list or anonymous FTP sites of in-progress drafts that people can consult to decide if an activity is relevant.

Instead, there are two ways of obtaining information about public standards bodies. You can join the club (or make friends with somebody in the club), in which case you can receive drafts of documents of committees you participate in. The other choice is to go to a commercial group like Omnicom and buy drafts.

Keeping the process closed is actually a design decision by many standards groups. One of the requirements in the public standards process is that only people that are "significantly and materially concerned" participate. Achieving consensus on technical standards is tough, and one can argue that closing access makes it easier to produce workable standards.

Of course, it is easier (but never easy) to achieve a consensus when monetary requirements limit the process to those who can afford to make a substantial investment in it. Limits on access mean that the people participating in the standards process are increasingly the same—diversity, in the form of small, innovative companies and bright graduate students at universities, is shut out. Limiting the process makes standards easier to produce, but the standards that are produced are not nearly as good.

Even the participants of the standards process realize how closed access is to their work. The chairman of a major international standards development committee acknowledged that he had easy access to any documents he wanted, but if his parent corporation was not actively committed to his standards-making activities, this would not be the case. In fact, at this same very large computer company, engineers frequently complain they are unable to get key documents, including standards that have been incorporated into the company's own products.

It is interesting to observe that limiting access has not really served its purpose. The standards coming out of groups like ISO and ANSI take a great deal of time to produce, making them less relevant when they come out. The inbreeding from large corporate families means that the standards are often a lowest common denominator compromise between large players instead of an innovative technical solution.

A members-only club that produces documents is one model of the standards process. The IETF is another model for producing standards. Both are standards. Their acceptance is judged on whether people actually adopt them. (One can argue that large vendors have a very definite advantage over others, but we leave the question of undue monopoly power for another time.)

Once standards are produced, however, the public standards process really starts to fall apart. Not only is it hard to participate in the process, it is extremely expensive to find out about the standards.

The reason is because standards bodies publish their standards with a copyright on them. You may not copy an ANSI, ISO, or CCITT document without infringing the copyright, at least if you believe the copyright notice on the covers, which states in no uncertain terms that the owner of the document retains all rights.

Who Owns Them?

Who owns a standard is an interesting issue. Sun published the NFS specifications and retains clear ownership of the documents. You can implement NFS from the specifications without Sun's permission, but you could not develop a new product and call it NFS without infringing on their copyright.

International standards are funny beasts. Throughout their development, they are in the public domain. Anybody who wants can make copies and distribute them. In fact, Omnicom has made quite a business of finding these public domain drafts and selling them. Making the documents available means that organizations do not have to be part of the inner circle to track standards status. Even making drafts available has not been without controversy. The International Telecommunications Union protested when Omnicom started selling draft documents in the U.S.

Once a document passes a magic point in the standards-making process, however, copyright is asserted. For ISO, this magic point is when a standard reaches Draft International Standard (DIS) status. For the CCITT, this point is when the standard is formally adopted and "published" by the ITU.

Groups like ISO and ITU are international bodies. For the ITU, copyright on a document is through a special protocol which was appended to the 1972 Universal Copyright Convention allowing specialized agencies of the United Nations to obtain the national equivalent of copyright protection for "works published for the first time." Notice the language "for the first time." There is great doubt as to whether the ITU can legally claim copyright protection.

ISO, with no international governmental status, is in an even more dubious legal position for asserting copyright protection. Not only are the documents in the public domain until they reach a stable status, but ISO has no formal status under the Universal Copyright Convention like the ITU.

Internal reports at the ITU and ISO have raised this point to senior management at both organizations. An internal report for one of the groups stated "as a legal matter, it is particularly doubtful whether [we] could claim that any standard which it publishes is actually [our] original creative work and not already in the public domain."

Both CCITT and ISO standards are rarely original work. They come from existing proposals, enter the public domain status, and only then become official copyrighted publications. If any copyright can be claimed, it is only on those minor changes that occur just before publication.

The reason for asserting copyright by the CCITT and ISO is simple—control. They both want the revenue and control that come from being able to decide who makes copies and who does not. For ISO, for example, standards are sublicensed in the U.S. to ANSI which sells them for a very high price, subsidizing ANSI activities.

Who Owns Standards?

For the ITU, high prices are the results of inefficiency and cross-subsidization of other ITU activities. The standards are printed and packed and mailed in Geneva, one of the most expensive printing centers in the world. The ITU spends $2.30 to print, bind, pack, and send every page of a standard, a cost three times greater than in the U.S. (also an expensive printing center). Printing alone costs the ITU 84 cents per page.

After the documents are produced, various internal cross-subsidies are added to come up with a final cost. These fairly vague costs include things like temporary staff even if they are not directly involved in producing the standards. Next, out of every 1800 copies printed, 400 are taken off the top and used for giveaways to an unspecified population of people and organizations. Finally, a 41% overhead tax is added on.

The result is significant. CCITT standards cost at least 50 cents per page. If you want anything like a complete set of the *Blue Book*, the 1988 compilation of CCITT standards, you are looking at an expenditure of around $10,000.

ISO documents are equally expensive. In the U.S., you must buy the documents through ANSI, the exclusive licensee for document sales in the country. ANSI, not known for its responsiveness, requires orders to be pre-paid to non-ANSI members and they do not accept credit cards or rush orders.

ANSI has some sub-licensees for ISO documents in the U.S., notably Omnicom. Omnicom, located in Reston, Virginia, can sell all ISO standards. However, the price they are allowed to charge is fixed as part of their ANSI agreement. When a new standard is produced, Omnicom has to call ANSI to find out what price to charge. This practice is usually known as price-fixing, but we leave that issue to the FTC.

The cost for documents from Omnicom is not cheap. One- or two- page addenda run $10 or $20. Longer documents are also expensive. Getting the FTAM specifications, for example, is a good $200. A random order to Omnicom for OSI specifications came to a total of $1350. When the order was shipped, it came in a box four inches high, yielding a cost for OSI standards of $388 per inch.

The cost of documents should be compared to other forms of information. After all, even books are expensive. Typical professional reference books are in the range of $25 to $100 per inch. Even manuals from corporations are substantially less than $388 per inch.

One could ask if the high prices are necessary to subsidize the standards activities. In the case of the CCITT, this is definitely not the case. Document sales are a minor part of its total budget (possibly because of the very high production costs). ANSI and ISO, when asked about their profits on document sales, refused to comment, stating that the matter was "proprietary."

One must remember that the companies participating in the standards process have already spent a great deal of money. The ITU estimates that the collective cost to member groups for participating in a major CCITT Study Group meeting is a private-sector expenditure of more than 5 million dollars.

In the ANSI/ISO world, the costs by participants are likewise quite high. Member companies pay for the staff time of their employees, including many trips to exotic locations. When the document sales are compared to the total expenditures for the standards process, document sales are a minor component.

Making standards available at a reasonable price—covering production costs—is one argument for easing access barriers to standards documents. A more radical argument is that any public standard should be available free of charge or for a very minor charge based solely on telecommunications costs to download the document or copy charges for a duplicating machine.

Selling standards for high prices has had a major effect on the acceptance of those standards. A strong case can be made that one reason for the slow acceptance of OSI is that people are simply unable to find enough information at reasonable costs. A question was posted on various mailing lists on the Internet and Usenet asking if the high cost of international standards documents was impeding the acceptance of those standards.

The response was overwhelming. Over 300 people sent back detailed replies. These people were the engineers and programmers responsible for building network support into their respective companies' products. Many were professors at major universities, responsible for training the next generation of engineers.

Almost without exception, people said the unavailability of documents was impeding their knowledge, and thus their implementations, of OSI and related standards. Professor Douglas Comer, for example, is one of the leading instructors on TCP/IP. He said that his students know very little about OSI precisely because of the high cost of standards documents.

High costs do not just stop universities and non-profit groups. They stop major corporations. Companies like Digital, Sun, and others typically give their engineers top-notch equipment to work on, including high-end workstations and the documentation necessary to be productive.

When you go into these organizations, however, you quickly see that the engineers do not have easy access to OSI information. OSI standards are kept in specialized libraries. Because the information is not on-line, it is fairly difficult to quickly check a standard to make sure you are in line with it.

An interesting outcome of keeping standards proprietary is that the information about them gets filtered. Many people who buy networks or use them learned about OSI from Marshall Rose's *The Open Book*.

The Open Book is an excellent book. However, Marshall Rose is known for his rather earthy assessments of the relevance of much of the international standards bureaucracy. By limiting standards distributions, ISO has ensured that most people learn about their work through interpreters like

Marshall Rose, one of the more prominent critics of the standards process.

The key is allowing, in the words of Jon Postel, Editor of the Internet, "random people" to access standards. The result of their work often makes a tremendous difference. Phil Karn, for example, is a researcher at Bell Laboratories. He developed a freely available implementation of TCP/IP for the PC and other low-end platforms. Karn's work has been supplemented by many others, resulting in much broader use of TCP/IP on PC-based systems, including broader acceptance for commercial PC TCP/IP products from companies like FTP Software.

The investment by a corporation in a standards process will ultimately be recouped by selling software, hardware, and networks. Corporations will not recoup their investment by having documents sell for higher and higher prices. People will simply use other sources of standards.

Access to standards documents must be easy and free. Standards define the rules of the games. If we are to use networks effectively, those rules cannot be hidden. Users need to know how their networks are built if they are to use them in a sophisticated manner.

Keeping standards secret and inaccessible hurts the industry much more than it hurts the users. Withholding knowledge about how things are built only works if you have a piece of technology that is suboptimal. If a standard is good, the exponential growth from a new market will far exceed the potential revenue from keeping the technology secret. After all, why participate in an old-technology market with a growth of 20% annually when you could be sharing a strong position in a market with 100% annual growth?

Without exception, the technologies in the field of computer networks that have the greatest long-term relevance are open technologies. The whole point of computer networks is connecting the maze together at increasing levels of functionality. Networks only make sense if their scope becomes universal.

Who Owns Standards?

Open access to standards is certainly important to the general public, but it is equally important to the standards bodies themselves. If they wish to avoid becoming standards dinosaurs, they must produce work that is broadly accepted and actively used.

After all, what good is a standard if nobody knows about it or nobody uses it? Opening up the standards process and making all standards available at minimal cost is the key to progress both for the computer industry as a whole and for the standards bodies themselves.

Glossary

10BASE2	10 Mbps/baseband/200 meters. IEEE standard for thinwire Ethernet.
10BASE5	10 Mbps/baseband/500 meters. IEEE standard for thickwire coaxial Ethernet.
10BASET	10 Mbps/baseband/twisted pair. IEEE standard for twisted pair Ethernet.
370 architecture	IBM architecture for mainframe computers, including the 3090 processors.
4.3BSD	*4.3 Berkeley Software Distribution* The current version of the Berkeley family of UNIX products.
4GL	*See fourth-generation language.*
802.2	IEEE standard for the Logical Link Control.
802.3	IEEE standard for CSMA/CD (Ethernet) medium access method.
802.4	IEEE standard for the token bus medium access method.
ACK	*Acknowledge* A network packet acknowledging the receipt of data.
ACL	*Access Control List* A security feature in operating systems that allows security on objects to be specified as a list of permitted actions for particular lists of users.
ACM	*Association for Computing Machinery.*

Glossary

ACS   *See Application Control Services or Access Control Set.*

ACSE   *See Association Control Service Element.*

address   There are two separate uses of this term in internet networking: "electronic mail address" and "internet address" [RFC1177].

Address resolution protocol   A TCP/IP protocol to translate an IP address into a MAC address (e.g., an Ethernet or SMDS subnetwork address).

address space   A collection of addresses that form a unified collection such as an internetwork.

addressing authority   The group responsible for assigning addresses within a domain.

ad hoc   Latin phrase meaning for a specific instance. Used in computing to refer to functions not previously planned.

advertising   The process by which a service makes its presence known on the network. Typically provided through some form of LAN-based multicast.

agent   Network management term for the portion of an entity that responds to management functions.

AIX   *Advanced Interactive Executive* IBM's version of UNIX [RFC1177].

alias   A name that is translated into another name.

allocation   Concept used in the transport layer protocols. An allocation is the amount of unacknowledged traffic that may be outstanding at one time.

AlterNet   A commercial TCP/IP-based network run by the people that run the UUNET commercial UUCP service.

American National Standards Institute   Private organization that coordinates some U.S. standards-making. Represents the U.S. to the International Standards Organization.

Glossary

ANSI   *See American National Standards Institute.*

API   *See application programming interface.*

AppleTalk   Apple's network protocol.

AppleTalk Filing Protocol   The protocol in AppleTalk used for remote access to data.

application   A program that performs functions for a user. Order entry systems and word processors are both examples of applications.

Application Environment Specification   OSF specification for a common operating environment on a desktop workstation.

application layer   The top layer of the network protocol stack. The application layer is concerned with the semantics of work. For example, getting a certain record from a file by key value on a foreign node is an application layer concern. How to represent that data and how to reach the foreign node are issues for lower layers of the network.

application programming interface   Specification of the calling structure between two programs. Usually between a general application program and a specific support service, such as communications support.

ARCNET   Hardware and software data link components manufactured by Datapoint and other companies that allows computers to form a 2.5-Mbps local area network with a star topology.

Areas   A term used in the routing layer. Level 1 routers are used to route within a single area. Level 2 routers route between areas. Up to 1023 nodes may be in an area, up to 63 areas in a DECnet.

ARP   *See Address Resolution Protocol.*

ARPANET   *Advanced Research Projects Agency Network* A DoD-sponsored network of military and research organizations. Replaced by the Defense Data Network. The ARPANET was officially retired in 1990.

Glossary

AS   *Autonomous System*   A set of routers under a common technical administration.

ASCII   American Standard Code for Information Interchange. A standard character set that assigns an octal sequence to each letter, number, and selected control characters. The other major encoding standard is EBCDIC.

ASE   *Application Service Element.*

ASN   *Abstract Syntax Notation*   The language used in the OSI presentation layer to define complex objects.

ASN.1   *Abstract Syntax Notation One*   OSI presentation layer protocol.

Assigned Numbers   Those numbers officially assigned as part of the Internet standards.

Association Control Service Element   Core set of facilities in the OSI application layer which allow application entities to form an association.

Async   *Asynchronous*   A data transmission method that sends one character at a time. Contrasted with synchronous methods which send a packet of data and then resynchronize their clocks. Asynchronous also refers to commands, such as in a windowing environment, that may be sent without waiting for a response from the previous command.

asynchronous   FDDI term for data transmission where all requests for service contend for a pool of ring bandwidth.

asynchronous event   Events occur asynchronously on a system when you cannot predict which one will happen next.

ATM   *Asynchronous Transfer Mode or Automated Teller Machine*   Asynchronous transfer mode is also known as "fast packet." A method for dynamic allocation of bandwidth on a cell basis.

attenuation   The level of signal loss, usually expressed in units of decibels.

Glossary

attribute

A "perceived property" of some entity that can be read, and maybe modified. Attributes are used in network management as well as in naming services. An example would be the password attribute of the object user. In a relational database, attribute is another name for a column in a table. In a data dictionary or other information model, an attribute is attached to a relationship or entity.

authentication

The function of verifying the identity of a person or process.

authorization

Determining if a person or process is able to perform a particular action. Contrast with authentication.

autobaud

The ability of a modem on the receiving end of a call to automatically detect the speed of transmission used by the calling modem.

backbone

A networking term used to refer to a piece of cable used to connect different floors or departments. Contrasted with a departmental network or work area network.

backup

Making a copy of stored information to use in case the original repository (usually a disk drive) becomes corrupted. To be contrasted with the alternate meaning of the word, "to overflow," which is usually used in the context of plumbing and sewage.

bandwidth

The amount of data that can be moved through a particular communications link. Ethernet has a bandwidth of 10 Mbps.

BASIC

Beginner's All-purpose Symbolic Instruction Code A programming language.

baud

A term used with older (slower) modems to refer to each modulation of an analog signal. A 300-baud signal modulates 300 times per second. A more explicit term for faster modems is bits per second, as several bits can now be carried on one modulation of a signal.

BBN

Bolt, Beranek, and Newman, Inc. The company responsible for development of the ARPANET.

beacon

A token ring packet that signals a serious failure on the ring.

241

Glossary

BER   *Basic Encoding Rules. See ASN.1.*

best-effort   A network module, such as the network layer IPX, that
delivery   attempts to deliver data but will not try to recover if
service   there is an error such as a line failure.

big endian   A computer that stores a multi-octet data structure
                   with the lowest addressed octet as being the most sig-
                   nificant. *See also endian and little endian.*

binding   Concept used in remote procedure calls. Two remote
                   programs bind with each other by starting a connec-
                   tion and then exchanging command requests.

Bisync   A synchronous protocol used in older IBM teleprocess-
                   ing environments. *See also BSC.*

bit mapped   A graphics term in which all bits of a display station
                   are controllable in contrast to a character-oriented ter-
                   minal.

BITNET   *Because It's Time Network* BITNET has about 2,500
                   host computers, primarily at universities, in many
                   countries. It is managed by CREN, which provides ad-
                   ministrative support and information services. There
                   are three main constituents of the network: BITNET in
                   the U.S. and Mexico, NETNORTH in Canada, and
                   EARN in Europe. There are also AsiaNet, in Japan,
                   and connections in South America. *See CREN*
                   [RFC1177].

block   A unit of I/O on computers. A block often ranges
                   from 512 bytes to eight kbytes.

blocking   The suspension of the execution of an application
                   process until some specified condition is satisfied.
                   Blocking occurs in synchronous processing. This term
                   is frequently used to describe the suspension of execu-
                   tion of a client application process until a remote pro-
                   cedure returns [Netwise RPC Tool].

bps   *Bits per second* Transmission speed on modems,
                   phone lines, and other data communications devices.

Glossary

bridge · · · · · · · · A device used to connect two separate Ethernet networks into one extended Ethernet. Bridges only forward packets between networks that are destined for the other network. Term used by Novell to denote a computer that accepts packets at the network layer and forwards them to another network.

broadcast · · · · · · Sending information to all users of a particular service. An Ethernet broadcast, for example, sends an Ethernet packet to every address on the network.

brouter · · · · · · · *Bridge/router* Device that forwards messages between networks at both network and data link levels.

BSC · · · · · · · · · *Bisynchronous. See bisync.*

BSD · · · · · · · · · *Berkeley Software Distribution* Term used when describing different versions of the Berkeley UNIX software, as in "4.3BSD UNIX" [RFC1177].

buffer · · · · · · · · A portion of main memory on a computer used to hold data.

bursty traffic · · · · Data communications term referring to an uneven pattern of data transmission.

bus · · · · · · · · · The part of a computer that connects peripheral devices so that they may communicate with the CPU and memory. IBM's Micro Channel Architecture is an example of a peripheral bus architecture. Also refers to any non point-to-point network with a multiple access characteristic, such as an Ethernet or Token Bus.

CA · · · · · · · · · *See Certification Authority.*

cached · · · · · · · · A piece of information that is retained in main memory instead of being flushed to disk. Keeping information cached alleviates the need to go to the disk to retrieve the data.

CACM · · · · · · · · *Communications of the ACM*

cartesian product · · Given two lists of data, the cartesian product is the set of every possible combination of the two lists.

Glossary

CASA — One of five gigabit testbeds in the Internet. This project involves WAN links between Los Alamos National Laboratory, Caltech, the Jet Propulsion Laboratory, and the San Diego Supercomputer Center.

CCITT — *Comité Consultatif International Télégraphique et Téléphonique* (Consultative Committee for International Telephone and Telegraph). Standards-making body administered by the International Telecommunications Union.

CCR — *Commitment, Concurrency, and Recovery* A part of the OSI Common Application Service Elements that allows the coordination of multiple users that access data on multiple nodes.

CERFnet — *California Education and Research Federation Network.*

certification authority — A network-based software process used in X.509 or RSA (public-key) authentication schemes. The certification authority maintains the public keys for users.

channel — An IBM term referring to a direct high-speed connection into a 370 architecture machine. A "channel attach" device operates at speeds of up to three Mbps, as opposed to more traditional devices that attach to a communications controller at 56 kbps.

CIC — *Certificate Integrity Check* A certificate integrity check is a quantity used to verify that certificate contents have not been changed.

circuit — A term used in networking that refers to a logical stream of data between two users of the network. A single physical link may have several virtual circuits running on it.

client — A module that uses the services of another module. The session layer is a client of the transport layer, for example.

CLNS — *Connectionless Network Service* One of two options for the OSI network layer. *See also CONS.*

Closed User Group — Data communications concept for CCITT (X.25 and ISDN) where only certain users (network addresses) can access a local connection.

Glossary

CN   *Common Name* Abbreviation used for X.400 addresses.

CNRI   *Corporation for National Research Initiatives.*

COBOL   *Common Business-Oriented Language* One of the first standardized computing languages. *See CODASYL.*

concentrator   A node on an FDDI ring which provides connections to additional stations. Known as a multi-station access unit or MAU in 802 token rings.

concurrency   When multiple users attempt to access the same resource. A lock manager addresses the problem of maintaining the integrity of resources in a concurrent environment.

congestion   Too much traffic for a given circuit.

CONS   *Connection Oriented Network Service.*

core gateway   Historically, one of a set of gateways (routers) operated by the Internet Network Operations Center at BBN. The core gateway system forms a central part of Internet routing in that all groups must advertise paths to their networks from a core gateway [RFC1177]. The core has been replaced by a set of Autonomous Systems.

COS   *Corporation for Open Systems.*

CPE   *Customer Premises Equipment.*

CREN   *Corporation for Research and Educational Networking* BITNET and CSNET have recently merged to form CREN [RFC1177].

CSMA/CD   *Carrier Sense–Multiple Access/Collision Detect* A control method for a network. Ethernet is an example of a CSMA/CD type of data link protocol.

CSNET   *Computer + Science Network* A large data communications network for institutions doing research in computer science. It uses several different protocols including some of its own. CSNET sites include universities, research laboratories, and commercial companies. *See CREN.* [RFC1177]

Glossary

CTERM   *Command Terminal Protocol* Part of the virtual terminal service in layer 6 of the Digital Network Architecture. An alternative to the CTERM services is the Local Area Transport Architecture (LAT) or Telnet.

CUG   *See Closed User Group.*

daemon   A UNIX term referring to a process that is not connected with a user but performs services, such as a mail daemon. The equivalent VMS term is a detached process.

DARPA   *Defense Advanced Research Projects Agency* A Department of Defense agency that has helped fund many computer projects including Arpanet, the Berkeley version of UNIX, and TCP/IP.

Data Access Protocol   A protocol used in the Digital Network Architecture in Layer 6. Provides a rich set of functions used for exchanging data between two nodes of the network. *See also File Access Listener.*

data country code   An ISO-administered format for unique OSI addresses based on geographic location. The codes are defined in ISO 3166.

Data terminal equipment   An X.25 term referring to the interface to user equipment as opposed to the DCE interface to the network.

datagram   The unit transmitted between a pair of internet modules. The Internet Protocol provides for transmitting blocks of data, called datagrams, from sources to destinations. The Internet Protocol does not provide a reliable communication facility. There are no acknowledgments either end-to-end or hop-by-hop. There is no error control for data, only a header checksum. There are no retransmissions. There is no flow control. *See Internet Protocol* [RFC1177].

DCA   *Document Content Architecture or Defense Communications Agency* Document Content Architecture is an IBM architecture similar in function to DEC's Compound Document Architecture (CDA). The Defense Communication Agency is responsible for the Defense Data Network.

DCC   *See Data Country Code.*

Glossary

DCE   *Data Circuit-terminating Equipment or Distributed Computing Environment* A Data Circuit-terminating Equipment is a device used in X.25 networks on the edge of the network that accepts and initiates calls. The DCE is, in turn, connected to a DTE which communicates with the user. The Distributed Computing Environment is the Open Software Foundation's modules for networking support.

DCL   *Digital Command Language* The user interface in the VMS operating system. Similar to the C shell in the UNIX operating system.

DDN   *Defense Data Network* A network for the Department of Defense and their contractors based on the TCP/IP and X.25 networking protocols.

DECconnect   A DEC cabling architecture used for facilities wiring.

DECnet   An implementation of the Digital Network Architecture by DEC, as opposed to implementations of DNA by other vendors.

DEK   *Data Encrypting Keys* Used for encryption of message text and (with certain choices among a set of alternative algorithms) for computation of Message Integrity Check (MIC) quantities. DEKs are generated individually for each transmitted message; no predistribution of DEKs is needed to support privacy-enhanced message transmission [RFC1113].

DES   *Data Encryption Standard* Federally sponsored encryption scheme.

designated router   A dynamic routing concept. A given broadcast circuit (such as an Ethernet) will have a designated router, which is used by end nodes to forward all packets which will need routing decisions.

Digital Network Architecture   DEC architectures for networking. DECnet is an implementation of DNA.

DIS   *Draft Information Standard* The step before becoming a formal international standard in the ISO process. At this point the standard is considered to be technically correct and only minor corrections are anticipated.

247

Glossary

DISOSS	*Distributed Office Support System* An IBM product that serves as a distributed library of documents. *See also DIA and DCA.*
distinguished name	An X.500 concept for the unique name of an object derived from its location in the Directory Information Tree.
distributed naming service	Network-based service to allow a user to find the current address of a given resource, such as a printer or file system.
DLAL	*Dual Letter Acronym Listing. See also MLAL.*
DNA	*See Digital Network Architecture.*
DNA Naming Service	A distributed naming service used heavily in DNA Phase V.
DNANS	*See DNA Naming Service.*
DNS	*See Domain Name System.*
Domain Name System	The Domain Name System is a mechanism used in the Internet for translating names of host computers into addresses. The DNS also allows host computers not directly on the Internet to have registered names in the same style [RFC1177].
Draft Standard Protocol	Classification for Internet standards. "The IAB is actively considering this protocol as a possible Standard Protocol. Substantial and widespread testing and comment are desired. Comments and test results should be submitted to the IAB. There is a possibility that changes will be made in a Draft Standard Protocol before it becomes a Standard Protocol" [RFC 1140].
DSAP	*Destination Service Access Point* The address for the destination user of a service. A remote IPX process would be considered the DSAP from the point of view of the local data link module.
DTE	*See Data Terminal Equipment.*
Dual Attachment Station	FDDI term for a node that is attached to both the primary and secondary fiber optic cables (as opposed to a node that is connected to the ring via a concentrator).

248

Glossary

dual-porting	Making a disk drive available to two different computers.
E.163	CCITT numbering scheme for public switched telephone networks.
E.164	CCITT standard for numbering in an ISDN environment.
EARN	*European Academic Research Network.*
Easynet	DEC's internal communications network.
EBCDIC	*Extended Binary Coded Decimal Interchange Code* A character code scheme used in IBM environments. *See also ASCII.*
Ebyte	*See exabyte.*
ECMA	*European Computer Manufacturers Association* A leading European standards body.
EDI	*See Electronic Data Interchange.*
EDIFACT	*EDI for Administration, Commerce, and Trade* Emerging international EDI standard.
EDUCOM	A trade association for universities located in Washington, D.C., specifically interested in computers and networking.
EGP	*Exterior Gateway Protocol* A protocol that distributes routing information to the routers and gateways which interconnect networks [RFC1177].
EIA	*Electronic Industries Association* Trade association recently renamed the Telecommunications Industries Association (TIA). Develops standards such as RS-232-C.
Elective Protocol	Protocol status for Internet standards. "A system may or may not implement an elective protocol. The general notion is that if you are going to do something like this, you must do exactly this. There may be several elective in a general area, for example, there are several electronic mail protocols, and several routing protocols" [RFC 1140].

Glossary

electronic mail
A collection of programs that allow users to exchange messages across a network.

email
Electronic mail.

End System
An OSI system on which applications run. An End System has full seven-layer OSI functionality. Basically equivalent to an Internet Host [RFC 1136].

endian
How a computer stores a multi-octet piece of data (e.g., a four-byte integer). *See big endian.*

ES
End system as defined by OSI: an OSI network layer entity that provides the OSI network layer service to a transport layer [RFC 1070].

ES-IS
End System to Intermediate System Protocol defined in ISO 9542 to allow end systems and intermediate systems on the same subnetwork to communicate.

Ethernet
A data link protocol jointly developed by Intel, Xerox, and DEC and subsequently adopted by the IEEE as a standard. Several upper-layer protocols, including DECnet, TCP/IP, and XNS, use Ethernet as an underlying transport mechanism. Ethernet is to be contrasted with other data link protocols such as token ring, DDCMP, and SDLC.

Ethernet controller
A device controller that gives a computer access to Ethernet services. Typically, the CSMA/CD protocols are built into the controller so the CPU doesn't have to worry about the details of the protocol.

Ethernet Version 2.0
The second version of the original specification for Ethernet, which differs slightly from the IEEE 802.3 standard.

Ethertype
Field in Version 2.0 of Ethernet that indicates the type of user (DECnet, NetWare, or TCP/IP, for example).

EUnet
European UNIX Network The European network based on UUCP.

exabyte
One billion gigabytes.

Glossary

Experimental Protocol	Classification for Internet standards. "Typically, experimental protocols are those that are developed as part of an ongoing research project not related to an operational service offering. While they may be proposed as a service protocol at a later stage, and thus become proposed standard, draft standard, and then standard protocols, the designation of a protocol as experimental may sometimes be meant to suggest that the protocol, although perhaps mature, is not intended for operational use" [RFC 1140].
External Data Representation	Presentation layer protocol developed by Sun Microsystems as part of NFS.
F.60	CCITT standard for telex services.
F.69	CCITT standard for telex addresses.
F.110	CCITT standard for maritime mobile service.
F.160	CCITT standard for international public facsimile services.
F.200	CCITT standard for teletex services.
F.201	CCITT standard for internetwork teletex and telex services.
F.300	A set of CCITT recommendations for Videotex systems.
F.401	CCITT standard for the naming and addressing for public message-handling services.
F.410	CCITT standard for the public message transfer service.
F.415	CCITT standard for intercommunication with public physical delivery services.
F.420	CCITT standard for the public interpersonal messaging service.
F.421	CCITT standard for communication between the X.400 interpersonal messaging service and telex service.
F.422	CCITT standard for communication between the X.400 interpersonal messaging service and teletex service.

Glossary

F.500
CCITT standard for international public directory services.

fax
Facsimile A messaging service based on transmitting bit maps of 200 dots per inch across dial-up telephone lines.

FDDI
See Fiber Distributed Data Interface.

Fiber Distributed Data Interface
A 100-Mbps fiber optic local area network standard based on the token ring.

file system
The portion of an operating system that is responsible for storing and retrieving pages of data onto a disk.

FINGER
Finger Protocol Elective Internet protocol defined in RFC 742.

FIPS
Federal Information Processing Standard.

FOO
A common variable used in examples. Derived from the military term FUBAR (F*d Up Beyond All Recognition).

fourth-generation language
A group of new languages often linked with database packages such as Ingres or Oracle. In contrast with FORTRAN and other third-generation languages.

frame
A series of bytes of data encapsulated with a header. The data link layer sends frames of data back and forth. "Frame" is often used interchangeably with "packet," although technically a packet refers to data from the network layer of the protocol stack. A packet is thus usually contained inside a frame.

FTAM
File Transfer, Access and Management The OSI application layer service that provides access to virtual file stores on foreign systems. Similar to the DNA DAP protocols in purpose.

FTP
File Transfer Protocol The Internet standard high-level protocol for transferring files from one computer to another [RFC1177].

full name
A unique, unambiguous name in the name space.

Glossary

full-duplex A data communications term that indicates that both ends of a communications link can transmit simultaneously. Contrasted with half-duplex, where only one side can transmit at one time.

Gateway There are two somewhat conflicting definitions of gateway, both used in networking. In the general sense, a gateway is a computer that connects two different networks together by performing protocol translation. Usually, this means two different kinds of networks such as SNA and DECnet. In TCP/IP terminology, however, a gateway used to be a link between two packet networks. This second meaning has been supplanted by "router."

Gbps *Gigabit per second.*

Gbyte *Gigabyte* One billion bytes of data.

Gflop *Billion floating operations per second.*

gigabytes *Billion bytes of data.*

GOSIP *Government OSI Protocols* U.S. government version of the international OSI standards.

granularity A term used in lock managers on an operating system. When the lock manager locks an entire file, it locks with a course granularity. When the lock manager locks a single record, it locks with a fine granularity. Granularity is one of the factors that influences the performance of a particular application, such as a DBMS.

half-duplex *See full-duplex.*

HDTV *High Definition Television.*

header The portion of a packet, preceding the actual data, containing source and destination addresses and error-checking fields [RFC1177].

heterogeneous Different.

253

Glossary

heterogeneous network   A network consisting of different network protocols or kinds of computers. A network combining SNA and DNA protocols using an SNA gateway to connect the two is a heterogeneous network.

hierarchical routing   Routing based on domains. Interdomain routers are responsible only for getting data to the right domain. There, an intradomain router takes responsibility for routing within the domain.

hop   A term used in routing. A hop is one data link. A path to the final destination on a net is a series of hops away from the origin. Each hop has a cost associated with it, allowing the calculation of the least cost path.

host number   The part of an internet address that designates which node on the (sub)network is being addressed [RFC1177].

HIPPI   *High Performance Parallel Interface*   An emerging ANSI standard which extends the computer bus over fairly short distances at speeds of 800 and 1600 Mbps. HIPPI is often used in a computer room to connect a supercomputer to routers, frame buffers, mass-storage peripherals, and other computers.

I.120   CCITT description of ISDN.

IA   *Issuing Authority*   A concept in Privacy Enhanced Mail that indicates which group is vouching for the integrity of a given certificate.

IAB   *Internet Activities Board*   The IAB is the coordinating committee for Internet design, engineering and management [RFC1177].

ICMP   *Internet Control Message Protocol*   Protocol used by the IP layer of TCP/IP for exchanging routing control messages.

IEEE   *Institute for Electronic and Electrical Engineers*   A leading standard-making body in the U.S., responsible for the 802 standards for local area networks.

IESG   *Internet Engineering Task Force Steering Group*   The governing body of the IETF.

Glossary

IETF

Internet Engineering Task Force A volunteer group that helps develop new technology for use in the Internet. An alternative definition proposed by Marshall Rose is "many fine lunches and dinners."

IGP

Interior Gateway Protocol A protocol such as RIP used within an administrative domain. Contrast to EGPs which are used to exchange information between administrative domains.

Ingres

A popular relational database management system that runs on a variety of operating system platforms. Previously a famous 19th century French painter.

Integrated Services Digital Network

An emerging international communications standard that allows the integration of voice and data on a common transport mechanism.

interchange key

A cryptographic key shared by two or more parties.

Intermediate System

An OSI system that performs routing and relaying functions in order to provide paths between End Systems. Intermediate Systems have no functionality above the Network Layer (although a practical realization of an OSI router will have some amount of End System functionality for network management functions, among other things). Basically equivalent to an Internet Router [RFC1136].

International Organization for Standardization

International standards-making body, responsible for the Open Systems Interconnect network architecture.

Internet

A collection of networks that share the same namespace and use TCP/IP protocols. The Internet consists of at least 4000 connected networks. The Internet should not be confused with an internet (lowercase) which refers to any interconnected set of networks. All members of the Internet use TCP/IP, although the system is in transition to a multi-protocol environment. It operates in over 26 countries and has over 300,000 hosts.

Glossary

internet | Any interconnected set of networks. Often refers to the vague mix of heterogeneous networks that are accessible by electronic mail using gateways.

internet address | An assigned number which identifies a host in an internet. It has two or three parts: network number, optional subnet number, and host number [RFC1177].

Internet Autonomous System | An autonomous system consists of a set of gateways, each of which can reach any other gateway in the same system using paths via gateways only in that system. The gateways of a system cooperatively maintain a routing database using an interior gateway protocol (IGP) [RFC1136].

Internet Protocol | The network layer protocol for the Internet. It is the datagram protocol defined by RFC 791 [RFC1177].

internetwork | A collection of data links and the network layer programs for routing among those data links.

internetwork address | An address consisting of a network number and a local address on that network. Used by the network layer for routing packets to their ultimate destination.

INTEROP | A biannual technical conference and trade exhibition sponsored by INTEROP, Inc. INTEROP is known for interoperability demonstrations that feature real-world demonstrations of emerging technology and standards.

IP | *See Internet Protocol.*

IPMS | *Interpersonal Messaging System* The protocols used for two user agents to exchange information.

IRTF | *Internet Research Task Force* The IRTF is a community of network researchers, generally with an Internet focus. The work of the IRTF is governed by its Internet Research Steering Group (IRSG) [RFC1177].

ISDN | *See Integrated Services Digital Network.*

IS-IS | *Intermediate System to Intermediate System* OSI protocols for routers.

ISO | *See International Organization for Standardization.*

Glossary

ISODE
: *ISO Development Environment* Software developed by Marshall Rose of PSI International that allows OSI services to use a TCP-based network.

JANET
: *Joint Academic NETwork* JANET is the primary academic network in the United Kingdom, linking about 1,000 computers at about 100 universities and research institutes. JANET has a domain name system similar to that of the Internet, but the order of the domain name parts is opposite (with the top-level domain on the left). [RFC 1168].

JNT
: *Joint Network Team* The group that maintains JANET.

Kb
: *Kilobit* 2^{10} bits of information (usually used to express a data transfer rate; as in, 1 kilobit/second = 1 kbps = 1 kb) [RFC1177].

KB
: *Kilobyte* A unit of data storage size which represents 2^{10} (1024) characters of information [RFC1177].

kbps
: *Kilobits per second* Thousand bits per second.

kbyte
: *Kilobyte* Thousand of bytes of information.

KDC
: *Key Distribution Center* An entity that distributes symmetric keys to two parties. Used in Kerberos.

keep alive message
: A message sent over a network link during periods when there is no traffic between users. The message tells the remote node that this computer is still in operation.

Kerberos
: A component of MIT's Athena project. Kerberos is the security system, based on symetric key cryptography. Contrast with the RSA public key cryptography techniques.

Kermit
: A popular file transfer protocol developed by Columbia University. Because Kermit runs in most operating environments, it provides an easy method of file transfer.

KIS
: *Knowbot Information Service* Internet service developed by CNRI to find electronic mail addresses.

257

Glossary

knowbot   An intelligent program that can access remote services in a Digital Library System.

LAN   *Local Area Network* Usually refers to Ethernet or token ring networks.

LAP   *Link Access Protocol* A protocol for accessing a data link. Examples are LAP B used in the X.25 environment and LAP D used in the ISDN environment.

LAPB   *Link Access Procedure, Balanced* A subset of the HDLC data link standards.

LFN   *Long, Fat pipe Network.* A network with high bandwidth and long delay, resulting in a large number of unacknowledged bits. This type of network is known as an "LFN," which is pronounced elephan(t).

Logical Link Control   The upper portion of the data link layer, defined in the IEEE 802.2 standard. The logical link control layer presents a uniform interface to the user of the data link service, usually a network layer. Underneath the LLC sublayer of the data link layer is a media access control sublayer. The MAC sublayer is responsible for taking a packet of data from the LLC and submitting it to the particular data link being used (such as Ethernet or token ring).

LSP   *Link State Packet* Routing control information message exchanged in a Phase V DECnet or OSI IS-IS routing domain.

MAC   *See Medium Access Control or Macintosh.*

Macintosh   A computer made by Apple Computer that is characterized by the graphical, intuitive user interface.

MAC-layer bridge   A device that connects two or more similar data links in a way that is transparent to the user of the data link service (the network layer).

Mailbus   A DEC architecture which provides a common message-handling system on a DECnet.

MAU   *See multistation access unit.*

Mbps   *Million bits per second.*

258

Glossary

Mbyte   *One million bytes.*

MCI Mail   Commercial electronic messaging service.

medium   The physical cable, such as coaxial cable, used on a network.   Somebody who can speak to the other world.

Medium Access Control   The bottom half of the ISO data link layer.   *See also Logical Link Control.*

message-handling system   A system of protocols, such as X.400, used to exchange messages, such as electronic mail.

Message Integrity Check   A quantity sent along with a message that is derived from the message contents.   The MIC is used to verify that the message has not been changed.   The MIC has the characteristic of giving very different results when small changes are made to the message contents.

Message Router   DEC product which implements the MAILbus architecture.   Message Router is analogous to the X.400 Message Transfer Agent.

message transfer agent   An X.400 term referring to the collections of network members responsible for transferring messages.   The final MTA delivers the message to a user agent which is concerned with reading, editing, and other types of interaction with the end user.

MHS   *See Message Handling Service or message-handling system.*

MIB   *Management Information Base*   A set of definitions of information that a managed object makes available to directors.

MIC   *See Message Integrity Check or Media Interface Connector.*

MILNET   *Military Network*   A network used for unclassified military production applications.   It is part of the Internet [RFC1177].

Glossary

MIPS

Million instructions per second. Architectures use different instruction sets, so comparisons of MIPS across products is highly misleading. MIPS also do not take into account the mix of other resources such as bus speeds, I/O processors, disk drive throughput, main memory, network controllers, and other components of a system. MIPS have been defined by Gerard K. Newman as a "meaningless indication of processor speed" and "marketing information to promote sales."

MIPS year

The computational resources consumed by a 1 MIP machine working for one year. Used as a benchmark of the computational complexity of a problem.

MIS

Management Information System A database system used to provide information to managers in an organization. The term has come to refer to the department in an organization responsible for computing.

MLAL

Multiletter acronym listing. See also DLAL.

Modem

Modulator/demodulator A device that takes digital data from a computer and encodes it in analog form for transmission over a phone line. Modems are also used to connect computers to an analog broadband system.

MOTIS

Message Oriented Text Interchange System Formal name for the 1988 CCITT X.400 standards.

mount

The process of making a remote file system available to a local node. A mount system call is used to inform the kernel about a new file system. If the file system if remote, the NFS or distributed file system mount protocol is used.

MTA

See message transfer agent.

MTU

Maximum Transmission Unit.

multicast

An address to which several nodes will respond. Contrast to broadcast, where all nodes on a network will respond.

Glossary

Multicasting A term used in Ethernet addressing. A multicast address is a group address that is meant for a certain subset of users on the Ethernet. LAT nodes communicate their current status with each other using a multicast address. To be contrasted with a broadcast address which is received by all users on the Ethernet.

multiport repeater An Ethernet repeater, typically for thinwire networks, that connects several segments into a multisegment Ethernet.

multiport transceiver Several Ethernet transceivers built into one device. Can operate as a concentrator on a cable or as a standalone Ethernet (known as Ethernet in a can).

multisegment Ethernet Several segments of Ethernet connected with repeaters. All signals broadcast on a multisegment Ethernet are received by all other nodes; in contrast to the extended Ethernet, where the MAC-layer bridge forwards only those packets destined for the other Ethernet.

multistation access unit A token ring device used to connect several stations to the ring. Similar to the multiport transceiver for the Ethernet.

multithreaded An operating system feature that allows a process to maintain several threads of execution, each under the control of the parent process. OS/2 is an example.

MVS/TSO *Multiple Virtual Storage/Time Sharing Option* MVS is an IBM operating system. TSO is the interactive subsystem, as opposed to a system like JES used for batch processing.

MX *Mail Exchange* A DNS resource record type indicating which host can handle mail for a particular domain.

NAK *Negative Acknowledgment* Response to nonreceipt or receipt of a corrupt packet of information.

namespace A commonly distributed set of names in which all names are unique.

NASA *National Aeronautics and Space Administration.*

Glossary

National Bureau of Standards   *See National Institute for Standards and Technology.*

National Institute for Standards and Technology   U.S. governmental body that provides assistance for standards-making. Formerly the National Bureau of Standards.

NBS   *National Bureau of Standards* See National Institute for Standards and Technology.

NCS   *See Network Computing System.*

NEARnet   *New England Academic and Research Network.*

NetBIOS   Network Adapter Basic Input/Output System. A Network protocol that allows a client program to find a server process and communicate with it. Similar to Named Pipes.

NETBLT   *Bulk Data Transfer Protocol* Obsolete Internet high-speed block transfer protocol defined in RFC 998.

NetWare   The networking components sold by Novell. A collection of data link drivers, a transport protocol stack, workstation software, and the NetWare operating system.

NetWare Core Protocols   Protocols used to obtain the core services offered by a NetWare file server. Includes a variety of facilities such as file access, locking, printing, and job management.

network address   The number of the network that a user is on. Each network (data link) in an internetwork has a number assigned to it. The full address of a station is the network address plus the local address of the node on that network.

Network Computing System   Apollo's computing architecture. The DEC RPC mechanism is derived from the NCS RPC architecture.

Network File System   A distributed file system developed by Sun Microsystems and widely used on TCP/IP systems.

Glossary

network number	The part of an internet address which designates the network to which the addressed node belongs [RFC1177].
NeWS	*Network Extensible Window System* A windowing environment from Sun Microsystems based on the Postscript language and a proprietary window control protocol.
NFS	*Network File System* A network service that lets a program running on one computer to use data stored on a different computer on the same internet as if it were on its own disk [RFC1177].
NIS	*Network Information Services* A set of services in Sun's Open Network Computing family that propagates information out from masters to recipients. Used for the maintenance of system files on complex networks. Yellow Pages are known in marketing-speak as the Network Information Services.
NIST	*See National Institute for Standards and Technology.*
NOC	*Network Operations Center* An organization which is responsible for maintaining a network [RFC1177].
node	An individual item in a set. An Ethernet node, for example, is a device attached to the cable with a transceiver, including a repeater, bridge, or computer. A file system node is a directory or individual file.
Novell	Makers of NetWare software for networks.
NREN	*National Research and Education Network.*
NSAP-address	Network Service Access Point address, or an address at which OSI network services are available to a transport entity [RFC 1070].
NSF	*National Science Foundation.*
NSFnet	*National Science Foundation Network* A high-speed internet that spans the country, and is intended for research applications. It is made up of the NSFnet Backbone and the NSFnet regional networks. It is part of the Internet [RFC1177].

Glossary

NSFnet
Regional

A network connected to the NSFnet Backbone that covers a region of the U.S. It is to the regionals that local sites connect [RFC1177].

NSI

NASA Science Internet NASA's wide-area network.

NSP

See Network Services Protocol.

NYSERnet

New York State Educational and Research Network An internet which serves NY educational and research institutions. It also serves as the NSFnet regional network for New York State [RFC1177].

OCR

Optical Character Recognition.

ONC

See Open Network Computing.

Open
Network
Computing

Sun marketing term for the family of protocols that includes the Network File System.

Open
Software
Foundation

Non-profit organization founded by Digital, IBM, and four other vendors to develop specifications for an open software environment.

Open Systems
Interconnection

The ISO's standards for a heterogeneous, open network architecture.

O/R Address

Originator/recipient address A valid X.400 address.

OS

Operating system.

OSF

See Open Software Foundation. One wag has suggested that OSF also stands for "Obliterate Sun Forever."

OSI

Open Systems Interconnection A set of protocols designed to be an international standard method for connecting unlike computers and networks. Europe has done most of the work developing OSI and will probably use it as soon as possible [RFC1177].

OSI Reference
Model

An "outline" of OSI which defines its seven layers and their functions. Sometimes used to help describe other networks [RFC1177].

OSTP

White House Office of Scientific and Technical Policy

Glossary

OU   *Organization Unit*   An X.400 address attribute indicating a sub-unit of an organization.

packet   The unit of data sent across a packet switching network. The term is used loosely. While some Internet literature uses it to refer specifically to data sent across a physical network, other literature views the Internet as a packet switching network and describes IP datagrams as packets [RFC1177].

Packet Assembler/ Disassembler   Special-purpose computer on an X.25 network that allows asynchronous terminals to use the synchronous X.25 network by packaging asynchronous traffic into a packet.

packet switching   A network that has packaged data into packets. A computer can handle many more virtual connections with packets than it can with dedicated connections (known as circuit switching). Packet switching forms the basis for X.25, as well as most network-layer protocols.

PAD   *See Packet Assembler/Disassembler.*

Paging   A memory management technique in a virtual memory operating system. Only a few parts (pages) of a program are actually in memory. When a new part is needed, it is paged into memory.

path   As a file system concept, the path indicates what set of folders or subdirectories a file is stored in. In the networking sense, a path is the route that a packet takes from the source to the destination. The path is a series of data links or hops.

PBX   *Private Branch eXchange*   A telephone switch which is installed at the customer premises.

Pbyte   *See petabyte.*

PDU   *See Protocol Data Unit.*

permanent virtual circuit   A circuit that is kept up permanently, as in the case of a dedicated leased line on the telephone network.

petabyte   One million gigabytes.

Glossary

PHIGS   *See Programmer's Hierarchical Interactive Graphics System.*

piggybacked   Added on to. A term used in protocols that require the acknowledgment of prior packets. The acknowledgment can often be piggybacked into the same packet as data that are headed in that direction.

POSIX   *Portable Operating System Interface for Computer Environments* IEEE-developed standards to provide a common interface to an operating system, thus making applications more portable.

PostScript   A page description language used on printers such as the Apple LaserWriter and on computer displays used in workstations from companies such as NeXT and Sun Microsystems. Similar in function to Xerox's Interpress.

POTS   *Plain Old Telephone Service* As opposed to ISDN, Call Waiting, or any other modern marvels.

presentation syntax   A standard method of representing data in a heterogeneous environment. The Abstract Syntax Notation 1 (ASN.1) is an example of a presentation syntax.

PROFS   *Professional Office System* IBM office automation package for the VM/CMS operating system.

Programmer's Hierarchical Interactive Graphics System   Imaging system providing sophisticated capabilities such as hidden-surface removal, shading, and depth cueing.

protocol   A formal description of message formats and the rules two computers must follow to exchange those messages. Protocols can describe low-level details of machine-to-machine interfaces (e.g., the order in which bits and bytes are sent across a wire) or high-level exchanges between allocation programs (e.g., the way in which two programs transfer a file across the Internet) [RFC1177].

Glossary

protocol data unit A layer communicates with its peer by sending packets. Each packet has a header that contains information that the peer will work with, such as addresses or acknowledgment requests. It also contains data, the protocol data unit, that is passed up to the client of the layer.

PSI *Packet-switch interface or Performance Systems International* Packet-Switch Interface is DEC software to allow a VAX to participate in an X.25 network. Performance Systems International is a network service provider and an active participant in the areas of ISODE, X.500, and SNMP.

PSN *Packet Switched Network* Typically an X.25 network.

PSTN *Public Switched Telephone Network.*

PTT *Poste Téléphone et Télégraphe* A government provider of communications functions in most European countries.

public domain Intellectual property available to people without paying a fee. Most computer software developed at universities is in the public domain.

Q.700 Introduction to CCITT SS No. 7.

Q.701 The message transfer part of Signalling System No. 7.

Q.711 Signalling connection control part of Signalling System No. 7.

Q.721 Telephone user part of Signalling System No. 7.

Q.761 The ISDN user part of Signalling System No. 7.

RAM *Random Access Memory* Dynamic memory, sometimes known as main memory or core.

RCL *Revoked Certificate List* A list used in X.509 security to specify which certificates are no longer valid.

RDA *Remote Data Access.* An international standard for access to databases in a heterogeneous computing environment.

Glossary

remote
procedure call

A set of network protocols that allow a node to call procedures that are executing on a remote machine. The Netwise RPC Tool, HP/Apollo RPC, and Sun's NFS RPC are examples of such protocols.

repeater

An Ethernet device used to connect two or more segments of cable together. The repeater retimes and re-amplifies the signal received on one segment before resending it on all other segments.

Request for
Comment

The Internet's Request for Comments documents series. RFCs are working notes of the Internet research and development community. A document in this series may be on essentially any topic related to computer communication, and may be anything from a meeting report to the specification of a standard [RFC1177].

resource
discovery

An area of research in computer science that attempts to find network-based resources. *See KIS.*

restricted
token

A special mode of asynchronous access in FDDI where the bandwidth is dedicated to an extended dialogue between two users.

RFC

See Request for Comment.

RIP

See Routing Information Protocol.

RISC

Reduced Instruction Set Computer Generic name for CPUs that use a simpler instruction set than more traditional designs. Examples are the IBM PC/RT, Pyramid minicomputers, Sun SPARCstations, and Digital DECstations.

RJE

Remote job entry Facility for submitting a job to a computer for execution. Card readers were early RJE stations. Today, the term usually means software that emulates RJE stations.

RMS

Record Management Services A common I/O interface for VMS used for access to local data via QIO calls and remote data via the DAP protocol.

root

UNIX superuser. The one account on a UNIX system that has privileged access.

Glossary

Routers	Dedicated hardware used to route traffic on a network. The alternative is to use a portion of a general purpose system such as a Sun or VAX.
routing directory	A database maintained by the network layer to determine which paths to use to get to particular networks.
Routing Domain	A set of End Systems and Intermediate Systems which operates according to the same routing procedures and which is wholly contained within a single Administrative Domain [RFC1136].
Routing Information Protocol	One protocol which may be used on internets simply to pass routing information between gateways. It is used on many LANs and on some of the NSFnet regional networks [RFC1177].
RPC	*See remote procedure call.*
RPC Tool	The RPC mechanism sold by Netwise, including the RPC compiler.
RS-232-C	A physical interface standard, used frequently for connecting asynchronous devices such as terminals. Developed by the Electronic Industries Association to define the electrical and mechanical link between a DTE and DCE.
RSA	*Rivest, Shamir, and Adleman* Developers of a patented public key cryptography method that forms the basis for the Internet Privacy enhanced mail as well as X.509 directory security.
RSADSI	*RSA Data Security, Inc.* The firm founded by RSA to commercialize their research.
RTT	*Round Trip Transmission* A measure of the current delay on a network.
SAA	*Systems Application Architecture* IBM Architecture to present common user, communications, and programming interfaces across multiple hardware platforms and operating systems.
SACK	*See Selective ACK.*
SAS	*See Single Attachment Station.*

269

Glossary

SCALE   The TCP window scaling option. Allows window information to be interpreted as being scaled by 1 to 16 powers of 2, thus increasing the size of the effective window [RFC1072].

SCCP   *Signalling Connection Control Part. See Q.711.*

SDLC   *Synchronous Data Link Control* IBM's data link protocol used in SNA networks.

search path   A mechanism in DOS, UNIX, and other operating systems that allows a user to specify a command without knowing which directory it is stored in. The operating system will search each of the directories in the search path for the command until it finds the file.

selective ACK   A TCP option which is used to convey extended acknowledgment information over an established connection. Specifically, it is to be sent by a data receiver to inform the data transmitter of non-contiguous blocks of data that have been received and queued. The data receiver is awaiting the receipt of data in later retransmissions to fill the gaps in sequence space between these blocks. At that time, the data receiver will acknowledge the data normally by advancing the left window edge in the Acknowledgment Number field of the TCP header [RFC1072].

sequence number   A unique number for every packet on a particular connection maintained by a reliable transport layer service. The sequence number allows the transport layer to see if any packets were lost or delivered out of sequence by the underlying network and data layers.

server   A program on a computer that provides services to workstations. File, database, print, and communications are just a few kinds of servers.

session   Networking term used to refer to the logical stream of data flowing between two programs communicating over a network. Note that there are usually many different sessions originating from one particular node of a network.

SGI   *Silicon Graphics, Incorporated.*

SGML   *See Standard Generalized Markup Language.*

Glossary

SIGCOMM   *ACM Special Interest Group on Data Communication* The professional society for people interested in computer communication.

single attachment station   FDDI term for a station attached to a ring via a concentrator.

SLIP   *Serial Line IP* A simple protocol for running IP over serial lines, defined in RFC 1055.

SMDS   *Switched Multi-megabit Data Service* A datagram-based public data network service developed by Bellcore and expected to be widely used by telephone companies as the basis for their data networks.

SMI   *Structure of Management Information* Recommended Internet protocol defined in RFC 1155.

SMT   *See Station Management.*

SMTP   *Simple Mail Transfer Protocol* The Internet standard protocol for transferring electronic mail messages from one computer to another. SMTP specifies how two mail systems interact and the format of control messages they exchange to transfer mail [RFC1177].

SNA   *See System Network Architecture.*

SNADS   *SNA Distribution Services* An architecture used for transferring messages in an SNA environment, similar to X.400.

SnailMAIL   The traditional non-electronic postal service.

SNAP SAP   *Subnetwork Access SAP* A special form of Service Access Point where the first five bytes of the information field in the Logical Link Control data serve as the protocol identifier.

Sniffer Network Analyzer   Network General product used to monitor many different upper- and lower-layer network protocols.

SNMP   *Simple Network Management Protocol* The standard network management protocol used in TCP/IP networks.

Glossary

socket   An entry point to a program, used extensively in the BSD version of UNIX as the entry point to the network.

SONET   *Synchronous Optical Network*   Standard for fiber optic-based circuits operating in multiples of 51.840 Mbps up to 48 Gbps.

source address   The origin of a data packet on a network.

SPARC   *Scalable Processor Architecture*   A reduced instruction set (RISC) processor developed by Sun and licensed by several vendors, including AT&T and Texas Instruments.

SPF   *Shortest Path First. See OSPF.*

SQL   *See Structured Query Language.*

SS7   *Signalling System 7*   Protocol related to ISDN. Directs how the interior of an ISDN network is managed.

standard   A convention that people know about and use. The nice thing about standards is that there are so many to choose from.

Standard Generalized Markup Language   ISO standard for the representation of revisable form text.

stored upstream address   Token ring concept. Each node on the token ring stores the address of the neighbor from which it receives data.

stream head   The entry point to a stream, a series of software modules connected with the STREAMS mechanism.

stream-oriented   A type of transport service that allows its client to send data in a continuous stream. The transport service will guarantee that all data will be delivered to the other end in the same order as sent, and without duplicates. Also known as a reliable transport service.

272

Glossary

STREAMS An AT&T mechanism developed for the UNIX operating system. STREAMS is a way of connecting a series of software modules, letting them send messages to each other.

Structured Query Language International standard language for communicating with relational database systems.

stub A piece of code that is used in RPCs. The stub appears like the called or calling procedure, thus masking the details of the RPC implementation from the calling or called procedures.

subnet A term used to denote any networking technology that makes all nodes connected to it appear to be one hop away. In other words, the user of the subnet can communicate directly to all other nodes on the subnet. A subnet could be X.25, Ethernet, a token ring, ISDN, or a point-to-point link. A collection of subnets, together with a routing or network layer, combine to form a network.

subnet number A part of the internet address which designates a subnet. It is ignored for the purposes of internet routing, but is used for intranet routing [RFC1177].

Sun Microsystems Makers of workstations and the Network File System.

superuser *See root.*

SVC *See switched virtual circuit.*

SVID *System V interface definition* AT&T-sponsored definition used to determine the compatibility of different implementations of System V.

switched virtual circuit A virtual circuit that is set up on demand, as in the case of a dial-up telephone line or an X.25 call. *See permanent virtual circuit.*

SWS *Silly Window Syndrome* A phenomenon found in TCP/IP whereby the available window is reduced to zero. Described by Dr. David Clark in RFC 813.

273

Glossary

synchronous   An FDDI service class where each requester gets a pre-allocated maximum bandwidth, and hence a guaranteed response time.

System Network Architecture   IBM's networking architecture.

T1   A term for a digital carrier facility used to transmit a DS-1 formatted digital signal at 1.544 Mbps.

T3   A term for a digital carrier facility used to transmit a DS-3 formatted digital signal at 44.746 megabits per second [RFC1177].

T.4   CCITT standard for group 3 facsimile transmission.

T.6   CCITT standard for group 4 facsimile transmission.

TCP   *See Transmission Control Protocol.*

TCP/IP   *Transmission Control Protocol/Internet Protocol* This is a common shorthand which refers to the suite of application and transport protocols which run over IP. These include FTP, Telnet, SMTP, and UDP (a transport layer protocol) [RFC1177].

Telenet   Packet switched network service offered by US Sprint.

Telex   Messaging mechanism that predates fax and electronic mail.

Telnet   The Internet standard protocol for remote terminal connection service. Telnet allows a user at one site to interact with a remote timesharing system at another site as if the user's terminal was connected directly to the remote computer [RFC1177].

terminal emulator   A program that allows a computer to emulate a terminal. The workstation thus appears as a terminal to the host.

terminator   Device on each end of an Ethernet cable to prevent reflections.

terabyte   One trillion bytes.

Glossary

THT   *Token Holding Timer* Token ring and FDDI term for the amount of time a node can transmit data before sending the token back out the ring.

TIA   *Telecommunications Industry Association. See EIA.*

TLI   *See Transport Level Interface.*

token bus   An alternative to token ring and Ethernet local area networks. Used in the MAP protocols. The token bus uses a multiple access protocol, but the device that "owns" the token is the only one that can send data.

token ring   A local area network protocol in which computers are connected together in a ring. A node waits until a token is passed around the ring, at which point it may send data. When it has finished sending it releases the token and passes it to the next node. *See FDDI.*

topology   A network topology shows the computers and the links between them. A network layer must stay abreast of the current network topology to be able to route packets to their final destination.

tower   DNA Phase V term for the sequence of protocol identifiers and associated address information through which a particular module can be accessed.

transceiver   A term used in Ethernet networks. The transceiver is the hardware device that connects to the Ethernet media, often a piece of coaxial cable. The transceiver is then connected to an Ethernet controller on the host system.

Transmission Control Protocol   The transport protocol in TCP/IP used for the guaranteed delivery of data.

Transport Level Interface   AT&T-developed specification for the interface between the transport layer and upper-layer users.

twisted pair   A pair of wires (or several pairs of wires) such as is used to connect telephones to distribution panels. Twisted pair is also being used as a physical transmission medium for Ethernet, token ring, and other forms of data links.

275

UCL	*University College London* A UK research center which is quite active in the area of X.500 directories and X.400 message-handling systems.
UDP	*See User Datagram Protocol.*
Ultrix	Version of UNIX sold by Digital.
Unibus	A peripheral bus used on 11/780 and 8600 VAX processors.
UNIX	Operating system developed and trademarked by American Telephone and Telegraph. UNIX is a pun on the Multics operating system, developed by MIT in the 1960s.
Usenet	Network of UNIX users. A somewhat informal network of loosely coupled nodes that agree to exchange information in the form of electronic mail and bulletin boards.
User Datagram Protocol	Part of the TCP/IP protocol suite. UDP operates at the transport layer and, in contrast to TCP, does not guarantee the delivery of data.
UUCP	*UNIX-to-UNIX Copy Program* The standard UNIX utility used to exchange information between any two UNIX nodes. Used as the basis for Usenet.
V.21	CCITT standard for 300 bps duplex modem over the general switched telephone network.
V.22	CCITT standard for 1200-bps duplex operation over the general switched telephone network.
V.22 bis	CCITT standard for 2400-bps duplex modems over the general switched telephone network.
V.23	CCITT standard for 600/1200-baud modems.
V.24	CCITT standard for the definition of circuits between a DTE and DCE.
V.27	4800-bps modem over leased circuits.
V.27 bis	CCITT standard for 4800/2400-bps modem over leased telephone-type circuits.

Glossary

V.27 ter   CCITT standard for 4800/2400-bps modem over general switched telephone networks.

V.29   CCITT standard for 9600-bps modem over 4-wire leased telephone circuits.

V.32   CCITT standard for a family of 2-wire modems operating up to 9600-bps over general and leased telephone circuits.

V.33   CCITT standard for 14.4-kbps modems over leased circuits.

V.35   CCITT physical interface standard for high-speed data transmission.

VAX   *Virtual Address eXtension* Hardware series made by Digital.

virtual circuit   A service offered usually at the transport layer. The user of a virtual circuit is able to send data to a remote user and not worry about putting data in packets, error recovery, missing data, or routing decisions.

VISTAnet   A gigabit testbed project located in North Carolina.

VMS   *Virtual Memory System* A DEC proprietary operating system for VAX computers.

VMTP   *Versatile Message Transaction Protocol* A transport layer protocol defined in RFC 1045.

WAD   *Walk Away in Disgust* Assembly language opcode.

WAN   *Wide area network* Sometimes also used to mean work area network or a small subnetwork for a work group.

WBI   *Water Binary Tree* Assembly language opcode.

WHOIS   An Internet program which allows users to query a database of people and other Internet entities, such as domains, networks, and hosts, kept at the SRI/DDN NIC. The information for people shows a person's company name, address, phone number, and email address [RFC1177].

277

Glossary

WKS *Well-known service* A service on TCP or UDP that uses a well-known port number and can thus be accessed without a priori knowledge of which port the application may be using at a given time.

work group Trendy term for people who work together. Several computers may be isolated on a small network, known as a work group network. Whether anything is accomplished is another matter.

WUPO *Wad Up Printer Output* Assembly language opcode.

X.3 CCITT standard for a packet assembler/disassembler (PAD).

X.12 ANSI committee for Electronic Data Interchange.

X.21 CCITT standard for circuit-switched networks.

X.21 bis Use of synchronous V-series modems over public data networks.

X.25 CCITT standard for the interface between a DTE and DCE for terminals operating in packet mode and connected to the public data network with a dedicated circuit.

X.28 CCITT protocols for an asynchronous terminal to communicate with an X.3 PAD.

X.29 CCITT protocols for a synchronous DTE (a host) to control and communicate with an X.3 PAD.

X.75 CCITT standard for interconnecting separate X.25 networks.

X.81 Internetworking between ISDN and public (e.g., X.21) circuit-switched networks.

X.110 CCITT standard for routing principles on public data networks.

X.121 CCITT numbering plan for public data networks.

X.200 CCITT version of the OSI reference model.

X.208 CCITT version of the OSI ASN.1.

Glossary

X.209	CCITT version of the OSI ASN.1 Basic Encoding Rules (BER).
X.211	Physical service definition for OSI for CCITT applications.
X.212	Data link service definition for OSI for CCITT applications.
X.213	Network layer service definition for OSI for CCITT applications.
X.214	Transport service definition for OSI for CCITT applications.
X.215	Session service definition for OSI for CCITT applications.
X.216	Presentation service definition for OSI for CCITT applications.
X.217	ACSE definition for OSI for CCITT applications.
X.218	CCITT equivalent of ISO 9066-1: Text communication - reliable transfer.
X.219	CCITT equivalent of the ISO Remote Operations Service Element (ROSE).
X.220	CCITT specification of the use of X.200-series protocols in CCITT applications.
X.223	Use of X.25 to provide the OSI connection-mode network service.
X.400	CCITT standard for message-handling services.
X.402	CCITT message-handling system: Overall architecture.
X.403	CCITT message-handling system: Conformance testing.
X.407	CCITT message-handling system: Abstract service definition conventions.
X.408	CCITT message-handling system: Encoded information type conversion rules.

Glossary

X.411   CCITT message-handling system: Message transfer system: abstract service definition and procedures.

X.413   CCITT message-handling system: Message store: Abstract-service definition.

X.419   CCITT message-handling system: Protocol specifications.

X.420   CCITT message-handling system: Interpersonal messaging system.

X.500   CCITT standard for directory information.

X.509   CCITT directory: Authentication framework.

X.511   CCITT directory: Abstract service definition.

X.519   CCITT directory: Protocol specifications

X.520   CCITT directory: Selected attribute types

X.521   CCITT directory: Selected object classes.

XDR   *See External Data Representation.*

Xerox Network System   A set of network and transport protocols (and a few applications) typically used in conjunction with Ethernet. An alternative to DECnet or TCP/IP. The network and transport layers of XNS form the basis for several networks, including Novell's NetWare.

XID   *Exchange Identification* An HDLC frame used when a new node attaches to the physical medium. The XID frame contains information such as the node ID or a verification password for the connection.

XNS   *See Xerox Network System.*

Yellow Pages   *See Network Information Service.*

zone   An AppleTalk concept. A zone is a collection of computers, which together make up an internetwork. Isolating operations within a zone limits the number of devices, such as printers, that a user has to choose from.

INDEX

Access networks, 25
ACORN project, 194-97
  compared to CASA, 197
  Linear Lightwave Network
    architecture, 195-96
Address Resolution Protocol (ARP),
  73, 91, 111
Address space, diminishment of, 105
Advanced Networks and Services
  (ANS), 32-33
Agents, 176-77
AlterNet, 27, 29-30
American National Standards
  Institute (ANSI), 145, 217-19, 227,
  229, 230
Andrew File System (AFS), 12, 135,
  142
ANSnet, 20
AppleTalk Filing Protocol (AFP),
  10-11, 148
Application layer networks, 24-25
ARCnet, 136, 147, 174
ARP, *See* Address Resolution Protocol
  (ARP)
ARPANET, 20
Asynchronous Transfer Mode (ATM),
  5-6, 72, 75-78, 87-88
  adaptation layers, 76-77
  as a LAN, 77-78
  as cell division technique, 76
  definition, 75
Authentication, and Privacy
  Enhanced Mail (PEM), 164
Authority and Format Indicator (AFI),
  106
Autonomous System Path, 125
Autonomous systems (AS), 116, 122

Backbones, 20-21
BI-BUS, 216
B-ISDN networks, 70-72
BITNET, 24-25, 33-35, 105
Border Gateway Protocol (BGP),
  125-26, 174, 225
Border routers, 122

CA*net, 20
California Institute of Technology
  (Caltech), 185
CASA, 185-94
  compared to ACORN project, 197
  quantum chemical reaction
    dynamics application, 187-88

3-D seismic profiling application,
  189-91
  weather modeling application,
    186-87
CERFnet, 20, 29-31
Certificates, PEM, 168-73
  Certificate Revolution List (CRL), 173
  cross-certification, 172
  hierarchies, 168-73
  RSA Data Security, Inc. (RSADSI),
    170-72
Classes of IP networks, 105
Commercial networks, 29-33
Common Management Information
  Protocol (CMIP), 157, 173-74
CompuNet, 25
Confidentiality, and Privacy
  Enhanced Mail (PEM), 163
Connectionless Network Service
  (CLNS), 119
Connection-Oriented Network Service
  (CONS), 119
Core backbones, 20-21
Core networks, 25
Corporate networks, 22-23, 25
Corporation for National Research
  Initiatives (CNRI), 29
Couriers, 205
Cray Research Inc., 101-4
Cross-certification, 172-73
CSnet "InfoServer," as source of
  RFCs, 18
Customer Premises Equipment (CPE),
  80-81

DARPA, *See* Defense Advanced
  Research Projects Agency (DARPA)
Data Access Protocol (DAP), 10, 12, 16
  protocols, 149
  and towers, 97
Data Encryption Key (DEK), 167
Data Link Connection Identifier
  (DLCI), Frame Relay, 73
Data link layer, components of, 39
Data link protocols, 26
DECnet, 3, 4, 6, 8, 10, 23-24, 35, 37,
  96-97, 118, 120, 151, 158
  routing exchanges, levels of, 118
  running TCP/IP simultaneously, 150
DECnet/OSI Phase V, 92, 96-98, 118,
  149-52
  CTERM protocol, 149
  Data Access Protocol (DAP), 149, 151

281

INDEX

283

INDEX

MCIMail, 24-25, 27, 143
Medium Access Control (MAC), 39-40
  extended Ethernets, 114
  MAC-level bridges, 40-41, 99, 217
    disadvantages of exclusive use of,
    40-41
Message integrity assurance, and
  Privacy Enhanced Mail (PEM), 164
Meta-networks, 25
Metropolitan Area Networks (MANS),
  standard for, 80
MIB, *See* Management Information
  Base (MIB)
Morris worm, 155
MOTIF, 6, 135, 139
Multistation Access Unit (MAU), 48, 52

Naming services, 140-41
NASA-Ames, 45-48
  architecture of, 48
NASA's Science Internet (NSI), 19, 20
National Gigabit Testbed, 8, 181, 184,
  197
Navigation tools, 33-35
Neighbor acquisition protocol, 120
Netfind, 210
NetWare, 95, 116, 136, 147-49
  Core Protocols, 12, 24, 130
  and NFS, 147-48
  Portable Netware, 147
Network addresses, classes of, 105
Network applications, categories of, 16
Network architecture, 1-2
Network Control Program (NCP),
  112-13
Network Extensible Window System
  (NeWS), 132-33, 139
Network File System (NFS), 1, 10-17,
  23, 93-94, 130-31, 141-42, 222, 224,
  228
  as a standard, 216-17
  definition, 141
  External Data Representation (XDR),
  15
Network Information Services (NIS),
  131
Networking protocols, vs. protocol
  suite, 24
Network management, 173-77
  agents, 176-77
  decentralized approach to, 174-75
  Management Information Base
  (MIB), 174-75
  SunNet Manager, 175-77
Network managers:
  issues facing, 26-27
  needs of, 40
Network security infrastructure, 156
Network Services Protocol (NSP), 97
  approach to data representation, 15

coexisting with FTAM, 16
  independent locking mechanism, 15
  stateless approach of, 15-16
NFS, *See* Network File System (NFS)
NIC, *See* Network Information Center
  (NIC)
NIS, *See* Network Information
  Services (NIS)
NORDUnet, 20
North American Numbering Plan
  (NANP), 82
Novell networks, 6, 91
  Netware, 95, 116, 136, 147-49
  IPX, 147
NREN, 27-29, 33
  architecture, 33
  interim NREN, 29
NSFnet, 20, 24, 27-28, 32-33
NSP, *See* Network Services Protocol
  (NSP)

Objects, definition, 205
Office Document Architecture (ODA),
  204, 207
ONC, *See* Open Network Computing
  (ONC)
Open Book , The (Rose), 137-38
Open Look, 133, 139
Open Network Computing (ONC), 7,
  93, 129-33
  computing environment, 132
  creation of, 130-31
  naming service, 140-41
  and Network File System (NFS),
  130-31
  Network Information Services (NIS),
  131
  windowing systems, 132-33
Open Shortest Path First (OSPF)
  protocol, 119, 121-22, 174, 225
Open Software Foundation (OSF), 6,
  7, 129-30, 133-35
  Distributed Computing
  Environment
  (OSF/DCE), 134-35, 139, 142, 151
  environmental stack, 134-35
  formation of, 133-34
  and IBM, 144-45
  naming service, 140-41
  standards, 221-24
    compared to IAB standards, 222
    Request For Technology (RFT),
    222
Open systems:
  managing, 173-77
  and standards, 215
Open Systems Interconnection (OSI),
  1, 2, 8, 11, 24, 38, 96, 98-99, 121,
  129-30, 135-37, 144, 150-51, 230
  addresses, 106

INDEX

INDEX

286

For Further Information

ANSI Sales Department
1430 Broadway
New York, NY 10018
Voice: (212) 642-4900

Bell Communications
Research (Bellcore)
Customer Service
60 New England Avenue
Piscataway, NJ 08854
Voice: (800) 521-CORE
Fax: (908) 699-0936
Telex: (908) 275-2090

CCITT
International Telecommunications Union
Place des Nations, CH 1211
Geneve 20, Switzerland
Voice: (44) (22) 730 51 11
Fax: (44) (22) 733 72 56

Corporation for National
Research Initiatives (CNRI)
1895 Preston White Drive
Suite 100
Reston, VA 22091
Voice: (703) 620-8990
Fax: (703) 620-0913
Email: rkahn@nri.reston.va.us

Corporation for Open Systems
International
1750 Old Meadow Road, Suite
400
McLean, Virginia 22102-4306
Voice: (800) 759-COSI
Fax: (703) 848-4572

IEEE Computer Society
345 East 47th St.
New York, NY 10017
Voice: (202) 371-0101
Fax: (202) 728-9614

Internet Activities Board (IAB)
Robert Braden, Executive Director
USC – Information Sciences Institute
4676 Admiralty Way
Marina del Rey, CA 90291
Voice: (213) 822-1511
Email: braden@isi.edu

Internet Engineering Task
Force (IETF)
Steve Coya, Executive Director
CNRI (see above)
email: scoya@nri.reston.va.us

For Further Information

Interop, Inc.
480 San Antonio Road
Mt. View, CA 94040
Voice: (415) 941-3399
Fax: (415) 949 1779
Email: info@interop.com

Open Network Computing
Attn: Dennis Freeman
Sun Microsystems, Inc.
Voice: (415) 336-0955
Email: dennisf@Corp.Sun.Com

Open Software Foundation
11 Cambridge Center
Cambridge, MA 02142
Voice: (617) 621-8700
Fax: (617) 621-0631

Special Interest Group on
Data Communication
(SIGCOMM)
Association for Computing Ma-
chinery
11 West 42nd Street
New York, NY 10036
Email: craig@bbn.com

SPARC International
535 Middlefield Road, Suite 218
Menlo Park, CA 94025
Voice: (415) 321-8692

UNIX International
20 Waterview Blvd., 3rd Floor
Parsippany, NJ 07054
Voice: (908) 263-8400

X/Open
1010 El Camino Real, Suite 380
Menlo Park, CA 94025
Voice: (415) 323-7992
Fax: (415) 323-8204

An Interop Publication

CONNEXIONS®
The Interoperability Report

BUSINESS REPLY MAIL
FIRST CLASS MAIL   PERMIT NO. 166   MT. VIEW, CA

POSTAGE WILL BE PAID BY ADDRESSEE

INTEROP INC
480 SAN ANTONIO RD STE 100
MOUNTAIN VIEW CA 94040-9925